19/12

KENSINGTON TO
ST VALERY EN CAUX

KENSINGTON TO ST VALERY EN CAUX

PRINCESS LOUISE'S KENSINGTON REGIMENT, FRANCE AND ENGLAND, SUMMER 1940

ROBERT GARDNER

In Memorium
Ted Simmons

First published 2012
by Spellmount, an imprint of The History Press
The Mill, Brimscombe Port
Stroud, Gloucestershire, GL5 2QG
www.thehistorypress.co.uk

© Robert Gardner, 2012

The right of Robert Gardner to be identified as the Author
of this work has been asserted in accordance with the
Copyrights, Designs and Patents Act 1988.

British Library Cataloguing in Publication Data.
A catalogue record for this book is available from the British Library.

isbn 978 0 7524 6880 8
Typesetting and origination by The History Press
Manufacturing Managed by Jellyfish Print Solutions Ltd.
Printed in Malta.

CONTENTS

ACKNOWLEDGEMENTS

My thanks are due to the following:

Ann Ash, *née* Simmons, who provided copies of official records relating to her father Ted Simmons. Richard Ashton, who read the manuscript and made valuable suggestions. Peter Gardner, for the account of the death of Charles Frost and for providing photographs of him. Richard Hills, my oldest friend and fellow HAC gunner, for writing the foreword. Mrs Vera Knott, *née* Simmons, for the account of Ted Simmons arriving at Bournemouth. Professor Philip M'pherson, who read the manuscript and gave advice. Linda Parker, who suggested the book's title. Brian Simmons, son of Ted Simmons, who provided the photographs of B Company at Reculver in August 1940, and of the sergeants' mess at Hothfield Place and gave permission for them to be reproduced. John Simmons, for providing background information about his brother Ted. Dr Allan Spence, for contacting Mrs Wood on my behalf, for providing tables of officers and copies of battalion orders, and for providing the photograph of machine-gun training in 1939. *The Daily Telegraph*, for permission to reproduce the photograph of machine-gun training in 1939. Mrs Marjory Wood, for permission to quote freely from the diary of her late husband Col B.R. Wood OBE, SBStJ., TD, DL and for permission to reproduce the two photographs of Lt Wood (as he then was) and the photograph of five officers of A and D Companies when prisoners of war. My thanks also go to Major R.J. Cannon MC and the Princess Louise's Kensington Regimental Association for permission to quote extracts from the regimental history *The Kensingtons*; to The National Archives, Kew, Surrey, for providing copies of war diaries and other documents and giving guidance on their use; to HMSO for guidance on the use of Crown Copyright publications; and to Andrew Bradford for permission to quote from *Escape from St Valery*. Finally I must thank my wife for her support and much-needed sense of humour.

LIST OF ILLUSTRATIONS AND MAPS

GLOSSARY AND ABBREVIATIONS

AFV Armoured Fighting Vehicle, e.g. tanks and armoured cars.

Artillery Wheeled large-calibre guns, in 1940 always towed by gun tractors not self propelled, capable of firing explosive shells long distances. Artillery regiments are either heavy, medium, field or anti-tank regiments.

Battalion An infantry formation of about 750 men, divided into companies and commanded by a lieutenant colonel.

Battery A sub-unit of an artillery regiment. There were usually three batteries to a regiment, each having two troops of four guns.

BEF British Expeditionary Force. The British Army in France. By early October 1939 four British divisions grouped into I and II Corps were moving into forward positions. By May 1940 the BEF had expanded to ten divisions in three corps, a total of 394,000 men.

Bn Abbreviation for battalion.

Bofors gun A light, quick-firing anti-aircraft gun of Swedish origin, in service with both the British and German armies. Sometimes used against ground targets.

Bren gun British light machine gun of Czechoslovakian design. It fired a magazine of thirty standard rifle rounds, though to prevent jamming many preferred to load only twenty-eight. Rate of fire was 500 rounds per minute. Usually fired from the prone position.

Brigade In 1940 a formation of three infantry battalions or armoured regiments. Commanded by a brigadier.

Carrier Lightly armoured, open, tracked vehicle in service from 1939. Used in a multiplicity of tasks, carriers had originally been designed to carry a light machine gun with a crew of two in addition to a driver.

CO   Commanding Officer. The senior officer in charge of a battalion or regiment, usually a lieutenant colonel.

Colour Sergeant   Infantry rank, one rank above sergeant. Same as staff sergeant in non-infantry units.

Company   A sub-unit of an infantry battalion, commanded by a major or captain. Usually five to a battalion. A machine-gun battalion had four machine-gun companies of twelve guns each plus a HQ company.

Company Cmdr   The officer in command of a company.

Corps   A formation of two or more divisions commanded by a lieutenant general. In May 1940 there were three corps in the BEF.

Coy   Abbreviation for company.

CQMS   Company Quartermaster Sergeant. Infantry rank, in charge of issue and control of all stores in his company and responsible to the regimental quartermaster sergeant (RQMS). Equivalent to the squadron quartermaster sergeant (SQMS) in armoured and signals regiments or battery quartermaster sergeant (BQMS) in the artillery.

CSM   Company Sergeant Major. One per company, a WO2.

Defensive Fire   Usually artillery fire laid down on previously identified positions, the co-ordinates of which have been surveyed and

(DF)   recorded to allow instant fire in defence of own troops. Guns not in action, e.g. during periods of rest, are often 'laid' loaded on the co-ordinates of a DF target ready to be fired instantly if required.

DR   Despatch Riders. DRs on motorbikes carried out a variety of tasks such as carrying reports and orders from battalion headquarters, escorting convoys and reconnaissance. When the battalion left Ilminster, the column of 183 vehicles included sixty-one motorbikes.

Division   In 1940 an infantry division was a formation of three brigades together with supporting arms, e.g. artillery, signals, medical and supply units, commanded by a major general.

DCM   Distinguished Conduct Medal. Highly prestigious gallantry award for non-commissioned ranks.

DSO   Distinguished Service Order. Award for commissioned ranks showing gallantry or exceptional leadership.

Echelon   B Echelon is most frequently referred to, usually meaning the formation of cooks, storemen and other personnel supporting troops. A Echelon is the transport for replenishment of the battalion's forward troops during or after action. F Echelon is the immediate fighting equipment of the battalion such as carriers.

FOO — Forward Observation Officer. A Royal Artillery officer, usually a subaltern, who identifies a target and directs fire on to it.

GSO1 — General staff officer 1. A senior officer (lieutenant colonel) at Divisional HQ.

HQ — Headquarters.

IBD — Infantry Base Depot.

LAD — Light Aid Detachment. A Royal Electrical and Mechanical Engineers (REME) formation attached to a battalion or regiment to provide assistance to MT such as breakdown repair.

Lee-Enfield — The standard British-issue .303in single-shot bolt-action rifle.

MC — Military Cross. Commissioned ranks' gallantry award.

MGTC — Machine Gun Training Centre.

MM — Military Medal. Non-commissioned ranks' gallantry award.

MMG — Medium machine gun (see Vickers).

MO — Medical Officer. A doctor attached to the battalion or regiment from the RAMC.

Mortar — An infantry weapon resembling a drainpipe on a stand, which could lob high-explosive shells called bombs in a high trajectory at low velocity. The 2in mortar could manage a rate of fire of eight bombs per minute over a range of 500 yards. British mortars were generally considered to be outclassed by German versions.

MT — Motor Transport of a battalion.

MTO — Motor Transport Officer. The officer in charge of all aspects of a battalion's motor transport, such as servicing and repair.

NCO — Non-Commissioned Officer (lance corporal, corporal, sergeant, colour sergeant, staff sergeant).

OC — Officer Commmanding, as in 'OC B Company'. It does not mean the same as commanding officer, which is the battalion's most senior officer and commands it.

Pioneers — Soldiers whose main duties are labouring, e.g. digging trenches.

Platoon — An infantry formation of about thirty soldiers commanded by a subaltern. In a machine-gun battalion there were three platoons to a company with four guns in each platoon.

Pn — Abbreviation for platoon.

POW — Prisoner of war.

Provost — Regimental police, frequently used for traffic control.

PSM — Platoon Sergeant Major. A warrant officer class 3 commanding a platoon. Discontinued after 1940.

QM — Quartermaster. An officer, frequently in the rank of captain. Has overall responsibility for all battalion stores. Assisted by the RQMS.

RA   Royal Artillery, nicknamed 'the gunners'.

RAMC   Royal Army Medical Corps.

RAP   Regimental Aid Post. This would be set up by the battalion medical officer at a secure location behind the front line, but close enough to receive battalion casualties and give treatment.

RAOC   Royal Army Ordnance Corps. Military engineers and fitters concerned with maintenance of explosives, ammunition and firearms.

RASC   Royal Army Service Corps. Supply and transport of most supplies including rations, fuel, ammunition and general stores. Also troops.

RE   Royal Engineers, nicknamed 'sappers'.

Recce   Reconnaisance.

RNF   Royal Northumberland Fusiliers. A machine-gun regiment similar to the Kensingtons.

RHA   Royal Horse Artillery. An elite regiment of the Royal Artillery.

RQMS   Regimental Quartermaster Sergeant. A warrant officer class 2. In charge of issue and control of a battalion's or regiment's stores. Responsible to the quartermaster and senior to the individual company quartermaster sergeants (CQMS).

RSM   Regimental Sergeant Major, a warrant officer class 1. There is only one RSM in every regiment or battalion. It is the highest non-commissioned rank, and the RSM always works in close touch with the commanding officer.

RV   Rendezvous. A pre-arranged location at which troops or vehicles will meet.

Section   In infantry a sub-division of a platoon, being eight men commanded by an NCO. There were three sections to a platoon. In machine-gun battalions there were two guns to a section, which were sometimes divided into two sub-sections of one gun each. In artillery a section is a sub-division of a troop.

Squadron   A sub-unit in armoured, signals and other regiments. Equivalent to a battery (in the artillery) or a company (in the infantry). Commanded by a major.

SSM   Squadron Sergeant Major. A warrant officer class 2. Equivalent to a BSM (artillery) or CSM (infantry).

Staff Sergeant A rank in non-infantry regiments. One rank above sergeant but below sergeant major. It is the equivalent of an infantry colour sergeant.

Sub-Unit   A general term to describe component parts. A company is a sub-unit of a battalion. A platoon is a sub-unit of a company.

Subaltern   A lieutenant or second lieutenant, often commanding a platoon.

TA   Territorial Army.

Troop A sub-unit of an artillery battery or an armoured squadron.

Unit Generic term for groups such as regiment, battalion, squadron, company, battery, troop. They can all be a 'unit'.

Vickers gun Medium machine gun, belt fed, water cooled, firing .303in ammunition. Rate of fire 500 rounds per minute, range approx 4,000 yards. Crew of two, gunner and loader, augmented by a third if battalion up to full strength. Entered service in 1912. Still in service in 1960s.

FOREWORD

History is a tale about people that has no beginning and no end. Dates and place names merely put men's actions and thoughts into a logical structure and sequence. Sadly and too frequently historians kill wonderful tales by drowning them in unnecessary clutter and forgetting that it is only men who make history. In this book Rob Gardner has told a gripping story of one regiment of the British Army and the actions of its men over a few months from their arrival in France in April 1940 to the regiment's near destruction two months later, followed by its anti-invasion role. This is a difficult story to tell because the reader must be given a considerable amount of information in order to understand what is going on and to keep pace with the unfolding action. Despite this necessity Rob has kept the story alive and intimate by drawing on the diaries, memories and anecdotes of the men who made this history.

My association with Rob goes back to September 1979. While lining up to give a blood sample as part of the induction process into the Honourable Artillery Company (HAC), an ancient City of London territorial regiment, the man behind me lent forward and whispered, 'make sure they don't take a pint'. We became firm friends, and over the next few years took it upon ourselves to enjoy the HAC experience as much as we could while trying equally hard to be effective while battling against the sometimes astonishing decisions of our superiors.

Rob's natural gift for understanding how the army works and how to control this vast machine from the bottom up must spring from his Civil Service background. Taking orders absolutely at face value could cause considerable confusion, as could asking ridiculous questions with a straight face, for example after a lecture on the relief of Ladysmith: 'Where exactly were the Germans again, sir?' I can only imagine that in war the ability to laugh at all around you must be the single most important ingredient that allows men to do the impossible and be willing to face overwhelming odds.

The story of the Kensingtons comes to life for me because of the human side of this tale. Not only is this book a scholarly work that any serious historian would be proud of, but it is also living history – real men telling us what they were thinking at the time. It reveals the confusion, the fear and the sadness – that nearly overpowering brew of human emotions that only men fighting for their country's survival can endure.

Richard Hills
Guernsey

PREFACE

I wrote most of this book during the seventieth anniversary year of the events described in it. One day during the early summer I was astonished to hear a young-sounding woman being interviewed for BBC radio saying that she had never heard of the Battle of Britain. A question about the Dunkirk evacuation could easily elicit the same response, although there will probably be some who will know that Dunkirk was the port from which the army was rescued in 1940, and you may even be told about the part played by the 'little ships'. Ask about St Valery en Caux, however, and hardly anybody will have heard of it or of what happened there over seventy years ago. From the end of April until 12 June 1940 the 51st (Highland) Division was in almost continuous action many miles away from the rest of the British Expeditionary Force (BEF), first in Lorraine, then on the Somme and finally in Normandy. It was still carrying out a fighting withdrawal along the Normandy coast almost two weeks after the successful conclusion of the Dunkirk evacuation. Sadly there was to be no Dunkirk for the Highland Division. Held back by the need to support the slow-moving French, whose transport was largely horse-drawn and whose infantry were mainly footsloggers, the division lost the opportunity to reach Le Havre and safety. With its back to the Channel at St Valery en Caux, exhausted, heavily outnumbered, short of food and, above all, of ammunition, and with German tanks and artillery commanding the clifftops overlooking the burning town, the division surrendered.

One of the individual units that made up the Highland Division was the 1st Princess Louise's Kensington Regiment. Two companies of the battalion were present at St Valery; the remaining three reached Le Havre and safety. Of those two companies at St Valery, totalling some 240 men, only a handful escaped. The rest were killed or taken prisoner. This book is my account of six months of war fought by this now little-remembered but typical London Territorial Army battalion, from its arrival in France in April 1940 to the catastrophe of St Valery in June, and the climax of the Battle of Britain in September.

The period covered was originally to have been from April to June 1940. During the writing process, however, I gradually came to the decision to extend it. The book therefore now includes the part played by the Kensingtons in the extraordinary events of July to September 1940, the summer that became our 'finest hour'. I had initially been disinclined to take this course, feeling that it would somehow detract from the conciseness of the story of how a London Territorial Army regiment was pitched untested into three continuous months of total war. On reflection I felt that the later events of the summer of 1940 were so unprecedented that I should include those months as a postscript to the events in France. I have therefore included a chapter describing the experiences of the remnants of the battalion as they were deployed along the 'invasion coast' of east Kent during the critical months of July, August and September 1940.

I was extremely fortunate to be given permission by Mrs Marjory Wood to quote freely from the diary of her late husband, Col Reg Wood, who served as a platoon commander in A Company of the Kensingtons. The diary is particularly detailed and is all the more valuable because of the relative scarcity of material relating to the regiment.

Other important primary source material has been the Kensingtons' war diary from the National Archives, which contains not only the battalion's daily diary of events but also an extensive cache of maps, operations orders, reports and messages. Amongst these papers I was lucky to find a four-page typed report on the final hours at St Valery by the officer commanding A Company, Kensingtons, and a report by the second lieutenant commanding two platoons which were cut off behind enemy lines. In addition to the war diary a small amount of other material also came from the National Archives, namely a recommendation for the award of a DCM and a report of an escape from a prisoner-of-war column and their subsequent return to England. The war diary happily survived the evacuation from France unlike some others that fell into enemy hands or were destroyed.

The war diary and Reg Wood's diary provided a foundation on to which I have applied material from secondary sources such as Eric Linklater's 1942 publication *The Highland Division.* This was written immediately after the events it describes and included in its list of consultees are senior officers of the 51st Division, officers such as Brig. Stanley-Clarke, the commander of 154 Brigade and subsequently of Ark Force. Major Ellis' *The War in France and Flanders* (HMSO 1953) and Basil Collier's *The Defence of the United Kingdom* (HMSO 1957) are two other works that I have found invaluable.

In recent years authors have enjoyed the huge benefit of access to material that was previously classified and therefore unavailable. Now this material can often be accessed via the internet without the author needing to travel at all; indeed in my own case photocopies of the war diaries were most efficiently made and despatched to me by the staff of the Record Copying Department of the National Archives. I have also been helped by a number of recent publications (all are listed in the Bibliography); the most extensive and detailed of these is, in my opinion,

Saul David's definitive work *Churchill's Sacrifice of the Highland Division*. Published by Brassey's in 1994, it took three years to research and write. David was meticulous in tracing and interviewing more than 100 survivors of the campaign.

I must also mention *The Kensingtons*, an account of the first and second battalions during the Second World War, published in 1952 by the Regimental Old Comrades' Association as a tribute to those who died while serving with the regiment.

What I have written is not an attempt to produce another detailed account of the campaign fought by the Highland Division in 1940. My intention was simply to present as detailed a record as possible of the part played in the war from April to September 1940 by the 1st Battalion Princess Louise's Kensington Regiment. To do this I have had to balance the relatively scarce amount of available material relating to the Kensingtons against the considerable volume of material relating to the division and to other units in it. Some of the latter was obviously essential to the reader's understanding of the Kensingtons' part in the campaign, but if too much had been included the main subject matter would have been swamped. It was a question of balance, and deciding what had to be excluded presented a continuous challenge. In the end I included virtually everything that related specifically to the Kensingtons and excluded anything else that I thought was not essential to an understanding of the progress of the campaign. Much that I would have liked to include about other units, such as the exploits of the fighting patrols in the Saar and the gallant work of the Lothians and Border Yeomanry, has therefore regrettably been left out. The result, I hope, is a balanced book in which the story of the Kensington Regiment in the battle for France remains the prime subject.

I have explained how, in writing the book, I have grafted material from other sources on to the framework created by the war diaries; much of this material is in the form of direct quotations. The danger in this approach, as will be appreciated, is that the author can easily be regarded as simply a compiler and editor. Nevertheless, I hope that writing in this way presents a clearer picture to the reader together with a sense of actually being present at the time, which can result from the use of contemporary material. Above all I hope that I have been able to add to the account rather than detracting from it. All such sources have been cited and referenced and please note that all original spellings have been retained in the direct quotations.

Finally, some personal comments. I have been inspired in the writing of this account by my admiration and affection for my late uncle Edward Simmons, who served in the Kensingtons and escaped from St Valery, and for his young TA colleagues such as Charles Frost (my aunt's brother) who served with him over seventy years ago. As a result of the 1940 campaign alone, many of them spent five long years as prisoners of war and eight, including Charles Frost, were killed in action. Others died of wounds or died in captivity.

Like Ted Simmons, I joined a London Territorial Army unit when a young man. That is now over thirty years ago and yet those years seem to have passed in a moment. In my experience it was not usual for people to discuss what motivated them to join the TA. Nobody ever suggested to me that it was out of a sense of patriotic duty and yet in reality that was probably the most common reason. In 1980 the Cold War with the USSR was still continuing and the country lived under the shadow of the 'four-minute warning', the length of time from the sounding of the warning sirens to the arrival of the first ballistic nuclear missile. In 1937 the perceived threat was similar but Armageddon was expected to be delivered from a sky black with German bombers. I had just returned from three years abroad in a country where young men were conscripted for twelve months and it had prompted a desire in me to follow the example of my father, two grandfathers and two uncles and make my own, albeit inadequate, contribution. I am relieved to see that the British Army does not appear to have suffered any lasting damage as a result.

Ted Simmons transferred to the Royal West African Frontier Force in November 1940, joining his new regiment in West Africa and later serving with the West African forces during the bitter fighting of the South-East Asia campaign. After the war he chose not to accept a commission and to remain in the regular army, and was transferred to the Army Reserve. His military conduct was assessed as exemplary and his testimonial reads as follows:

C/Sgt Simmons, who began his military career as a territorial in 1937, has served continuously since august 1939. He embarked for overseas service in November 1940 and served in W. Africa and the S.E. Asia campaign until his return home in May 1945. His commanders in the field have reported very favourably on his services and, since joining this unit, his work has been first class.

He has performed a very difficult administrative job in a very creditable manner and has proved beyond doubt that he is in every way efficient, honest and thoroughly trustworthy. I am pleased to recommend him as a man of pleasant personality who will certainly prove an asset to any employer.

He was a member of D Company and was present when Charles Frost was killed on the night that B Company relieved D in the Bois de Busch on the Saar. He also escaped from St Valery and the best guess is that he was among the group from D Company who escaped from Veules les Roses in a rowing boat with CSM Satchwell. That is all there is to tell and my inevitable regret is that this book was not written twenty years ago before the memories of so many personal experiences were lost forever. Ted Simmons died on 23 September 1992 at the unfairly early age of seventy-two. Patriot, exemplary soldier and good friend, he served his country in the dark days of 1940, later in the swamps and jungles of West Africa, and finally in the bitter fighting in the Arrakan, Burma, against a ruthless enemy.

It is to his memory that this book is dedicated.

Robert Gardner
Isle of Ely

JOINING THE BEF

The history of the Kensington Regiment – Kensingtons converted to a machine-gun bat-talion – Declaration of war and mobilisation of the Territorial Army – Illminster, Somerset – Kensingtons move to France and are attached to the 51st (Highland) Division – Strengthening the 51st (Highland) Division – A brief assessment of the BEF's equipment – Move to the Saar region and positions forward of the Maginot Line – Topography of the Saar region and tactics for troops deployed.

THE HISTORY OF THE KENSINGTON REGIMENT

Princess Louise's Kensington Regiment, known in two world wars simply as 'The Kensingtons', was originally a volunteer infantry battalion. In 1908, as a result of the well-known army reforms of Richard Haldane, Secretary of State for War in the Liberal government, the Territorial Force was formed. All yeomanry and volun-teers became part of the new TF, which in 1921 became the Territorial Army (TA). The Kensingtons had become closely associated with Queen Victoria's sixth child, Princess Louise, who lived in Kensington Palace, and in 1914 had adopted the title '13th Princess Louise's Kensington Battalion, The London Regiment', which later became 'Princess Louise's Kensington Regiment'.

KENSINGTONS CONVERTED TO A MACHINE-GUN BATTALION

Like all territorial units, the Kensington Regiment was formed of paid part-time volunteer soldiers whose basic military commitment was to attend a minimum of twenty evening drill nights each year and a fortnight's annual camp. For this the soldier received, in addition to pay for drill nights, an annual 'bounty', which in 1938 was £5. The Kensingtons were at this time a rifle battalion, but in 1938 it was announced that they were to be converted from a standard infantry unit to a fully mechanised machine-gun battalion. This is therefore an obvious point at which to examine both the organisation and function of machine-gun battalions in 1938. A battalion was organised into five companies: a headquarters (HQ) company and four machine-gun companies. The latter were each equipped with twelve Vickers medium machine guns. Each machine-gun company was divided into three platoons of four guns each, with each platoon sub-divided into two sections of two guns each. In addition to the forty-eight Vickers guns the battalion had eighteen Bren light machine guns and, as personal weapons, 175 pistols and 559 rifles. The full complement was about 740.[1] The function of a machine-gun battalion was to provide firepower in support of other units, either offensively or defensively. In practice this meant that the Kensingtons hardly ever fought together as a single unit of four machine-gun companies, if at all. Sub-units, usually at company strength, would be deployed as required by the division or brigade. They in turn would deploy their three platoons to the unit or units being supported, and the platoons would very likely provide that support by sections or even sub-sections of guns in different locations determined by the circumstances. It will be seen that these tactics meant that at times units of the Kensingtons could be very widely spread, and companies and platoons could be under pressure to change locations quickly to meet new threats at times when the enemy was attacking in strength. Eric Linklater wrote:

> Both on the Saar front and later ... the two machine-gun battalions, Northumberland Fusiliers and Kensingtons, were for tactical purposes divided among the brigades, and because they did not fight as a whole it is difficult to assess or describe their work. But wherever the infantry were in action there were machine gunners to support them, and perhaps it is sufficient to say that the battalions which had Kensingtons attached to them speak well of the Kensingtons, while those which were assisted by the Northumberland Fusiliers were convinced that they had the better support. The conclusion is that both were good.[2]

By February 1939 tension was rising. German troops entered Prague on 15 March 1939, and the dreadful prospect of a second European war in twenty-one years seemed to creep closer. On 29 March the Secretary of State for War announced that the strength of the TA was to be doubled and that each TA battalion or regiment was to raise a 'duplicate'. Soon after this conscription was introduced, but any man who joined the TA was exempted. For the Kensingtons this meant the creation of a second battalion. It may perhaps emphasise the seriousness of the situation if it is looked at in the context of the following extract from Collier:

The British Government responded by joining the French in guarantees to Poland; taking measures to bring the twelve divisions of the Territorial Army up to strength and then double them; introducing conscription; and setting up a Ministry of Supply to find the weapons needed by a rapidly expanding army … Thereafter the home defences passed gradually from their peacetime state to one of readiness for war … Anti-aircraft formations of the Territorial Army were called out in four contingents for one month at a time and guns were moved to pepared positions in a belt twenty-five miles deep extending from Newcastle to Plymouth.[3]

Princess Louise's Kensington Regiment was undoubtedly a prestigious territorial battalion. Yet it was more than just a matter of normal regimental pride. Her Royal Highness Princess Louise herself, daughter of Queen Victoria, regarded the Kensingtons as her own regiment. She had presided over the ladies who worked the new colours presented to the regiment by King Edward VII in 1909. In 1913 she consented to the use of her name in the regiment's new title, and in 1928 to the use of her personal cipher as a design for a new collar badge. On returning from camp in 1936 the Kensingtons marched from Victoria station to Kensington Palace where Princess Louise inspected them, and on Armistice Day she laid a wreath at the drill hall and took the salute as the troops marched past the Cenotaph and the Kensington War Memorial. There was also a civic connection. The regimental cap badge depicted the arms of the Royal Borough of Kensington and the regiment played a full part in civic ceremonial, carrying out such duties as route lining, providing guards of honour and parading at the civic Sunday service. Sporting events included the Brigade Boxing Championship, which the Kensingtons won for the eighth time in 1937. The cadet corps of Latymer School was affiliated to the regiment. There was also a large and active Old Comrades Association, and in 1936 many of its members enrolled in the newly formed Kensington Defence Company, a predecessor of the Home Guard. Its function in wartime was to take over guard duties and similar work that would free up troops. Although not of ancient origin, the Kensingtons had a respectable lineage reaching back to the mid-nineteenth century, and a highly respectable war record from 1914–18 during which 1,205 Kensingtons were killed and thirty battle honours were awarded, including 'Somme 1916'. As the second war loomed they could be, and were, proud of their new role as a machine-gun battalion. Not one single facet of the battalion's life but the fusion of them all made the Kensingtons one of the country's finest territorial units. At the end of the war an inspecting officer was to write: 'there may be territorial regiments as good as this but there can be none better than the Kensingtons with their admirable history and high tradition.'[4]

DECLARATION OF WAR AND MOBILISATION OF THE TERRITORIAL ARMY

The TA soldiers resumed their civilian lives after the annual camp of 1939, but it would be just a fortnight before they were back in uniform and this time it would be for six years. Many of these young men became prisoners of war in 1940. Many others paid the ultimate price and would never return to their homes and families. TA anti-aircraft regiments were mobilised on 21 August as the relentless and seemingly inexorable drift to war continued. Finally Germany invaded Poland on Friday 1 September 1939 and at 3 p.m. that day mobilisation of the 206,000-strong TA commenced. Many were contacted at their homes by the military police with orders to report to their drill halls. Ted Simmons was woken at home in Chiswick at 2 a.m. by military police[5] and some soldiers were on duty before the end of August. On Sunday 3 September Britain declared war on Germany.

The Kensingtons' immediate role was to provide military support to the civil authorities, with each company attached to a police station. On duty at all times were a liaison officer and a despatch rider who would relay to company HQ any police request for military assistance in instances such as looting and rioting during air raids. This arrangement continued until late October, by which time there had been neither air raids nor rioting and the Kensingtons were placed on duties that involved guarding 'Vulnerable Points'.[6] The routine of those early days of the war was captured in his diary by Lt Reg Wood of A Company:

Sept 2nd. Advance Battn H.Qs at Hammersmith Police Station. Breakfast arrived supplied by Messrs Chance of Acton until we went onto R.A.S.C. rations. Food poor. Sgt Froblich made A/CSM. Relieved Mike at police station, met Inspector Fraser, D/Supt May, Det Sgts Cade, Green and Burns. 'Officers Mess' in room in basement. Detectives search foreigners and take down their particulars. In case of looting or rioting during air raids L.O's job at police station was to send back to Coy HQs for troops. Lunch at Crown Hotel opposite; Mrs Neil proprietor. Hammond relieved me at 15.00hrs. P.S.I. Sgt Parnell (Middlesex Regt) arrived attached to Coy. Big thunderstorm in evening. Scheme evolved of 1 P.C. on duty, 1 in reserve, 1 free – latter to go out in near area but to return at once on air raid warning.

Sept 3rd. Arms drill taken by Sgt Parnell in garden behind house. Announcement of Declaration of War on wireless at 11o/c. Air raid warning at 12.00hrs, six men of Coy without respirators. Mustard gas detectors fixed to sentries' bayonets. Lunch at Crown. Tom off to town to get black-out paint for windows. Went home in afternoon, put steel helmet, carried on shoulder, through bus window. Returned at 20.00hrs to sleep at police station. Air raid warning 03.00hrs, went into street.

Sept 4th. Relieved by Ham at 07.00hrs. David managed to obtain Cam House, Camden Hill Road (late millionaire's house) as a billet. Large lawn, Italian garden, garage, paved court yard. Moved in 11.00hrs. Large ballroom on first floor as our bedroom, camp beds etc set up. In future 1 P.C. and officer concerned to be off duty from 17.00hrs to 22.00hrs. Arms drill in morning, and PT. in afternoon. M.G. instruction in garden. At 18.00hrs guard mounted. 2 trucks per Coy, 1 to collect rations from Chances at Acton and for any other purposes, the other for driving instruction. David's car also taken over. Canteen opened, Truman's beer obtained by Mike, chocolates and cigarettes by Q.M.S. Minski from Harrods. Eardley left Coy to become O/C B Coy and Harley sent to M.G.T.C. Alderley.

Sept 5th. Early morning PT started at 06.15hrs. Cooker obtained from Gas, Light & Coke Co. Stones and Pyne sent to Depot. Sammy Lohan (T.A.R.O.) I.O.

Sept 6th. Air raid alarm 06.00hrs. David in bath – Coy, except sentries, go to basements. All clear 2 hrs later.

Sept 7th. Hammond to Netheravon with Wasey, Walker and Kent. J. Evans replaces him in our Coy. Ray Milton (transport Sgt) commissioned. Chimay on S.O. course. Beginning staff course Camberley. NCOs courses at L.D.S.I. Moor Park and Richmond. Parnell appointed C.S.M. A Coy. Few NCOs sent as instructors to depot and 2nd Middlesex at Gosport. ORs as batmen to GHQ France.

Sept 9th. David breaks ankle playing rugger – stays at Cam House. Duties at police station revised, only D.R. at police station during day but officer at night. M.G. training in full swing – route marches round Kensington. Lectures by Howard 2I/C 'Unexpected Always Happens in War' and 'The Regiment' etc.

Oct 21st. Leaving Kensington for V.P. (Vulnerable Point) duties at Stanmore aerodrome. Acting 2I/C took estate agent round Cam House – Damages £185. Gas, Light & Coke Co claimed we had bought cooker for £115, we said we hired it. Left in first coach for Stanmore to take over from E Coy 2nd Kensingtons. Arrived Stanmore 11.00hrs took over from Capt Belol. No sentry duties etc laid down, all very inefficient, Troops billets good – officers mess excellent, also bedrooms, central heating, H & C, telephone. O.I/C Station Wing Commander Bold (late Indian Army) referred to all youngsters in balloon barrage as useless wingless wonders, amongst them C. Gadney, rugger referee. Coy arrived at 14.00hrs. Took David round. Troops' duties fairly severe 48 hrs on, 12 hrs off, guarding Camp and Manor House (Air Ministry), Cipher station, also roving sentries at night. Officers duties practically nil but orderly officer had to go round posts at night, David, Ham and I shared this duty which meant that we were on duty all day and night one in three, otherwise we were free after lunch on the other two days. I used to go home some days which meant four changes of train or go up west with the other off duty. When O.O. I used to stay in mess playing cards, darts etc or listen to wireless to 00.15hrs then go round posts taking about half an hour, back to bed, then round again at 06.00hrs. After breakfast in the morning we attended Coy office, then did M.G. tactics by ourselves, then PT. No opportunity to give troops M.G. training as they were on guard always, and all kit given to D Coy who were running NCOs courses at Chiswick under Capt Garston, Middx. Very inefficient but Howard thought wonderful. On Tuesdays and Fridays dances were held which were very well attended. On Wednesday night an E.N.S.A. show. Troops food excellent, three hot meals a day. Our mess also excellent.

Oct 23rd. Orderly Officer. E.N.S.A. show. Renee Hunter came over to Sgts mess afterwards. Squadron Leader in plain clothes tried to get into Manor House. Nearly shot by guard. Told him not to try to be clever with us.

Oct 26th. Went to dinner at Berkeley with David, Eardley and Muriel and then on to Cabaret club.

Oct 30th. E.N.S.A. show. Jack Buchanan.

Oct 31st. Refereed boxing contests at R.A.F. vs ourselves. Howard, Laurie and Bryar came over to watch.

Nov 3rd. Mike returned from L.D.S.I. course and Ham went in his place.

Nov 5th. Went over to Depot at Mill Hill and met Howard's and my old Pl Sgt who is now instructor there and Jimmy Nevin, England rugger international, also Howard Pyne and Dennis Stones.

Nov 6th. Went with Mike to first night of George Black's show 'Black Velvet' at Hippodrome. Danced with Rosa Beaumont. Had dinner at Regents Palace afterwards and met two girls.

Nov 7th. Told on telephone that Security police wished to know what information I had given girl the previous evening – None. Turned out later to be Sammy Lohan who knew girl well.

Nov 9th. Went to Windmill theatre with David. Dinner at Piccadilly.

Nov 11th. David & I went to St Mary Abbots church for Armistice Day service and had lunch at Battn HQ.

Nov 13/15th. 48 hrs leave. Went to Trocadero.

ILLMINSTER, SOMERSET

On 17 November Lt Col Hancocks relinquished command of the battalion and Lt Col Howard took over. On the same day it was announced that the Kensingtons were to move to Ilminster, Somerset, joining 44th (Home Counties) Division. Other ranks younger than 20 years old and those earmarked for officer training were posted to the 2nd Battalion. It could be inferred from this that overseas service was imminent. Reg Wood described in his diary the battalion's journey to Somerset and the settling-in period:

Nov 19th. Parade 06.15hrs. Group Captain Bold said how sorry they all were we were going etc etc. March to Stanmore station. Arrived at Mill Hill station and joined up with B and C Coys. Scots Guards dug out Captain smoking cigar in turban and teddy bear coat, R.T.O. Got on train next stop Addison Road to be joined by D Coy, HQ Coy, and Battn HQs. Large crowd on platform. Col Campbell, Lt Col and Mrs Hancocks, Col Sir D. Banks, Mayor of Kensington etc. Hands shaken all round. Train drew out at 10.00hrs for Ilminster. David, Mike, Charles, Eardley, John Smith and myself in one carriage. Good luncheon baskets. Played Vingt et un. Arrived Taunton at 15.00hrs, tea. Ilminster 16.00hrs. Troops marched from station to large shirt factory in main square, taken over as billet, and given hot meal. D Coy officers and Sgts had arrived week earlier to do the billeting. C and D Coys with Battn HQs and HQ Coy to be billeted in Ilminster in old factories, schools, etc. Officers in George hotel, Howard, Hoare and Chimay in Shrubbery Hotel. Cookhouse in old blacksmiths forge in main square. Sgts mess in old hall. R.A.P. in disused house, hospital in old chapel staffed by V.A.D. nurses. Battn HQ in empty house. After meal A and B Coy officers and men left in coaches for South Petherton, village about 8 miles away just off Ilminster–Yeovil road. Troops then billeted in village halls, skittle alleys etc. A Coy had 4 Pl in hall of Crown hotel, 5 Pl in hall and skittle alley of Wheatsheaf and 6 Pl in old school. Troops had to sleep on palliases only. Mike and I billeted in Crown hotel in main square of village, Proprietors Mr & Mrs Wood. Fairly comfortable and improved as we stayed on. Cookhouse and messing hall in large empty garage. Coy offices in second floor of empty house. QM and MG stores with guard room on ground floor.

Nov 20th et seq. Efforts were made to make men more comfortable by hiring gas heaters and putting in electric light etc. Lectures were arranged to take place in dance hall of George hotel, Ilminster every evening except Friday at 17.15hrs given by Tregonning and Chimay on what they had learnt, obviously very little. Officers from South Petherton went over in a truck and we were generally late, incurring Howard's displeasure. Chimay had had colossal row with Proprietors of George hotel over the taking over of the hall and Howard had ordered all the officers to leave there and go to the Shrubbery or find other billets. The bar was also put out of bounds to all ranks. During the week drafts arrived of conscripts, reservists and regulars from K.R.R. depot, Y & L, E Yorks, Beds & Herts etc. All the reservists were ex machine gunners. Whilst our trained Sgts took the men on gun drill, classes in fire orders etc were arranged for the NCOs. Mike, Ham, Laurie and myself took these classes at South Petherton in requisitioned rooms of Coy HQ billets etc, and although we had all been on courses it meant a good deal of swotting so we had little time in the evenings for ourselves. In afternoon, route marches, respirators drill, PT, guard mounting with regimental band on alternate days at Ilminster and South Petherton took place in the respective squares. Rather a farce at South Petherton with buses and sheep always getting in the way. This was later stopped by the Major Gen. The Toc H in the village opened a canteen and the locals all invited our troops and also gave them baths as no public baths were available. Dances were held every Saturday night in local hall and at Ilminster Sgts mess held a dance in George hotel dance room for full Corporals and above but of course bar could not be used. Every Wednesday night an ancient film was shown in the local hall at South Petherton but Ilminster had one flea-pit of a cinema.

Training was started:

Dec 9th. All Coy Cdrs went off with C.O. to Batcombe Down to carry out recce for Divisional digging exercise the next week. Our Coy was to be in position on Monday morning, dig M.G. emplacements etc, stay in position the whole night and be relieved the following night at 20.00hrs by B Coy and so on. Meanwhile Mike, Peter and myself went into Yeovil to the cinema, had dinner at the Mermaid and then went on to Montacute.

Dec 10th. Although a Sunday, David wanted to do recce with Pl Cdrs for scheme on Monday – rather annoyed as wanted to go to Montacute. Mike was O.O. and acting 2 I/C of Coy so I took David and Ham in car. No 5 Pl was in reserve and would not be digging. On arrival at Batcombe Down decided on platoon positions. One of my sections was to be in hedge just off main road, the other about 100 yards away in hedge in field, Pl HQs between the two at a track. Went down steep hill, brakes none too good, hair pin bend to place selected for Coy HQs. On way back puncture outside Crewkerne. David and Ham changed wheel. On return arranged details with Pl Sgt.

Dec 11th. At this time each Coy had only 8 trucks (2 per Pl, 2 Coy HQs) so coaches necessary to drive troops in. Civilian drivers very bolshy. Left at 08.30hrs for Batcombe Down, arrived one hour later. Platoon dig in and camouflage. Full network of emplacements likely to take 4 days to dig. Reservists excellent at this. Visit from Brig Steele in bren gun carrier emphasises not to make tracks walking between sections as visible from air. I look at tracks his carrier is making. Stew sent up from Pl HQs at 13.00hrs and water cart. Bitter wind, snow in early evening. After tea arranged sentries during night, patrols of our own supposed to be in front with bren guns, call for D.F. red over green and red. Settled down to cold night, stew brought up at 20.00hrs bad, sent D.R. back to Coy HQs who produced sausages. Cooked them by burning sign posts etc. Pte Rayner taken ill, gave him my greatcoat. No sleep all night, too cold and snow. General Osborne 'Snow White' came round positions at 09.00hrs said troops should do PT, silly fussy old dodderer. Howard arrived 10.00hrs, no criticism. Cold and windy all day, waited longingly for relief. At 19.00hrs first reliefs for infantry Battns came through. One Battn marched past my Pl HQs three times having lost their way!! Relief by B Coy supposed to have been completed by 20.00hrs eventually completed at 02.00hrs. Slept in coach all way back. Arrived South Petherton 03.30hrs. Troops given hot tea etc. Mike and I prepared some breakfast in hotel at 06.00hrs then went to bed.

Dec 18th. Conference of all officers at Battn HQs. Howard had been well brassed off by Div General. A Coy escaped censure as we had dug well and done a lot. B and D Coys got full benefit of Howard's tongue. Arthur Cower had apparently tried to argue with the Div Cdr. Eardley relieved of command of B Coy, to go as 2 I/C C Coy. Arthur Cower to go to Depot after Xmas leave and then hand over to Charles Mountford temporarily. Williamson of D Coy to come to us as 2 I/C. B, C and D Coys were to repeat exercise during day only. A Coy excused but officers would have map reading and questions by Howard and Hoare on Batcombe Down.

Jan 12th. Heard that A, B, C and D Coys were to go to Tidworth for a week of field and range firing, Bn HQs and Howard were to remain at Ilminster and HQ Coy were to look after our billets at South Petherton. Neville Hoare to be C.O. at Tidworth and I was to be Adjutant.

Jan 14th. Left for Tidworth. A and B Coys drawn up on Ilminster–Yeovil road. Long wait for C and D Coys who were, as usual, late. Finally moved off at 09.00hrs. I travelled in Neville's car – only took sufficient kit to last a week, rest left behind in my bedroom at the Crown. Arrived at barracks at 13.00hrs. Sammy Lohan recently returned from gas course was acting as messing officer, and had arrived there two days ago. Had good meal ready for the troops as well as excellent lunch for the officers. Troops very pleased to be billeted in proper quarters for the first time since the war began. Large Orderly room, Adjutants room and C.Os office. Barracks in peacetime occupied by 10th Lancers. We took over their mess and crockery etc, officers bedrooms, large with coal fires, comfortable beds, tables etc, H & C water. Saw troops settled in and then arranged next days shooting. Good mess dinner that night. First time that nearly all officers of Battn had dined together since outbreak of war.

Jan 15th et seq. Coys out all day. I stayed in office. D.R. arrived each night at 18.00hrs from Ilminster with Battn Orders etc. Very cold, snow on ground.

Jan 19th. Visit of Div Cdr. Took him in thick snow to see Coys firing at Netheravon. Sammy Lohan left for the depot. Very sorry as I liked him.

Jan 21st. Left Tidworth to return, at 09.30hrs. Snow on roads frozen hard, trucks break down, speed 8 mph. Travelled in Neville's car in rear of column in case of accidents. B Coy truck skids into house at Mere. Stopped at Wincanton for sandwiches and beer. Journey very slow, car breaks down, towed by Tregonning's truck. Outside Ilchester truck skids, slews round into ditch and overturns, we follow and do likewise. Much shaken, sheep killed. Tregoning breaks ribs. Phone for ambulance and L.A.D. from farmhouse. Neville goes on in another truck as has to attend C.Os conference. On arrival of ambulance and L.A.D. leave in Donald Roe's car for South Petherton and arrive there at 18.30hrs. After dinner had T.A.B. inoculation as did entire Coy.

Jan 24th/26th. Laurie Bryar on 48 hours leave so went to Battn HQs as Adjutant and stayed at Shrubbery hotel. Pleased as missed big Coy scheme, very cold and snow thick on ground. Had long talks with Johnny Dodge about Howard in evening and played table tennis with de Chimay. On 26th. Mike, David and R. Wasey (promoted Capt and 2 I/C B Coy in place of Tregoning) came to stay at Shrubbery for night as leaving at 05.00hrs next day for artillery demonstration at Salisbury. Rumour advance party leaving for France on Feb 12th. Crates of maps of France arrived.

Jan 28th/30th. Digging of pits continued. Mike went to Ilminster to take over C Coy for a couple of days as Garston and Holding ill. All those unfit for service overseas left Battn, including C.S.M. Parnell.

Jan 31st. Big Coy scheme in thick snow at Buckfast St Mary. Target obscured by mist. P.S.M. Darling made C.S.M. of A Coy.

Feb 3rd/4th. 48 hours leave. Did final shopping for France. Went to Piccadilly hotel for dinner, cabaret and dance. Met Arthur Carver there with his wife whom he had married that day, said he was joining 1/7th Middx Regt.

Feb 5th. Advance party consisting of Paul Beevor, 1 Sgt, his driver and batman left in Humber Snipe for France.

Feb 7th. King's inspection of Division outside Crewkerne. Battn formed up with officers facing inwards. King walked between. Neville Hoare acting C.O. as Howard was ill with jaundice. John Smith continuously questioned if it would take over three weeks, as Howard would then lose command. Rumour in evening that move to France off and Battn probably forming part of X force to assist Finland. Confirmed later in evening from Division that we would not be going to France on Feb 12th.

KENSINGTONS MOVE TO FRANCE AND ARE ATTACHED TO THE 51ST (HIGHLAND) DIVISION

Routine training continued during February, March and for the first days of April. Lt Col Howard relinquished command due to illness and was replaced by Lt Col Parker, a regular soldier from the Middlesex Regiment. A church parade was held as usual on Sunday 7 April but by then orders had been received from Movement Control that the battalion was to proceed overseas on 13 April. An advance party had already left on the 5th, followed on the 6th by the road party of five officers (including Reg Wood) and 193 other ranks and all the vehicles:

Apr 6th. Breakfast at 06.00hrs. Mrs Meltorn gave Peter and I large luncheon baskets with bottle of whisky each in them. Left George hotel at 07.00hrs in David's Humber Snipe. Joined column of transport drawn up from White Horse Inn on Yeovil road along Strawberry Hill and past the Shrubbery, 122 vehicles and 61 motorbikes. A/A trucks dispersed along column. Reported all correct to Chimay at 07.20hrs. Col Parker, his wife, Mrs Chimay, Laurie and Phyl Bryar and all Coy Cdrs there to see us off as well as local population. Move off at 07.30hrs. Main Dorchester Road, Sherbourne, Wimbourne, New Forest, Ringwood, Romsey (control point). Huge congestion of all types of army vehicles outside Southampton, wonderful chance for enemy bombers. After long wait waved on by M.Ps and then rushed through Southampton escorted and surrounded by M.Ps straight to the docks.[7]

Back in Ilminster, in the middle of all the preparations to leave, five new arrivals from the Machine Gun Training Centre (MGTC), posted to join the battalion, reported for duty on the 10th. They were just in time to join the rest of the battalion parading in Field Service Marching Order (FSMO) for the commanding officer's (CO) inspection. The next day baggage vans were loaded at Illminster station and on Saturday 13 April the main body of the battalion, seen off by almost the entire population of the little Somerset town, boarded two trains for Southampton where they embarked on SS *Amsterdam* for Le Havre, sailing with escorting destroyers and arriving there early on Sunday 14 April. Meanwhile, the road party had arrived at Le Havre on the 10th:

Apr 10th. Batman brought cup of tea at 06.15hrs. Visited troops and warned them to be ready to disembark at 09.30hrs. Had breakfast on board. E.S.O. came on board and said everyone except 1st Kens to disembark. Thought then that we were going to Norway after all but it was only to take us round in boat to other side of harbour where M.T. boat was. Disembarked there and met Paul Beevor, advance party to be billeted at chateau at Valliquerville, small village just off route Nationale from Le Havre between Bolbec and Yvetot. As trucks were unloaded, drivers to take them off to billet in batches of six. Our batman and Peter Smythe went in first truck to get things organised there. Stayed at Quai all morning and then went to the Transatlantique for lunch. Drew 800 Frs, 1/3 of month's allowance, from field cashier. In afternoon went round the town with Donald Rae in his car. A.M.Ps who were dockers in civvy life unloaded all the trucks and were very bolshy as got lower rates of pay than in peacetime employment. Docks closed at 16.00hrs so left for Valliquerville. Chateau in big grounds with large avenue of trees under which trucks were to be parked. Empty downstairs but upstairs rooms had beds in them. Beevor had got meal ready for troops having drawn R.A.S.C. rations which would be delivered to us in future. Guards arranged. After seeing men settled in, Chimay, Peter, Donald and myself drove into Le Havre in C.Os car which had been unloaded first. Ray did not come as he was tired. Excellent dinner at Frascati and then went to Cabaret shows.

Apr 11th. Had breakfast at Hotel de l'Europe, rue de la Poste, at Bolbec and then went to Le Havre. Drivers whose trucks had not yet been unloaded were driven down in two trucks. Air raid warning went on arrival but no one seemed to take any notice, All clear five minutes later. I had lunch again at Transatlantique and then went round town. After tea at Chateau, liaison officer to be attached our Battn arrived named Drouet. Took him into Yvetot to dine at Hotel des Grandes Victoires and played table tennis with daughter of proprietor. Chimay drove car on wrong side all the way home.

Apr 12th. Whilst last lot of trucks were being unloaded at docks and after breakfast at Bolbec, called on Mairie to arrange billeting of Battn. List of places obtained. I did A Coy, Peter, B Coy, and Paul Beevor and Drouet C, D and HQ Coy. Battn HQs were to be billeted at the chateau. Only barns available for troops but R.Es were to put up wash troughs etc. Mike and I were to have two large bedrooms in old lady's house near the church, Charles in room at baker's shop and David in nearby farmhouse whose owner made me drink his own distilled Calvados at 09.30hrs in the morning after a thick night. B, C and D Coys were billeted in farms and barns between Valliquerville and Yvetot. Spent afternoon and evening in Le Havre with Donald Rae visiting cabaret shows and had dinner at the Frascati, then more cabarets.

Apr 13th. All trucks off loaded and maintenance on them started. Had lunch at Hotel des Grandes Victoires in Yvetot again and afterwards were advised that Battn would be arriving at Yvetot station at 14.00hrs on Sunday April 14th. Spent evening in Le Havre again.

Apr 14th. All transport driven to Yvetot station after lunch to await arrival of Battn. Train steamed in at 14.00hrs. Drove Coy off to billets. Tea in Coy office, empty house in main street, then had conference. Anticipated stay at Valliquerville would not be long. Had dinner at Hotel des Grandes Victoires with David, Mike, Parker, Laurie, Eardley and Chimay.

The main body of the battalion had arrived at Le Havre on Sunday 14 April and that afternoon were moved by train to Yvetot, approximately 30 miles east of Le Havre, a journey that took one and a quarter hours. There they were met by the road party and shown to the billets that they were to occupy for the next thirty-six hours while general inspections and vehicle maintenance were carried out. What nobody could have realised then was the significance of a pretty little seaside town less than 20 miles to the north. Its name was St Valery en Caux. From Yvetot the battalion moved east to Blangy on the Bresle River, another town that was to assume a certain significance in less than two months' time. The advance party, consisting of the officer commanding (OC) of HQ Company and three other ranks, left on 15 April with orders to report to Lt Hanman, area commandant, Blangy. The main body, led by the recce party of regimental police and two motorcycle orderlies, was formed up on the main Havre–Yvetot road by 0845 hours on 16 April and left at 0900 hours for Blangy via Neufchâtel. A mechanised battalion on the move such as this involved a very large number of vehicles. Battalion HQ was the lead vehicle followed by HQ Company, D, C, B and A Companies, B Echelon (cooks, quartermaster etc.), LAD (mechanics of the Light Aid Detachment) and the Medical Section. All troops carried three days' hard rations, and vehicles travelled full and carried sufficient additional petrol for 200 miles. Anti-aircraft protection was provided by HQ Company, which allocated three trucks armed with Bren guns to C Company, A Company and the LAD. After an overnight halt at Blangy the column moved again at 0745 hours to Armentières near the Belgian border, arriving at 1400 hours on 17 April, and finally joining III Corps of the BEF.

Their sojourn at Armentières, however, was to be no more than a very temporary arrangement for the Kensingtons, since on 13 April, the very day that they had left Ilminster, there had been a development in France that was to have significant consequences for them. On that day Maj. Gen. Victor Fortune, general officer commanding the 51st (Highland) Division, also part of III Corps, was informed that his division, which had arrived in France at the end of January, was to move 180 miles south-east to the Saar region to occupy part of the sector in front of the Maginot Line. Additional units were to be attached to the 51st to strengthen it. One of those units was to be the Kensingtons. Unlike units stationed in the north, which were positioned on the French border with neutral Belgium, those on the Maginot Line were in direct contact with the enemy, dug-in on the German border with the French provinces of Lorraine and Alsace. Since December British units at brigade strength had been rotated in turn through the Saar section to gain combat experience. Now the commander-in-chief (C-in-C) of the BEF, General Gort, had decided to replace the brigades with entire divisions. The 51st was a famous division with a proud record from the previous war. It was composed entirely of territorial battalions. At the end of February GHQ decided to swap three of these TA battalions with regular ones serving elsewhere, ostensibly to provide experience and 'stiffening'. It is difficult to see how this was expected to work in practice without a closer integration of regular and TA soldiers in mixed battalions, which for many reasons would be impracticable. More likely it was an unjustifiable prejudice on the part of GHQ against TA units. Many TA units were to show stubborn bravery, including D Company 7th Norfolks on the western perimeter at St Valery en Caux, facing Rommel's 7th Panzer Division with nothing but rifles, and D Company 4th Borders who were still holding Incheville on the evening of 13 June, by which time the rest of the division had surrendered. Farther north, on 20 May two territorial divisions, 23rd and 12th, faced three panzer divisions at Doullons, Abbeville and Albert. The German war diary says they met British troops who fought tenaciously in spite of facing numerous tanks.[8] There are many other examples of the bravery and high morale of territorial units and we should recall part of the oft-quoted report by the German IV Corps:

> The English soldier has always shown himself to be a fighter of high value. Certainly the Territorial divisions are inferior to the regular troops in training, but where morale is concerned they are their equal.[9]

There also appears to have been a policy of replacing TA COs. The Lothians and Border Horse Yeomanry territorial CO had been replaced by a regular officer shortly before the regiment was attached to the 51st Division. The three swapped regular infantry battalions had regular COs and they replaced three TA battalions who had TA COs. On 15 May the territorial CO of the 5th Gordons was replaced by a regular on alleged medical grounds and on 8 June the CO of the 4th Camerons went. He was told that he was in need of a rest. He had been the last remaining non-regular CO of the nine infantry battalions.

STRENGTHENING THE 51ST (HIGHLAND) DIVISION

In common with all infantry divisions there were nine infantry battalions in the Highland Division. They were grouped into 152, 153 and 154 Brigades. These nine battalions were 1st and 2nd Black Watch, 2nd and 4th Seaforth Highlanders, 4th Queen's Own Cameron Highlanders, 1st and 5th Gordon Highlanders, and 7th and 8th Argyll and Sutherland Highlanders. Of these battalions three were regular, having been swapped with TA battalions as described above. In addition there were four artillery regiments (three field and one anti-tank), four companies of engineers, and also signals, medical corps, service corps and ordnance corps units. These units comprised the normal strength of an infantry division, but as we have seen it had been decided to increase the strength of the 51st for its move to the Saar. It was therefore substantially reinforced by attaching to it two machine-gun battalions (the Kensingtons and the 7th Royal Northumberland Fusiliers), two pioneer battalions (6th Royal Scots Fusiliers and 7th Royal Norfolk Regiment) and three artillery regiments (two field and one medium). There was also an additional engineer unit, service corps, medical units and ordnance units. The only armour in the division was provided by the 1st Lothians and Border Yeomanry, a Scottish territorial regiment that was also attached as part of the reinforcements. Their function was to carry out reconnaissance and to provide fire support for the three infantry brigades. They were equipped with forty-four Bren gun carriers as well as twenty-eight Vickers Mk VIb light tanks. It should be appreciated that infantry divisions did not normally include an armoured component and the Lothians had been allocated to 51st Division by GHQ, where they were GHQ troops in the 1st Light Infantry Reconnaissance Brigade. All the attached troops came either from III Corps or from GHQ. Corps troops, including the Kensingtons, were units under the command of III Corps but not part of any of its divisions. Similarly, GHQ troops were part of a pool of units held at the disposal of GHQ and were not part of any of the corps.

These additional troops increased the total strength of the division to around 20,000.

A BRIEF ASSESSMENT OF THE BEF'S EQUIPMENT

It may be helpful at this stage to consider briefly the strengths and weaknesses of the BEF's equipment. There had been some modernisation in recent years. Personal kit, for example, included the new battledress, and the 1937 pattern webbing. Some of the weaponry, however, would have been familiar to a soldier of the First World War and some of the newer equipment was inadequate when it was issued.

The personal weapons for the infantryman and other arms in 1940 were the Lee-Enfield .303 rifle and the Mills grenade, each of which had been in service, with minor modifications, since 1914. The Vickers medium machine gun was of pre-First World War vintage, having entered service in 1912, but it was such a reliable weapon that it stayed in service, unbelievably, until 1968. It was a .303in, water-cooled, belt-fed medium machine gun firing 500 rounds per minute over a maximum range of 4,500 yards. It had a crew of three and weighed a hefty 50lb. The 3in mortar with its weighty base plate also dated back to the First World War. New weapons included the .303 Bren light machine gun, which was an excellent and very reliable piece of equipment, firing 500 rounds per minute with a thirty-round magazine. It has to be said, however, that its German counterpart, the MG-34, had the edge over the Bren with a significantly higher rate of fire (900 rounds per minute) and a larger magazine (fifty rounds). The new .55in Boyes anti-tank rifle was heavy to carry and only effective against the most lightly armoured vehicles or soft-skinned trucks. The 2in mortar was a fifth of the weight of the old 3in weapon and was therefore far easier to carry. It had a maximum range of 500 yards and a rate of fire of eight bombs per minute. Like the Bren, the Vickers and the Lee-Enfield rifle it was to remain in service for many years after the war.

The Universal Carrier, sometimes used offensively in the role of Bren gun carrier, was a useful new light-tracked and lightly armoured general-purpose vehicle. Ellis describes the carrier as 'a lightly armoured, open, tracked vehicle designed to carry a light machine gun with a crew of two men and a driver. Having a good cross-country performance carriers provided highly mobile fire power and they were incorporated in both armoured and infantry units. As they proved to be a valuable means of cross country transport they were also used for many other purposes.'[10]

In regard to the Royal Artillery, new guns were coming into service, notably the 4.5in medium gun and the 25-pounder field gun. These superb guns remained in service for forty years, the 4.5 being modified to increase its calibre to 5.5in. The BEF's anti-tank capability was based on the 2-pounder gun. When it came into service in 1936 the 2-pounder gun was very good. By 1940 its performance against the Mk III and Mk IV panzers was less effective. Divisional anti-tank regiments were equipped with forty-eight 2-pounders.

Radio communication in all units was very limited. In a standard infantry division it only existed between divisional and brigade HQ and down to the individual battalion or regimental HQ. Communications between sub-units, from battalion HQ to company HQ, and thence to platoons, usually relied on field telephones and runners, both vulnerable to gunfire.

There were also some deficiencies in transport. The BEF, unlike the French and German armies, was fully mechanised, but the vehicles were not always up to the job. Some units had to rely on commandeered civilian vehicles, many of which were not four-wheel drive.

In this brief assessment of the British Army's equipment it would be an omission not to examine its tanks. This is not the place, however, to embark on a detailed analysis of the differing tactics in the use of armour employed by the protagonists, despite the fact that it was a critical success factor for the Germans. There were three types of British tank. The light tank was designed for reconnaissance. It was fast at 35mph, but very vulnerable because its armour was dangerously thin and it was armed only with two machine guns. The Cruiser Mk IV was designed to break through enemy lines and cause havoc in the rear areas. Again, it had the speed, 30mph, but neither adequate armour nor armament. The Matilda infantry tanks were designed to operate with the infantry. The Mk I Matilda was twice as heavily armoured as the Cruiser but very slow at 8mph and weakly armed with two machine guns. The Mk II Matilda was a considerable improvement, at 15mph almost twice as fast than the Mk I, and with 3.1in of armour it was more thickly protected than any German tank. It was armed with the 2-pounder gun.[11]

MOVE TO THE SAAR REGION AND POSITIONS FORWARD OF THE MAGINOT LINE

On the evening of the day of their arrival at Armentières the Kensingtons were given the news that they were to be attached to 51st (Highland) Division and would move to the Saar front as part of what was to be known as Saar Force. Next day the CO, Lt Col F.G. Parker, was ordered to report to Metz in the Saar district and left at 0900 hours on 19 April. There he was to meet the divisional commander, Gen. Fortune, and, with the brigade commanders and other unit commanders, to carry out a reconnaissance of the divisional area. On the same day other units of the 51st Division began to move to the Saar, but in the CO's absence the Kensingtons settled down to a routine of maintenance and training. Training of Motor Transport (MT) drivers took place by night. Officers and other ranks attended a demonstration on the use of rockets and Very lights. Company commanders carried out MT inspections. A church parade was held by the chaplain on Sunday 21 April, the battalion marching behind the regimental drums through Armentières from Place St Vaast to C Company billets. On the same day the adjutant and the quartermaster took a small party to visit the Kensingtons' cemetery in Laventie. Surprisingly, one of the party, Sgt Greenhill, had assisted in the burial of the first man to be interred in the cemetery twenty-five years earlier, in March 1915, and L/Cpl Waller, who was also in the party, had been serving with the Kensingtons at the time as well. Next day the battalion was visited by Lt Gen. Sir Ronald F. Adam, the commander of III Corps.

On Tuesday 23 April the CO arrived back from Metz at noon and gave orders for an immediate move to the Saar. The advance party of two trucks comprised

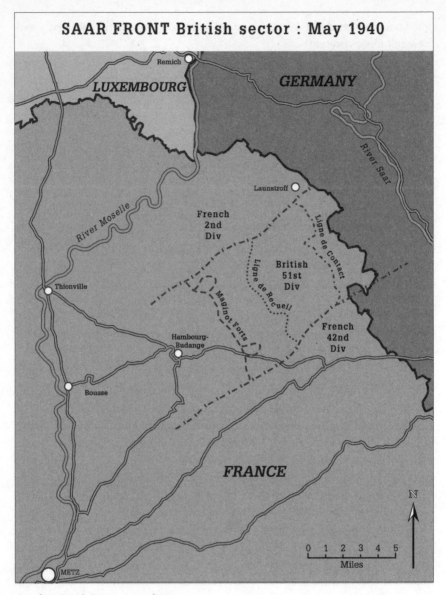

Saar front British Sector

Capt. Salmon and 2/Lt Wood, the RQMS Mr Edgecombe, a sergeant from each of HQ, B, C and D Companies, one batman and two drivers. They left Armentières at 0800 hours on Wednesday 24 April to report to the assembly areas of Hagondange and Talange near Metz. From these assembly areas the battalion was to move up to positions in front of the Maginot Line. It was raining as the advance party left and drove over cobbled roads past slag heaps in the industrial landscape. The aim was to do the 280 miles in two days and the scenery improved as they progressed. Reg Wood noted that they entered Lorraine and found beautiful valleys, rivers and woods. Metz seemed equally beautiful with wonderful buildings, good shops, and excellent bars and cabarets. After a 'tip top dinner' in the Royal Palace Hotel ('best in Metz') Salmon went to bed and Reg and Drouet (the French liaison officer) did the rounds of the cabarets. Billeting of the rest of the battalion was done over the next two days:[12]

Apr 26th. After breakfast, took one of the 8cwts into Talange with Salmon, Drouet and the R.Q.M.S. and called on the Mairie; there they sent us off to Hagondange to see the Town Major, a very old French Capt. He said that both villages and all surrounding ones were already full up with Scotsmen and he only had a few barns left. We explained to him we had 701 men, 122 vehicles and 61 motorbikes to put somewhere but he merely shrugged his shoulders but gave us a French Sgt. Sgt a decent chap and we soon had buildings earmarked for H.Q. Coy, an empty house for Battn H.Qs and barns etc for C and D Coys on outskirts of Talange. Had lunch at café on main road leading to Maizieres. After lunch we told Sgt we still had two more Coys to fix up and he said he knew of a school but French building laws did not allow these to be used. However he thought French billeting commission might accede to request as no other buildings available if we were to allow them to purchase some English cigarettes. This we were able to arrange and the school near the iron factory was taken over with ample accommodation for both Coys and covered – in court for the trucks. Most of the people being in large coal, steel and iron factories close by which were a mass of light at night, because, so they said, the Germans would not bomb what they themselves had built before the last war. The people born during and before the last war spoke German only and only those born since spoke French. They were supposed to be very anti-British but all those I met went out of their way to do me every kindness and the rest seemed apathetic. We decided to leave the officers' billets until the next day and returned to Metz. In the evening Drouet and I went to the Moulin Rouge and the Casino.[13]

The main body of the battalion formed up in the Place St Vaast, Armentières, at 0820 hours on 25 April. The recce party consisted of the intelligence officer, regimental police and three motorcycle orderlies. It moved independently of the main body. As mentioned earlier, a mechanised battalion took up a great deal of space on the roads and on this occasion the 51st Division's Provost Company was on hand to police routes in large towns throughout the move. In other respects the administrative arrangements were similar to those for the move from Yvetot to Blangy and Armentières. Arrangements were made for a daily delivery of fresh rations to the column and emergency rations were also carried. The water truck was to travel full and be kept topped up, and the troops' water bottles were to be filled. All vehicles were to travel on full petrol tanks and refuel at the petrol dump at La Fere. A second dump was available in the St Menehould area. More ominously perhaps, full issues of ammunition took place and the final approach to Talange was to be made under cover of darkness. The 280-mile road route from Armentières to the Saar took the troops near towns made famous during the First World War, and when on 27 April the battalion halted for a day at a hide at Florent en Argonne, near St Menehould, some 20 miles west of Verdun, there were tangible reminders of that earlier conflict 'the troops finding many relics of the last war in the woods'.[14]

The order of march for the main body was Battalion HQ, HQ Company, C Company, B Company, A Company, D Company, B Echelon, Medical Section, LAD. Anti-aircraft protection was to be provided by three trucks from HQ Company armed with Bren guns and allocated to B and D Companies and LAD. Speed was to be kept to 20mph and there would be fifteen-minute halts at 0945 hours, 1145 hours and 1345 hours. The main body left at 0845 hours on 25 April. The intention was to reach the assembly areas near Metz on 28 April. The route to be followed on the first day was via La Basse, Lens, Douai, Cambrai, St Quentine, La Fere. By the end of 25 April they had reached the La Fere area and established Battalion HQ in the village of Fressancourt.

The route for 26 April was via Laon, Corbeny, Rheims, Suippes, and by the end of the day the column had arrived in the St Menehould area, and had billeted troops and established Battalion HQ in the village of La Neuville du Pont. The next day was spent in the hide at nearby Florent en Argonne. From there the battalion moved at 1915 hours on 27 April for the final leg of the journey. This was via Clermont, Parois, Verdun, Abaucourt, Étain, Fleville, Briey and Aboue. The recce party rejoined the main column and the final approach to Talange and Hagondange was to be made in darkness. Vehicles were to move in platoon blocks with 20 yards between individual vehicles and 60 yards between blocks. Leading vehicles of blocks were to use dimmed headlights and the remaining vehicles were to use tail-lights only. Drivers had been warned to check tail-lights and to take all hills and corners steadily. Talange was reached at 0400 hours on 28 April.

TOPOGRAPHY OF THE SAAR REGION AND TACTICS FOR TROOPS DEPLOYED

The Maginot Line was France's defensive line along her eastern border with Germany. It consisted of large underground concrete forts with heavy-calibre guns that rose into their firing positions under hydraulic power. The line itself ran from Luxembourg in the north to Switzerland in the south, covering that part of the French border contiguous with the German border. It would, however, be a mistake to think of the line as a continuous barrier. The distances between the forts were considerable, sometimes up to 5 miles or farther. In between were block-houses, barbed wire and anti-tank obstacles. In addition there were supposed to be four other defensive lines. The Ligne de Contact was approximately 7 to 10 miles

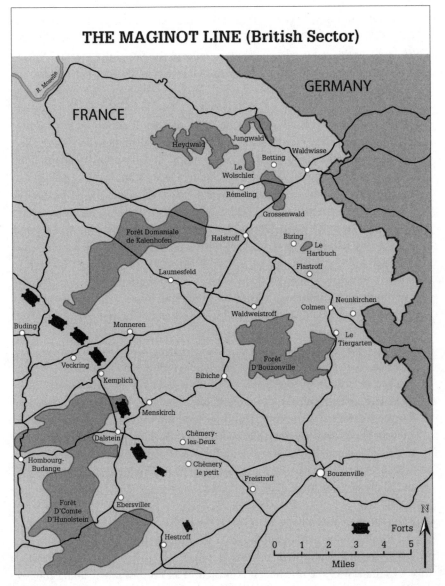

THE MAGINOT LINE (British Sector)

The Maginot Line

in front of the forts, and faced the German Siegfried Line across no-man's-land about 3 miles from the German border. It was supported in places by the Ligne de Soutien. The Ligne de Recueil was a defensive line in front of the forts, while the Ligne d'Arret was behind the forts and was intended to be the final holding position that would never be breached. It was, however, not yet complete.

The sector of the Ligne de Contact to be taken over from the French by the whole of the Highland Division ran from Heydwald wood to Wolschler,

Grossenwald, Grindorf, Hartbuch, Colmen and Neunkirchen, with the enemy actually in possession of the villages of Grindorf and Neunkirchen. The Ligne de Contact was at this point approximately 10 miles to the east of the Maginot fortress line itself. Lorraine had been taken by the Germans in 1871 and had only been restored to France in 1918, hence the proliferation of German place names. The 1:25,000 maps of the military area between the Maginot Line and the German border[15] depict closely drawn contour lines and swathes of deciduous forest dominated by the great sweep of the Forêt Domaniale de Kalenhofen. The eastern part of the province of Lorraine was a pastoral country of dairy farms, orchards, plum brandy and quiche lorraine. The area close to the German border was a rolling, forested landscape with small villages and farms connected by lanes and tracks through the woods. Winkelmerter wood, Hartbuch wood, Spitzwald wood, Grossenwald, Lohwald, Hermeswald wood, Grand Wolschler, Petit Wolschler, Heydwald wood: these were the names of some of the woods which would soon see vicious and determined fighting. Villages such as Waldweistroff, Betting, Bibiche, Rémeling, Grindorf, Colmen and Neunkirchen were scattered throughout the sector. Situated east of the Maginot Line these villages, together with farms and other settlements, had all been evacuated of civilians, with livestock and dogs abandoned. Linklater described the region as:

> … a rich green countryside of undulating hills, well watered by many streams, patched heavily with forest, sprinkled with orchards and numerous villages. The fields were wet, the ground soft, when the highlanders arrived, but the weather was improving, and before long the midday sun was hot enough. There was something like enchantment in the warmth and beauty of Lorraine. The woods were beech, and the huge pale trees were dressed in the brilliance of new leaves. The forest floor was patched with lilies of the valley, and all the orchards were in bloom.[16]

The division occupied what was known as the Hombourg–Budange sector, named after a hamlet some 3 miles behind, that is to the west of, the line of Maginot forts. The sector's front line or Ligne de Contact was about 6 or 7 miles forward, that is to the east of the fort line. It consisted of an outpost line running roughly north–south from the Heydwald to the Grossenwald, from the village of Rémeling to Grindorff-Ewig and on to the Hartbuch and from the village of Flastroff to Neunkirchen, which was in German hands. The line was divided into three brigade sectors, one for each of the infantry brigades in the division. Of the three infantry battalions in each brigade one manned the Ligne de Contact in its particular brigade sector, one manned the Ligne de Recueil and the third was held in reserve.

On 27 April the divisional commander, Maj. Gen. Victor Fortune, circulated to his unit commanders a secret document entitled 'Saar Defence Notes'.[17] In it he explained that the defence of what he described as 'the Maginot System' so differed from British methods that it was very important that every commander clearly understood the French plan of defence in case of a major attack. The report explained the functions of the defence lines, or '*Le Couverture*'. The Ligne de Contact, supported in places by a Ligne de Soutien, was roughly what the British would call an outpost line. It was expected to hold out to the last man, but troops could be withdrawn or thinned out by order of the corps or army commander if information of a major enemy attack was available. The Ligne de Soutien, where it existed, was to assist the Ligne de Contact to withdraw if ordered, or to act as a second line of defence if attacked. The Ligne de Recueil was the last defence line before the Maginot defences, and it was to positions behind this line that troops in the Ligne de Contact and the Ligne de Soutien would fall back if ordered. The defence notes went on to describe the Maginot defences as a system of underground forts of various sizes supported by fortress troops in blockhouses and defence works. In addition, field troops provided supporting artillery to cover the front of the defences and infantry immediately in front of the forts to break up an enemy attack.

The efficacy of this multi-million-franc defensive system was about to be tested to its limits.

2

OPERATIONS ON THE SAAR

C and D Companies deployed to the forward areas – Patrol activity by British and German troops – Movement within the operational area – Battalion HQ arrives at Bibiche – A and B Companies relieve C and D – PSM Frost becomes Kensingtons' first casualty – Enemy attack Heydwald and Grossenwald – Reports from front-line positions – Execution Z ordered: withdrawal to Maginot Line – Tactics and difficulties of withdrawal – Sgt Pratt awarded the Distinguished Service Medal – Positions in the French sector occupied – Disaster on the Meuse and German breakthrough at Sedan – The move south-west – Arrival at Foucarmont: evacuation of civilians begins – Enemy aircraft and parachutists

---

C AND D COMPANIES DEPLOYED TO THE FORWARD AREAS

The Kensingtons had arrived in the assembly area of Talange, slightly north of Metz, at 0400 hours on 28 April and were rested after their 280-mile journey from Armentières. Over the next two days the CO reconnoitred the operational areas allocated to 152, 153 and 154 Brigades, the divisional infantry brigades that the Kensingtons would be required to support. It was decided that two of the battalion's four machine-gun companies would be deployed in the forward area at any one time, with the remaining two held in reserve. C and D Companies were the first to go forward.

At 1900 hours on 29 April both companies left Talange for the Ligne de Contact in the forward operational area some 10 miles in front of the Maginot Line. Each column moved in vehicle groups of five with 40-yard intervals between vehicles and 250 yards between groups. As they drew closer to the operational area only tail-lights were permitted. One can imagine the thoughts of the young soldiers sitting in the back of the trucks as they crept slowly through the deepening dusk towards the front line and what for most of them was to be their first experience of action.

We know that Sgt Greenhill and L/Cpl Walley had served in the previous war and it is reasonable to assume that there were others. Many more, however, would have been too young to have served, while others would not even have been born until after the end of the Great War – the war to end war. It was May time, and the orchards of the deserted farms and cottages would have been heavy with pink and white blossom as the convoy passed. In such times every man has his own thoughts and fears. C Company was to move to Veckring via Rurange, Metzeresche, Kedange, Klang and Monneren. After leaving one platoon at Veckring, the rest of C Company was to proceed to Rémeling the next day. D Company was to move to Vigy via Ennery, Chailly and Antilly. After leaving one platoon at Vigy the rest of the company was to proceed to Hobling the next day. All these areas were well forward. Rémeling was only 1 mile behind the front line and accommodated the advanced HQ of the 1st Gordons. Hobling was actually a small fortification (*petite ouvrage*) of the Maginot Line itself, consisting of infantry and observation blocks.

PATROL ACTIVITY BY BRITISH AND GERMAN TROOPS

As a machine-gun battalion, the Kensingtons' role was to provide firepower in support of whichever infantry unit they were attached to. Initially the fighting on the Saar front was limited to nighttime probing of the enemy's defensive positions by infantry patrols of both sides. Both the British and the Germans generally patrolled in section strength, that is eight soldiers and two NCOs. Infantry defences in the front line were isolated strongpoints of barbed wire, dugouts and trenches with a machine-gun section at each end. It quickly became evident that some form of tacit agreement had existed between certain French units and the Germans. The French were keen to maintain a quiet life and generally refrained from night patrolling, shelling of German positions or any other aggressive actions. They were consequently very reluctant to support British moves to adopt a more assertive policy:

> Although the French had reported that the areas were quiet there was occasional shelling during the day and numerous attempts by the Germans to test the defences aggressively during the night. These attacks were repulsed using grenades, tommy guns and rifles, though not with machine guns which could only be used on fixed lines at night. During the day the opportunity was taken to repair any gaps in the wire and catch up on sleep, since everyone had to be alert all night.[1]

It should be appreciated that the whole province of Lorraine had been in German hands from 1871 to 1918. Linklater writes:

> The German troops who held the advanced positions of the Siegfried Line had the great advantage of knowing the country. Many were local men who

had poached the woods they now patrolled and were familiar with every yard of the ground. Their patrols were aggressive, and dominated the area. On a front so thinly held it was impossible to keep them out, and sometimes they penetrated as far as Waldweistroff. They made much use of trained dogs, and tricks to unnerve the defence, patrolled aggressively and with determination, and made their presence known by removing defensive tripwires and tapping telephone wires.[2]

The Scots infantry battalions were not impressed by their allies' lack of aggressive spirit. Neither were they intimidated by the enemy's patrolling techniques, and quickly established their own battle patrols:

Patrols went out to hamper and observe the enemy, to provoke him to fight. It was the Divisional policy that the routine patrol should be carried out in so enterprising a fashion as to make deliberate raiding unnecessary, and the nightly stalking of the enemy, with grenade and tommy gun and the patrol with their faces blackened was done with persistent energy and a high spirit.[3]

As the battalions took their turn in the Ligne de Contact the skirmishing there grew fiercer. A typical encounter would start with a few shots fired from the darkness into a platoon post, or the throwing of a grenade at a figure seen dimly in a forest ride, and from its explosion might flare a miniature battle. Very lights, splitting the darkness, would reveal the enemy beyond the coiling wire. If the attack were pushed, and reinforced, the green and white light of an SOS would bring a defensive curtain of artillery fire, or might summon the comforting noise of Bren-carriers. Our dawn patrols, searching the woods, would see where some German had lain wounded, or fallen dead.[4]

MOVEMENT WITHIN THE OPERATIONAL AREA

The arrangement for alternating two forward companies with two in reserve clearly required some administrative orders for travel to and within the operational area. These were issued on 29 April. Advance parties of units and detached sub-units were to be limited to one vehicle load and were allowed to proceed in daylight on the day of the move. All traffic routes east of the Maginot Line were under the control of the divisional provost company who had established traffic control points at Ennery, Bousse, Aboncourt, Kedange and Metzeresche. All relief movement to forward companies was to be carried out by night and was to be completed by 0500 hours. Any units failing to reach their destinations before 0500 hours were to lie up under cover and filter forward in small parties, making use of available cover. Road movement by day was to be reduced to essentials, and an interval of not less than 500 yards was to be maintained between vehicles. Transport not required in forward areas was to be detached during the forward move. During the period of relief of the forward companies, movement in the staging areas was to be reduced to the minimum and the strictest anti-aircraft defence precautions were to be taken. The water truck was to report to Battalion HQ daily at 1000 hours for instructions to proceed to forward companies.

On 1 May Maj. de Chimay came over from commanding HQ Company to take over as OC of A Company in place of Capt. Charles Mountford who remained as second-in-command (2i/c). De Chimay had little experience of machine guns and was frank enough to admit it. Fortunately Charles Mountford had a good grounding in the subject. That night de Chimay took Reg Wood and Mike Meikle (each a platoon commander) to dinner in the Hotel Meunie, Metz, and was forthright enough to reveal to them that he was going to need their help. Dinner was followed by the casino and Reg could not help noticing how the polished buttons and Sam Browne belts of the British officers stood out in strong contrast to the scruffy appearance of the French.[5]

Capt. Beevor took one platoon of C Company and one of D Company to Waldweistroff, and another platoon of D Company took over from 4th Cheshires in the Ligne de Soutien in 154 Brigade's area. The rest of C Company took over from the French 130th Regiment in the Ligne de Contact and Ligne de Soutien in 153 Brigade's area. Rémeling became C Company's HQ, covering the Heydwald to Grossenwald sector of the front line. The 1st Gordons took up forward positions in the evening. That night, as if to welcome the arrival of the Kensingtons, intense enemy patrol activity took place and all four C Company machine-gun posts retaliated with grenades and rifle and pistol fire. Next day C Company's two furthest-forward posts reported an intensification of enemy patrols during the night accompanied by some light machine-gun fire.

During the daylight hours of 2 May units continued settling into front-line positions. One platoon of C Company took over from the 7th Royal Northumberland Fusiliers (another machine-gun battalion) in the 154 Brigade area and D Company took over from the French in 152 Brigade's area and reported enemy patrol activity during the night. This pattern of relatively quiet days and active nights continued the next night. During the day, work continued at all positions to improve the defences, but during the night of 3/4 May D Company reported enemy patrol activity and some grenade throwing. C Company reported about 400 rounds of machine-gun fire, and one of their posts had the unnerving experience of hearing German voices on the telephone wire at 0030 hours and 0715 hours. During the day, work was continued at all posts to improve the machine-gun emplacements:

The typical platoon post comprised a group of what appeared to be log cabins within a dense perimeter of barbed wire. About the fringes of the woods the ground had been so wet that it had been scarcely possible to dig positions into it: they had to be built on top of it. The log cabins had been constructed by the French, and unfortunately they were not bullet proof. In open ground there were field trenches, sand bagged and revetted, but the French had created many more positions than the [British] could hold or thought desirable; and the surplus ones had to be flattened or the Germans might occupy them … With remarkable speed the log cabins were replaced by dug in positions of a more serviceable sort.[6]

BATTALION HQ ARRIVES AT BIBICHE

At 2030 hours on 3 May, Battalion HQ with HQ Company and A and B Companies moved east to Bibiche. This was a much farther forward position in the Ligne de Recueil. With halts for ten minutes every hour and speed restricted, the journey took four hours, with the leading vehicle arriving at 0030 hours on 3 May. It was a dark night with no moon, and although the leading vehicles were allowed sidelights for the first part of the journey from Aboncourt, as they drew closer to the operational area, tail-lights only were permitted. The advance party was led by Maj. de Chimay, OC A Company, who went ahead with the pioneer section, and two soldiers from each of A and B Companies, who would have provided some firepower if the party ran into trouble. The main body of the column was led by the recce party under the orders of the battalion intelligence officer (IO) and comprised the IO himself, the regimental police and all motorcycle orderlies. The recce party was followed by the CO, A, B and HQ Companies, the Medical Section and finally, bringing up the rear so as to be able to deal with any broken-down vehicles, the fitters of the LAD. Two days' worth of rations per man were taken, and the future ration supply point for the whole battalion would henceforth be at Kedange. Vehicles moved in their platoon groups, leaving 40 yards between each vehicle and 250 yards between each group. The route taken was via Ennery, Chailly les Ennery, Antilly, Bettlainville, Altroff, Aboncourt, Ebersviller, Dalstein, and Chemery les Deux. This route took the battalion through the Maginot Line itself where forts were situated near the villages of Budling, Veckring and Dalstein. Bibiche was only 4 miles as the crow flies from Veckring, but the route along winding forest roads was much longer. Lt Reg Wood, platoon commander in A Company, recorded the move in his diary:

> May 4th. At 12.00hrs left for Bibiche, I drove with Drouet beside me and Peach (driver) and Brackley (batman) in the back. Went through tertiary and secondary line of defences consisting mostly of trenches and pill boxes and after passing through Ebersviller reached very wooded country and proceeded into Maginot Line. Went through the Line at Dalstein and checked by control. Whole line here built into hills and woods, deep A/T ditch in front, large mine field and masses of barbed wire. Map reading now of supreme importance otherwise would find myself in enemy lines. Eventually Bibiche

reached, roads leading into and out of village mined at both ends. The place was incredibly filthy, manure and dung heaps piled up high outside the houses. Even the church was full of straw and manure. Reported all correct to Battn H.Qs and then found house in village which A and B Coys officers were sharing with Coy offices etc on ground floor. Troops in other houses and trucks in barns. Big cleaning up in process, straw being burnt and cartridges dropped by the French exploding right and left. Mike, Charles and I shared a large room and put up our camp beds. Ron in our Coy mess downstairs had bought large supplies of tinned food, beer, whisky and wine at Hagondange and N.A.A.F.I. at Metz. Meantime Chimay was out on recce of C Coys positions whom we were to relieve on Monday, May 6th, and we were to go round with him next morning. At night the sentries in the village were increased in case of penetration by German patrols although we were about three miles behind our advance posts. That night as we went to sleep we heard the chatter of guns in the distance.[7]

A AND B COMPANIES RELIEVE C AND D

With Battalion HQ now established at Bibiche, reports continued to come in from C and D Companies in the forward positions, confirming that while work on the positions continued during the day and evening, the enemy were still very active by night, with grenades being thrown and rifles fired from positions all along the divisional front. In the centre sector (152 Brigade) enemy snipers were active. D Company reported that at their post in the Bois de Busch two rifles had been damaged, one by a grenade and one by a round from a sub-machine gun. C and D Companies in the centre sections of the Ligne de Soutien and the Ligne de Contact had been in action for five days and were now due for relief by A and B Companies, which had been held in reserve. The troops had received their baptism of fire and the battalion's first rounds had been fired in anger. The swap over had not been attempted before and so was a potentially tricky exercise. The move was carried out in the following three phases on 6 and 7 May.

On 6 May A Company (less 5 Platoon) was to relieve C Company (less 12 Platoon) in positions in the Winkelmeter wood in the Ligne de Contact. 4 Platoon was moved in three 15cwt trucks to rendezvous with C Company guides at 0945 hours. 6 Platoon was moved to a different location and marched to the final rendezvous with C Company guides at 1100 hours. A Company HQ moved to Rémeling, arriving at 1100 hours. During the night one section reported hearing a motorcycle in Neunkirchen.

On 6 and 7 May 5 Platoon of A Company and 9 Platoon of B Company were to relieve 12 Platoon of C Company and 13 Platoon of D Company in the centre sector of the Ligne de Soutien and the Ligne de Contact. On 6 May one section of 5 Platoon was taken by truck to the rendezvous at a road and track junction, where they were met by C Company guides at 1000 hours and taken to 12 Platoon positions. Capt. Mountford and the second section of 5 Platoon moved to Waldweistroff, arriving at 1000 hours. On 7 May one section of 9 Platoon was taken by truck to a rendezvous in the Winkelmeter wood where they were met by a D Company guide and taken to 13 Platoon positions. The second section of 9 Platoon was taken by truck to Bizing where they were to be met by a guide.

Also on 7 May B Company (less 9 Platoon) was to relieve D Company (less 13 Platoon) in the Ligne de Contact. All of 7 Platoon plus one section of 8 Platoon were taken in six trucks from Bibiche to the South Dampont barrier at grid 41182832, where they were met by D Company guides at 0930 hours. The second section of 8 Platoon was taken in two trucks to the Bois de Waldweistroff where they were met by a D Company guide at 0945 hours. B Company HQ followed in two trucks to the South Dampont barrier where they were met by D Company guides at 1130 hours. At all locations machine guns, ammunition and equipment were taken over in situ and the trucks that had delivered the relieving troops brought C and D Company personnel back to Battalion HQ at Bibiche.

On 7 May artillery fire was reported by all posts, and A Company reported the dropping of considerable numbers of German propaganda leaflets, all written in French. Enemy patrols were active in all sectors.

Reg Wood continues:

May 5th. Chimay to have only two Pls under him, No 4 (mine) and No 6 (Mike). No 5 and one from B Coy were to be under Charles' command in the next sector with Coy H.Qs Waldweisstoff, ours to be at Remeling. At 09.15hrs Chimay, Mike and myself left in the Humber Snipe and drove to the Battn H.Qs of the 1st Gordons in a wood behind Remeling where Chimay saw Col Wright, the C.O. On leaving there we drove off to Remeling under enemy observation. After passing through intricate A/T barriers we arrived in Remeling showing some signs of enemy shelling and stopped at house which Padfield was using as Coy H.Qs. Had a drink with him and he said daytime was alright, but nerve-racking at night coping with enemy patrols and his platoons in front were firing most of the night. Went to the Heydwald wood about 1½ miles away to see J.Walker's position which Mike was taking over. These consisted of trenches with log dug-outs surrounded by masses of barbed wire on the edge of the wood overlooking the German positions. Nearby were Platoon positions of a Coy of 1st. Gordons. We then returned to Remeling and out to the foret Dominale where [there was a position] which I was to relieve. The position was on the edge of a wood overlooking Grindorf railway tunnel, the primary task, whilst the secondary was to prevent counter penetration on the left edge of the Grossenwald wood about 1000 yards in front. The guns were in log dug-outs surrounded by barbed wire and with a hut a few hundred yards back which served as Sec or

Pl H.Qs. All three emplacements shut themselves in at night and no movement could take place between them, even in the event of wounded. If we ever were seriously attacked we should be caught like rats in a trap. The other Section was in the right edge of the Grossenwald. To reach this we went down a road across open country screened from enemy observation where a road ran parallel to the foret Dominale back to Remeling. We struck across open country, the road we had come down leading up to the left edge of Grossenwald. Suddenly a whistling noise was heard, Chimay flopped down on his face, we followed suit and several shells burst nearby. We waited a few minutes and then continued. A marked path led us through the wood (as a lot of booby traps etc had been set) and we reached the Coy H.Qs of D Coy, 1st Gordons well dug into the side of a road going through the wood. Barbed wire was everywhere. After a call and drink then proceeded to the section position on the edge of the wood. Except for one log hut where those off duty slept, the gun positions were mere emplacements connected by trenches and very open to grenade throwing. An O.P. was also built out in front. A little in front of us and to the left, in a valley separating the Little Welschler, Big Welschler and Heydwald woods was the small village of Betting where another Coy of the Gordons was and which was a scene of lively activity at night as was the Grossenwald also. We returned down a screened road leading to Remeling on which snipers frequently fired and after arranging with Padfield about the take-over the next morning returned to a long overdue lunch at 16.00hrs at Bibiche. In the evening we held a conference and gave instructions to Pl Sgts, Sec Cdrs and Sec Cpls. Only two trucks were to be allowed up to the positions and these had to carry between them 33 men. The drivers were being left behind at Bibiche. The guns and equipment we were taking over from C Coy. Only small haversacks allowed and no packs. C and D Coys were to return to Bibiche, collect our guns and equipment and move into the ligne de recueil which the French had started to dig.[8]

May 6th. Left at 09.15hrs to relieve C Coy. I took large pack with change of kit, shirt, vest, pants, socks, boots, book, 500 cigarettes and a bottle of whisky. In addition I had two bottles of whisky in my greatcoat pocket. Trucks travelled 100 yards apart, route Halstroff, St Travois la Croix and then road leading into foret Dominale. Various tank barriers and mines laid in the roads had to be circled around and the two villages showed signs of enemy shelling. Just before entering foret Dominale saw dummy batteries made of logs and camouflaged with netting. Proceeded up road into wood as far as possible and then off-loaded Sgt Hewey's platoon in this wood, made my Pl H.Qs here during the day as good hut available. Spending the alternate nights at each position as sections were a mile apart and no communication possible except by telephone after dark. Leaving Sgt Milnes, my Pl Sgt, permanently at Grossenwald position. Checked stores with Page, put my platoon in position and in the picture and then with Henry Page took other section to Grossenwald, well spread out. Explained to Sgt Webb … to lay down defensive fire between Little and Big Welschler if former wood had to be evacuated by platoon there. Warned troops to get as much sleep as possible during day, necessity of shaving etc (in contrast to C Coy's scruffy appearance). Retired to Sgt Hervey's section who had done wonders already over installing a stove in Pl H.Qs hut. When the French had originally built these positions it had been autumn but now foliage etc screened field of fire and view which C Coy had done nothing about. Rations were brought up at 08.00hrs, 13.00hrs and 18.00hrs from Coy H.Qs at Remeling. Mail etc and stuff ordered from Rocky came up with evening rations. Clearing of foliage and wiring during afternoon. I liaised with platoon of Lothian and Border Horse nearby and also with platoon of B Coy on the other side of the road with whom we shared the duty of putting A/T barrier across road at night and down which A/T rifle was sighted. Lt Watt of Gordons came round after tea to give me route of his battle patrol he was taking out that night. At dusk left for Grossenwald. Milnes and I occupied O.P. and to do 4 hours on and 4 hours off but it always worked out we were both awake all night taking odd nips from my flask and also one at a time lying flat in the trench smoking a cigarette. Dark fell at 22.45hrs and dawn at 03.15hrs, 'stand to' half an hour before each. Activity at end of wood during night but nothing near us except when Cpl Fox threw a hand grenade at what he thought was a German and was only a rabbit and nearly hit Milnes and myself in the O.P. An hour after dawn the Gordons sent a patrol out to clear the wood and it was then safe to move about again.[9]

May 7th. Left for the other section at 07.30hrs. I had passed quiet night except when night firing lamp had been lit and illuminated the whole wood until Sgt Harvey crawled out and placed a piece of cardboard over it. Half of the section slept in the morning whilst the other half cleaned guns, improved wire etc and reversed it during the afternoon. I used to help with the wiring, read a book etc and tried to sleep in the afternoon but generally one side or other started shelling. Chimay used to come round at about 10.00hrs with C.S.M. Darling. This afternoon a French mobile battery appeared behind us, loosed off several shells and then quickly disappeared. 10 minutes later the enemy replied and a few shells landed on a newly set-up wire, much to the annoyance of all. Stayed night here. Unpleasant feeling being shut in these log emplacements. Johnny Rhodes of 1st. Gordons took out battle patrol and brought in 4 prisoners.[10]

May 8th. After breakfast went over to section in Grossenwald. Said they had heard a great deal of noise and lot of flashes from Little Welschler wood but no C.D.F. put up. Stayed there during morning and at lunch time walked down road to Coy H.Qs at Remeling and had lunch at Coy H.Qs. Met Rocky and ordered some whisky from him. Spent night at Grossenwald position. Severe shelling at 21.00hrs. Gordons had casualties. Patrols very active, opened fire three times and grenades thrown at party raiding Gordons platoon on our left who had casualties. Rumble of traffic behind German lines entire night, seemed as if they were bringing stuff up.[11]

PSM FROST BECOMES KENSINGTONS' FIRST CASUALTY

The relief of C and D Companies was completed by 8 May but the Kensingtons had suffered their first casualty of the war. In the words of the war diary:

... soon after midnight 7th/8th P.S.M. Frost, commanding no.8 Pln [B Company], who was with one section of his pln in the Bois de Busch 413286 (1:25,000 Waldwisse 5–6) was killed by sub machine gun fire. 6654365 P.S.M. Frost C W who enlisted in the Bn. on the 1st March 1938 was the first P.S.M. in the Bn. having been appointed on Dec 20th 1939. He was keen, capable and an excellent platoon commander. He was buried during the afternoon at Luttange (39662761).[12] This was our first casualty suffered by the Bn. in action.

He had been shot in the jugular vein by a sniper.[13] He must have decided to go with the section of 8 Platoon to the Bois de Waldweistroff on the basis that the other section could be left under the command of the platoon commander of 7 Platoon. In his civilian life Charlie had worked for one of the big department stores in Kensington High Street and had recently married. Harpur records the incident in the regimental history, but gives the date as 5 May:'... the first battalion casualty was on May 5th when P.S.M. Frost, of B Coy., a first class platoon commander, was killed in the act of throwing a grenade during an evening raid on his platoon, by a bullet from a tommy-gun fired at very close range.'[14] Harpur would appear to be incorrect since the war diary clearly gives the date as 8 May and this is the date engraved on PSM Frost's headstone.

During 8 May there was much enemy activity in the area of Damport Farm both during the day from the air and during the night from patrols. The next day positions in the Ligne de Recueil were reconnoitred, and reinforcements arrived in the person of 2/Lt G. Kent and forty-eight other ranks, which brought the battalion up to its war strength and provided an extra man for each machine gun. Enemy aircraft were active over the entire divisional front. At 1330 hours, post 75, manned by a section of B Company, was being shelled by German artillery.

One shell struck a machine-gun emplacement which was under the command of Cpl Huard, demolishing the emplacement and exploding a box of French hand grenades in the trench. Cpl Huard threw himself in front of one of his men,

Pte Wischhusen, as a result of which Huard sustained wounds in both legs and superficial cuts to the face. Due to this action Pte Wischhusen was only slightly wounded. Cpl Huard then ordered his men to vacate the damaged trench as many grenades were lying about with the pins half extracted. Wood:

May 9th. When Chimay visited me in foret Dominale in the morning he said there was a talk of our withdrawal through the ligne de recueil where C and D Coys were as the enemy had brought up large reinforcements opposite us and it would be impossible to hold the outposts. At 13.00hrs orders covering a withdrawal through ligne de recueil to Verkering in the Maginot came through. Code word was 'Alerte'. Two trucks would be sent up to foret Dominale to take away Sgt Hewey's section and all the guns and equipment. The section in Grossenwald was to retire down road to Remeling and take up position in a cemetery overlooking road and Betting and cover the withdrawal of Gordons from there. Bren gun carriers of L. and B. Yeomanry would then cover our withdrawal. Roads would be left open for us unless enemy penetrated behind when bridges would be blown and we should have to take pot luck. In afternoon did recce of this position, set 8 men digging two gun emplacements. R.I.A.S.C[15] were now bringing up our rations on mules. Some of my platoon, reservists, who had been in India got on well with them. Brought up first mail we had received since leaving Hagandange. Glad to get letters, 'Sketch' and 'Overseas Daily Mirror'. Shelling heavy at night, enemy patrols close, wire cut in several places.[16]

May 11th. Soon afterwards news came through that C Coy were going to relieve us. We were humbly relieved as it meant not having to take up the suicide position in the cemetery. One section was to be relieved in the afternoon and the other the following morning. I sent Sgt Milnes and two scouts off to Remeling to get a truck and recce the positions in the ligne de recueil and stay there. In the afternoon Sgt Webb's section in Grossenwald was relieved. Handed over to Henry Page and then left for my other section in the foret Dominale. Only slight patrol activity took place that night but our wire was again cut.[17]

May 12th. Relieved at 09.00hrs and left on truck for St Marguerite via St Francois-la-Croix and Hargarten. On arrival at Monneren where the road led straight up to Vekring in the Maginot tunnel turned right and half way along road to St Marguerite met a scout. Led us off road up a track into a copse. Met Milnes who said C Coy had not done much in their five days sojourn and took me forward to the positions. Trench system connecting two M.G. pits and O.P. and log dug-out at back. Trenches very shallow but Sgt Webb's men already digging and camouflaging hard as it was in the open on a small ridge overlooking road, Hargarten, Laumesfeld, Kalembourg about 600 yards away, on the right east end of foret Dominale, Hargarten railway tunnel and road leading up to Monneren. Targets of this platoon were enfilading fire on Hargarten railway tunnel up to half way of road to Monneren. Other section position 100 yards away, targets road from Hargarten to Kalembourg and edge of wood beyond. On their right was a Coy of 7th Norfolks in a wood. In between my two sections was a Pl of 1st Black Watch with two others in between Sgt Webb's section and St Marguerite. About 50 yards an A/T ditch and barbed wire. Behind us giving us a very confident feeling the guns of the Maginot. Pl H.Qs were established in the copse which also gave cover for our two trucks. Troops set to work improving positions, reported position to Coy H.Qs ¾ mile away at St Marguerite and liaised with Black Watch, Norfolks and A/T gunners. As we were in the support line only three men on duty in each section at night, one on each gun and one in O.P., rest rested in dug-out. At Pl H.Qs one sentry – all relieved every hour, this necessary in case of enemy patrols. I slept in truck.[18]

ENEMY ATTACK HEYDWALD AND GROSSENWALD

Deadly though patrol activity and skirmishing could be, and indeed had been, it was still essentially limited to the probing by each side of the opposition's line using light forces. On 10 May the situation changed suddenly and completely when Germany launched Plan Yellow (*Fall Gelb*), the attack on the west. Simultaneous attacks struck at northern France, Holland and Belgium, and Luxembourg. In the early hours large numbers of German bombers flew over the division's positions, heading west, and returned after attacking French airfields. In the expectation of a major attack the division was placed on full alert, the telephone message '*Mis en Garde* proper to be put into effect forthwith' being received at 0725 hours. The Kensingtons' Battalion HQ was ordered to withdraw to a position in the Forêt du Comte d'Hunolstein, approximately 5 miles west of Bibiche behind the forts. The next day enemy aircraft continued to be active in the early mornings and during the day there was spasmodic artillery fire, both Allied and enemy. At Battalion HQ on 12 May a church service was held in the forest while enemy aircraft continued to fly over divisional positions. German parachutists were reported to have landed in the vicinity but although both HQ staff and HQ Company provided patrols and doubled the guards, nothing was found. Enemy aircraft were active over the whole front and some positions came under mortar fire. An incendiary bomb fell on a house in the vicinity of Battalion HQ and burned for two days, and there was a further report of enemy parachutists being dropped.

On receipt of the message '*Mis en Garde*' C and D Companies were immediately deployed from reserve to previously arranged positions. Y Company was formed from men taken from C and D Companies and also took up defensive positions.

X Company was formed from one platoon each of C and D Companies, which had already been deployed together.

The following accounts describe the German attacks on the Heydwald, Grossenwald and Wolschler woods:

Harpur: At 16.00 hours heavy shellfire was put down by the enemy on the Heydwald and Grossenwald. Eventually the enemy, armed with flame throwers, attacked and captured the nearby Wolschler Wood but were prevented from crossing the gap to the Heydwald where 6 Platoon of A Company, commanded by Lt. Meikle, were awaiting them, by the cross fire from 4 Platoon, commanded by Lt. Wood, in the Grossenwald ... During this battle 4 Platoon Kensingtons nearly ran out of ammunition, but were saved by supplies brought up by the company cooks in a bren gun carrier along a fire swept road. In the meantime Betting village, occupied by a platoon of the 4th Black Watch, was surrounded and covering fire was put down by the machine guns to enable the Jocks to withdraw.[19]

Wood: May 10th. Friday. At 03.30hrs large fleets of enemy aircraft passed overhead and returned with several gaps a few hours later. At 08.00hrs Chimay rang up to say Belgium and Holland had been invaded. Every one on alert as push expected in our sector. In afternoon masses of enemy troops observed opposite Little and Big Welschler woods. Tremendous barrage on woods at 17.00hrs, then enemy attacked. Opened up with everything we had. Heavy mortar and shell fire on us. Gordons Coy H.Qs had several casualties. Little Welschler soon captured by enemy, opened up with enfilading fire when crossing over to Big Welschler. Attack then developed on Betting. Gordons trying to withdraw. L/Cpl Stokes and I took gun out in open to be able to fire over their heads down main street.[20] ... The Coy Cdr of the Gordons from Betting said that the noise of our bullets going over their heads was like music in their ears.

Ellis: At 04.00 on May 13th a heavy barrage opened on the central and northern sectors and extended to the southern end of the Hartbusch. It lasted for half an hour and was answered by British artillery firing its defensive fire tasks. As soon as the German barrage lifted the enemy attacked Wolschler wood and the Grossenwald and various posts between the two but the 2nd Seaforth Highlanders and the 4th Black Watch held their ground. North of the Grossenwald the enemy made other attacks but they too were defeated. The rest of the front was shelled and the French sectors on either flank were both attacked strongly. At 07.00 heavy shelling preceeded renewed attacks on the British front and close quarter fighting lasted for several hours, especially in the Grossenwald and Wolschler. All attacks were defeated except a small lodgement in the north of the Grossenwald. Two hours later a third barrage was laid down by the enemy and a third attack followed. This was also frustrated, though two posts which had been flattened by shellfire had to be evacuated. Meanwhile our artillery broke up enemy concentrating in Hermeswald orchards and pursued the retreating formation. The rest of the day was relatively quiet. There was renewed shelling and machine gun fire on the 14th but such attacks as were made were half hearted and were driven off. In and around the Grossenwald the 7th Argyle and Sutherland Highlanders spent the afternoon burying the enemy dead. [21]

Linklater: On the following morning [13 May], at five minutes past four, the enemy began to fire a heavy barrage along the whole battalion front and the 154th Brigade's front to the right. The Allied artillery replied. Behind the enemy's barrage came infantry armed with grenades, automatic guns and flame throwers. They made some progress round the right of the Grossenwald, but Heydwald and the Wolschler were held, and the lonely section that remained in Betting, surrounded and shelled again, was still lively. About nine o'clock at night, when the village was in flames, this section was rescued by Second-Lieutenant Rhodes leading a fighting patrol of the 1st Gordons. [22]

Note that it is unclear whether the attack occurred on 10 or 13 May. Harpur and Wood suggest 10 May, Ellis and Linklater 13 May. The war diary is silent on both dates!

REPORTS FROM FRONT-LINE POSITIONS

The following two reports from front-line units to Battalion HQ give a picture of conditions at the forward machine-gun posts: 2/Lt Page wrote of the twenty-four hours from 0600 hours on 13 May to 0600 hours on 14 May:

A fairly active day. Shelling continued until about 12.00 hours thoughout the section. No direct hits were recorded on either of my posts although several shells landed within 15 feet of the gun positions. No one was hurt and the men were very happy despite the sight of some nasty casualties sustained by other units. In the afternoon the Germans were seen carrying their wounded back to the Jungwald. A little after this a section appeared from the same point and started to make its way [forward]. After a burst from us these men went to earth and did not appear again. Later in the afternoon, at about 16.00 hours, about 20 men appeared between L'Eichien and the Jungwald. This body of men appeared to have prisoners amongst them and were waving white flags. At about 17.00 hours German patrols were reported in the area 41012918. We fired four bursts about this area from our alternative position.

The guns are now being kept outside the old gun post in order to be able to ward off close quarters attacks. A quiet night followed a hard day, no shells landing near the post. A certain amount of mortar fire was heard to the north … from 0330 hours to 06.00 hours.

Capt. Padfield, OC C Company, wrote on 14 May:

Last night was marked by intermittent heavy shelling which continued till about 07.00 hours. Low flying enemy aircraft continually reconnoitred with impunity both village and our lines and a visit is usually followed by shelling. All lines were again cut last night and in consequence I have up to now established contact with only two of my posts, runners are on the way to others. Yesterday morning's activity resulted in about 50 casualties, mainly wounded. One dead one wounded and one whole Bosch were brought into village. One dead German found inside our wire about 50 yards away from post (Betting Wood). His effects were collected and sent to Brigade Intelligence via Ingerville. His name was Karl Wankel. Owing to the haste in which I had to send his effects away I was not able to thoroughly examine them and in consequence could not establish his regiment. Several boxes of German machine gun ammo were also found outside this post. The cemetery at which it was originally thought to establish a machine gun post has been shelled out of recognition. I have reconnoitered the roads in immediate vicinity and except for a spot at … they are reasonably passable. A company of 5th Gordons relieved company of 4th Black Watch after dark last night. As a direct consequence the 5th Gordons lost one officer and an NCO wounded, fire being opened on them by the 4th Black Watch. This occurred outside post (Wolscher) and my men are apprehensive that similar happenings would occur to them if relieved by night. I have assured them that every endeavour would be made to effect a relief [by day]. They are a little jumpy but not more than is expected owing to shelling. Bosch gets round our post, calling out to the men to stop firing as they are the Seaforths. Each night here I have had jittery messages from the scots in forward positions stating that a general withdrawal was imminent. On each occasion I had to get it negatived by C.O. Scots. This makes the men rather unsettled. Hope long message understood. Please send urgently more telephone wire and 200 Players for self.

It is interesting to compare these two messages (which are to be found in the war diary). 2/Lt Page is a lowly platoon commander. His message is what we might now call 'up beat'. His men are cheerful despite the sight of some nasty casualties. Page does not want to appear negative. Capt. Padfield, however, is a company commander holding the MBE who may have seen active service in the Great War. He describes enemy aircraft flying unopposed over his positions as doing so 'with impunity'. He is quite willing to assess his men's morale as 'jumpy'. Each night the Germans prowl round the perimeter wire, calling out to the British troops who are becoming jittery. Already there has been a 'friendly fire' incident that has unsettled everybody. Padfield obviously has a sense of humour though. Not only does he describe the capture of a 'whole Bosche' but, being of equal rank to the recipient of the message, Capt. Bryar, the adjutant, he is quite prepared to end his message with a request for 200 cigarettes for himself.

EXECUTION Z ORDERED: WITHDRAWAL TO MAGINOT LINE

On 15 May the Germans launched a full-scale attack along the whole front and made several penetrations between the outposts. The war diarist records that during the evening Sgt Willmott was shot in the head by a German with a tommy gun, that one bullet pierced his steel helmet in two places but that 'fortunately the wound was not fatal and his progress was recorded as satisfactory'. Sadly this was incorrect as Sgt G.A. Willmott, aged 29, died on 17 May. He was almost certainly buried at Luttange. After the war he was reburied at Choloy War Cemetery.[23] Linklater:

On the 14th a company of the Black Watch, its communications cut, put up an SOS about half past five … it had held off for more than an hour a determined infantry attack, but now it was hard pressed. A troop of the Yeomanry was sent to investigate but one of its tanks was bogged in the soft ground about the fringes of the Grossenwald, and the other two were hit by anti tank fire and high explosive. Enemy machine guns and mortars were in action in the Hermeswald, their artillery was still lively, and some of our posts had been badly knocked about by eight inch shells. The Camerons had had a roughish time, losing a couple of section posts in the Tiergarten, and the brigade battle patrol had been isolated by fire in Spitzwald … During the early morning of the 14th, in the Gordons' sector, the Gemans fired 3,600 shells into a company front within an hour and a half: forty shells a minute, or thereabout. Telephone cables and defensive wire were cut, and German infantry followed the barrage … D Company of the 5th Gordons, on the extreme left of the Heydwald, had lost touch with two of its forward posts, and patrols sent over to re establish contact were driven back by heavy machine gun fire. At five o'clock on the morning of the 15th the Germans enclosed three posts of D Company, as if in a box, by concentrated artillery fire. At six o'clock their infantry attacked, and was driven off. Then the barrage came down again, and for another three hours the shelling lasted. No news came from the forward posts, and every attempt to reconnoitre was driven back by machine gun fire. Later in the day D Company reported it was holding its last position with twenty eight men and the wire was down … the forward posts had been captured and D Company, with nearly seventy casualties, had to withdraw under the covering fire of a fighting patrol … It had become evident that our advanced positions were untenable against the superior forces which the Germans were using.[24]

Gen. Fortune decided to abandon Heydwald, Grossenwald, Wolschler and Betting and withdraw to a new line along the ridge of Kalenhofen. Before this movement had begun, however, withdrawal was ordered to the Ligne de Recueil to conform with the movements of the French on either flank.[25] The code word for this withdrawal was 'Execution Z'.

TACTICS AND DIFFICULTIES OF WITHDRAWAL

Meanwhile, orders had already been given for A Company Kensingtons to take over from C Company in the Ligne de Contact and to establish their HQ at Rémeling. C Company was to occupy A Company's former positions in the Ligne de Recueil and set up HQ at St Marguerite. These orders were overtaken by 'Execution Z'. French troops on either side of the British sector had already fallen back from some positions, and on 15 May the French Army commander ordered the implementation of 'Execution Z', a full withdrawal to behind the Ligne de Recueil close to the Maginot Line forts themselves. This was not an easy task. For the forward companies of the Kensingtons, the order meant that their machine guns would have to cover the withdrawal of the infantry units.

When 'Execution Z' was initiated on 15 May all British troops began to withdraw from the Ligne de Contact and Ligne de Soutien. The Kensingtons' Battalion HQ moved just before midnight from the Forêt du Comte d'Hunolstein to Luttange, about 5 miles south-east of the old position, arriving at 0130 hours. They were joined there by B Echelon and the LAD.

The Kensingtons' C Company withdrew to Metzeresche, leaving two of its 15cwt trucks ditched en route. Apart from this and two cases of shell shock, the only mishap was the leaving behind of two officers and six men. One officer was reconnoitring other positions and the other went back to assist one section that had difficulty in getting out. The section was engaged right up to the last minute, giving covering fire to withdrawing infantry who were being fired on by German machine guns. One of the Kensingtons' guns knocked out one enemy gun with its first burst and effectively dealt with at least two others. Both officers and men got away and rejoined their company the following afternoon after a long march.

X Company withdrew to Luttange, the troops marching the greater part of the way. Their trucks had been sent back earlier in the operation and they had to march until trucks could be sent from Luttange to collect them.

D Company was to withdraw to Altroff and had the farthest to travel. Three 15cwt trucks were left behind after becoming bogged in the Forêt de Bouzonville. One section had been located in Colmen and took advantage of the arrival of mules of the Indian RASC which Sgt Greenhill had used to bring up rations (the first for three days). The animals were pressed into service to carry the guns and equipment for part of the journey as far as Dalstein, in the line of the Maginot forts. Altroff was over 2 miles farther on from Dalstein, but farther on forest tracks.

SGT PRATT AWARDED THE DISTINGUISHED CONDUCT MEDAL

During the withdrawal to Metzeresche, C Company earned the Kensingtons' first decoration of the war when Sgt Pratt's section put down covering fire in the Wolschler wood to enable a company of 5th Gordons, pinned down by enemy fire, to extricate itself. Sgt Pratt then withdrew his section without loss. The incident is touched on by Linklater in describing the difficulties of withdrawing while close to the enemy:

> To evacuate positions so near to the enemy's fluid line was by no means easy – a company of the 7th Argylls lost two sergeants and seven men killed by shellfire; a company of the 5th Gordons slipped out of the Wolschler, covered by a sergeant of the Kensingtons and his two machine guns and the defences of the Ligne de Recueil were by no means complete.[26]

For this Sgt Pratt was awarded the Distinguished Conduct Medal (DCM), a decoration for gallantry second only to the VC. The original recommendation for his DCM was dated 20 May 1940 and signed by Lt Col Gordon Parker:

> I wish to bring to notice the distinguished conduct of no. 2688669 Sgt. R. D. Pratt, 1st Bn. Princess Louise's Kensington Regiment (The Middlesex Regt). During the withdrawal from the Ligne de Contact on the evening of 15th May 1940 Sgt Pratt's machine gun section located in Wolscher Wood was withdrawing to Remeling. In the course of this withdrawal the OC of C Company 5th Gordons asked Pratt if he could give his company covering fire to get across the open ground. At least three German machine guns were in action against C Company 5th Gordons at that time. Sgt Pratt unhesitatingly got his section into action and immediately silenced at least one enemy machine gun and continued firing on the remaining guns until the Gordons passed through the section position. This action drew the enemy fire onto himself with the result that only one man of the Gordons was wounded during the encounter. The OC C Company 5th Gordons personally congratulated Sgt Pratt on his gallant action. Sgt Pratt handled his section with great skill and determination and set a magnificent example to his men. His conduct and initiative was all the more praiseworthy as his instructions were to get back to Remeling without occupying any intermediate positions. I wish to recommend Sgt Pratt for the Distinguished Conduct Medal.[27]

When this recommendation reached 154 Brigade HQ it was annotated by Brig. A.C. Stanley-Clarke: 'I do not consider that the action of this NCO merits the award of the Distinguished Conduct Medal and recommend that of the Military Medal' and was returned to Lt Col F. Gordon Parker, the CO of the Kensingtons. Gordon Parker's response is not recorded but can perhaps be imagined. The recommendation was then redrafted in the following terms:

> On 15th May 1940 Sgt. Pratt's machine gun section was ordered to withdraw to a rear locality without occupying any intermediate position. During the course of the withdrawal a company of a neighbouring battalion had to withdraw across some very exposed ground which was being swept by enemy machine gun fire. Sgt. Pratt unhesitatingly got his machine gun section into action and although by doing so he drew the enemy fire to his own position he so successfully engaged the enemy that the neighbouring unit withdrew with only one casualty. Had it not been for the imitative, skill and determination of Sgt. Pratt, heavy casualties would undoubtedly have been suffered. [28]

This document appears to have been forwarded directly to the divisional commander, Gen. Fortune. He approved it and Sgt Pratt subsequently got his DCM. Wood:

> **May 13th.** Rations came up as usual from Coy H.Qs. Improvement of positions. Chimay came round and invited me back each night to Coy H.Qs for dinner. Food obtained from Rocky and beer from Black Watch canteen in St Marguerite. Enemy planes active in morning. Went with Chimay in afternoon to visit Maginot. Much impressed by gun chambers, chart rooms etc and depth. In evening Farlander drove me to Coy H.Qs in farmhouse in St Marguerite. Coy transport parked in an orchard. Chimay produced champagne as well as excellent wine. Rocky arrived with rations and mail and I ordered some more whisky from him. Cigarette parcels also arrived. Shelling in the evening. [29]

> **May 14th.** Censored letters in my truck and ate some of Pte Farlander's birthday cake. Enemy recce planes over. Maginot A/A engaged them when they were out of range! Chimay arranged for baths by mobile bath unit at Vekring, half platoon to be away at a time. Left with first party at 14.00hrs, truck driven slowly so as not to raise dust and attract enemy observation on open road to Vekring. Showed pass at barrier and drove to shed in main street behind where bath unit was. Vekring was a garrison town and the new barracks were very clean. Most of civilians evacuated at start of war. Bought chocolate and champagne from French canteen. Saw 70 ton French tanks drawn up in 'Bois Militaire'. At dinner that night Chimay expressed the opinion that if the French had severe reverses he would never be surprised if they packed in. [30]

May 15th. All morning and afternoon enemy recce planes were active and heavy shelling could be heard from the front, so we were not surprised when at dinner we got the 'Alerte' through, Mike and I rushed back to our platoons as, when C and D Coys and those in front came through us to withdraw behind the Maginot, we should be the front line again. So much for our five days rest with all the digging, although it repaid us in fewer casualties.[31]

POSITIONS IN THE FRENCH SECTOR OCCUPIED

As darkness fell on 15 May there was considerable enemy activity, but the withdrawal had been successful and the battalion was in good spirits. C and D Companies had withdrawn from their forward positions in the Ligne de Contact but A, Y and B Companies remained in occupation of positions in the Ligne de Recueil. On 16 May the Kensingtons were ordered to occupy positions in the Ligne d'Arret behind the Maginot Line itself in a sector taken over from the French by 154 Brigade. The warning order specified that 154 Brigade, with the Kensingtons under its command, was to take over from the French behind the Maginot Line in the French 42nd Division sector. The positions to be occupied were in the Hestroff to Gomelage area some 2 miles south-west of the British divisional sector border. The moves were to take place before dark on 16 May. They would initially only involve C and D Companies, and company commanders and platoon commanders were to be prepared to reconnoitre the new positions sometime during the afternoon. C and D Company personnel attached to X Company were to rejoin their respective companies forthwith. A, Y and B Companies were to withdraw from the Ligne de Recueil and to move back to Metzeresch, Luttange and Altroff respectively by the routes already given and remain there until ordered to withdraw to the new positions. The new positions in the French sector were reconnoitred during the day by the CO and by the OCs of C and D Companies. During the night C and D Companies took up these positions and Battalion HQ moved from Luttange to Gondreville:

> **May 16th.** When dawn broke C and D Coys were safely behind us in the Maginot except for two trucks ditched in the A/T ditch in front of us, one at Kalembourg, the other at Laumesfeld. The troops had taken all the equipment etc out and carried them with them. At 06.00hrs enemy troops and a truck were observed at Hargarten railway tunnel. Later on a patrol was observed about half way up the road from Hargarten to Monneren in an orchard and they immediately (opened fire) with bad luck for the Black Watch who had some casualties. I went out with a covering party to Lamesfeld and Mike did the same at Kalembourg. It was tricky work picking our way through the minefields but after what seemed an eternity with the enemy possibly very close, the trucks were got out and driven off without hesitation to St Marguerite. Whilst at Coy H.Qs in the evening we saw a German officer and 2 O/Rs caught by

Johnny Rhodes and a patrol who were having a very good dinner with the Black Watch and were being well cared for. That night I was glad to get a large quantity of mail, magazines and cigarette parcels. Just before dusk the village was heavily shelled and one unexploded shell landed about 50 yards away from the Coy H.Qs which caused some qualms until the sappers cleared it away.[32]

The next day, 17 May, there was some air activity but on the whole things were quiet. One truck of C Company, left behind in the withdrawal, was recovered. The Germans had not followed up their attack and seemed to be content to leave the ground vacated by Allied troops to their own isolated patrols:

> **May 17th.** Except for shelling by an enemy mortar established in an orchard on Hargarten–Monneren road, nothing much happened the whole day except L/Cpl Parnell endeavoured to engage an enemy recce plane with a Boyes A/T rifle. At 20.00hrs severe shelling but most landed just in front or behind us until they ranged on Monneren and soon had it well alight. Soon afterwards the Maginot guns replied for an hour. That night patrols were active on our left and there had been talk earlier of shortening the line by pulling in the flank where Mike's [2/Lt A.R. Meikle] platoon and the Gordons met the French Division.[33]

On 18 May Lt Milton, the motor transport officer (MTO), managed to recover the second abandoned C Company truck. According to the battalion war diary the truck 'was most skilfully recovered … with the assistance of a bren carrier from the 1st Bn. Gordon Highlanders who were most helpful'. Lt Milton reported that sterling work was done by the small squad of MT drivers that he took with him to do the recovery and especially by L/Cpl Thompson. On the same day the OC of A Company, Maj. de Chimay, returned from a brigade conference with the news that the Kensingtons were to be relieved that afternoon by the 7th Royal Northumberland Fusiliers and that Company HQ was to move to Ebersviller. As well as this news, de Chimay brought back some choice wines and spirits and tinned food. The withdrawal of 4 Platoon (Reg Wood) appears to have been delayed and the column finally proceeded slowly and well spread to Monneren and crossed the Maginot Line at Veckring. The next day a despatch rider was sent to guide them to Ebersviller via Dalstein. At Ebersviller there were signs of civilians, who were being evacuated at only two hours' notice, and British troops were releasing tethered dogs and milking cows with agonisingly swollen udders. Here the word went round that the division was to rejoin the BEF and that the Kensingtons were to leave at 2200 hours for St Marie aux Chens, travelling by night. The three platoons came in at 2130 hours and the whole of A Company formed up in a line under the trees. The night was very dark and the roads were dusty and bombs were falling in the distance. Talange and Hagondange had been bombed and Metz had been shelled by long-range artillery.[34]

Around this time the battalion suffered another casualty. His name appears on the battalion roll of honour and a search on the Commonwealth War Graves Commission records reveals that his date of death was 'between 19th May and 23rd June 1940'. He may have been taken prisoner on 19 May and his death may not have been reported until much later. His name is listed on the Dunkirk Memorial, which commemorates those who were captured during the campaign and have no known grave. He was Albert William James Piggott, aged 23, the son of Lucy Piggott and stepson of Archie Woolmore of Greenford, Middlesex.[35]

DISASTER ON THE MEUSE AND GERMAN BREAKTHROUGH AT SEDAN

The respite for the Kensingtons was to be short lived. The French had experienced a major disaster on the Meuse River, which was to have consequences for the 51st (Highland) Division. When, on 10 May, the German Army commenced Plan Yellow – its assault on the west – von Bock's Army Group B struck at Holland and Belgium. The Allies had anticipated this, and British and French troops immediately crossed the Belgian border and advanced to previously identified defensive positions. What had not been anticipated, however, was the simultaneous strike farther south by von Runsted's Army Group A into southern Belgium and Luxembourg, driving through the Ardennes to the Meuse River and the French border. This was the *Sichelschnitt* or 'sickle cut'. If the panzer corps could penetrate the Ardennes and force the crossings of the Meuse the opportunity would be there for a drive west to the Channel. This would cut off the British and French in Belgium, into which they had been lured by von Bock, and cause them to be surrounded by Army Group B to the north and Army Group A to the south.

There are many accounts of the German breakthrough at the Meuse. They invariably stress the strength, and particularly the speed, of the assault. They show the inadequacy of the Allied response (notwithstanding the heroic but suicidal daylight strikes by Fairey Battles and Bristol Blenheims of RAF Bomber Command at the pontoon bridges over the Meuse). For the purposes of the present account, however, we need only consider the broad strategy of the German offensive and its consequences for the Highland Division, for those consequences were ultimately catastrophic.

At 0435 hours on 10 May Gen. Guderian's XIX Panzer Corps, with over 800 tanks grouped into three divisions, and with infantry, artillery and support troops, had crossed the German border with Luxembourg and thrust west through the Ardennes, arriving at the Meuse River at 1400 hours on 12 May. The first pontoon bridges were across the river by the early hours of the 14th and the tanks began crossing at 0200 hours with massive air support. Early on the 14th the French C-in-C Gen. Alphonse Georges burst into tears, exclaiming 'our front has been broken at Sedan'. Paul Reynaud, the French premier, telephoned Churchill and told him 'we are defeated, we have lost the battle'. By 19 May the three panzer corps had advanced 110 miles and were at the Canal du Nord, approximately 80 miles from the Channel. At nightfall on 20 May elements of the 2nd Panzer Division, after advancing an incredible 60 miles in a day, had reached the sea at Noyelles sur Mer near St Valery sur Somme.

Back on the Maginot Line one of the French divisions had been withdrawn on 17 May and belatedly sent north to support the effort to contain the breakthrough. On 20 May, the very day that German forces had arrived at the coast, the Highland Division was ordered to withdraw further and concentrate at the town of Étain, 20 miles west of Metz, prior to rejoining the rest of the BEF. The signal read: 'warning order. 51 Div is being withdrawn into reserve in ETAIN area. Move begins night 20/21. Details later but make all preparations.' On the same day a message for the Kensingtons arrived from Brig. George Burney, commander of 153 Brigade. Addressed to the CO, it read:

> I would like to express my appreciation of the excellent work done by the detachments of your battalion sent up to support units of this Brigade in the Ligne de Contact recently. They had a hard and difficult task which they carried out in a most commendable manner and their behaviour and cheerfulness were at all times deeply appreciated.[36]

It had been agreed that any British unit stationed on the Saar front would be returned to the BEF in the event of an enemy offensive. The arrival of the 2nd Panzer Division at Noyelles sur Mer on the Channel coast, however, now presented the unpleasantly inescapable fact that it had become physically impossible for 51st (Highland) Division to rejoin the BEF. The *Sichelschnitt* was complete and for the British, once reality dawned, it must have felt as though a massive iron gate had clanged shut on their hopes.

THE MOVE SOUTH-WEST

The bulk of the division moved on 22 May, and by the morning of 23 May was concentrated at Étain. Six of the infantry battalions were to travel by train, the remainder of the division by road. The destination for both groups was Pacy, 40 miles north-west of Paris. This, however, was the first of several French plans that were destined to be overtaken. Linklater sums up the confusion:

> The first intention of the [French C-in-C] had been to use the Fifty-First in the defence of Paris. Then, more urgently, the danger seemed to come from Montmedy and the Division was ordered to Varennes. But it did not stay. There was a day when plans were changeable as April weather, and every command was hotly pursued by countermand.[37]

The Kensingtons, meanwhile, had moved from Gondreville to St Marie aux Chenes, a distance of about 30 miles. A and C Companies, having farther to go, had moved via separate routes during the night of 20 May, followed the next night by Battalion HQ and HQ Company.[38] The LAD moved from Hessange and D Company from Drogny. All of these sub-units, with the exception of B Company, which was still at Menskirch, were reunited at St Marie aux Chenes.

From St Marie aux Chenes the battalion moved 25 miles to Hautecourt les Broville during the night of 22/23 May. The main column was preceded by an advance party under Maj. Walden, accompanied by the company quartermaster sergeants of HQ, A, C and D Companies. A recce party consisting of the regimental police and six motorcycle orderlies under the battalion intelligence officer also operated independently. The main column formed up ready to move at 2100 hours with Battalion HQ at its head followed by HQ, A, C and D Companies, the medical officer (MO) and the LAD. Vehicles travelled in groups of five, with 20 yards between vehicles and 250 yards between groups. No lights were shown save sidelights on group leaders and tail-lights on rear vehicles of groups. The route taken was via Auboué, Hatrize, Labry, Conflans, Buzy and Étain. Hautecourt was reached at 0300 hours. Happily, B Company now rejoined the rest of the battalion, having handed over to the French in the Ligne de Recueil, and moved from Menskirch to Hautecourt, where they arrived in the early hours. News arrived that the Germans had captured Calais and Boulogne, cutting the division off from the main BEF, but 1st Armoured Division had landed on 16 May and were along the line of the Somme with the French.[39] Two days were spent at Hautecourt, giving the chance to sort out machine-gun kit and make up deficiencies, but on the second day came disturbing rumours of the German breakthrough at Sedan which led to further rumours that armoured columns were close. Hautecourt was quickly put into a state of defence but no enemy appeared.

It was inevitable that the unprecedented speed of the German advance soon necessitated a change of plan, the first of several as the French High Command struggled ineffectually to contain the position. Plan two required that during the night of 24/25 May the Kensingtons were to move to Candy in the Varennes area, north-west of Verdun, together with the rest of the division, which was to support the French. Most of the division other than the rail party had arrived at Varennes by the early hours of 25 May, only for there to be a further change of plan by the French. Plan three reverted to the original decision to move the division to Pacy. An advance party left Varennes during the afternoon of 26 May with the remainder due to follow that night.

Many aircraft were seen and heard in the sky and it was decided to halt overnight in the grounds of a large château at Sezanne. Here they learnt of yet another change: plan four cancelled the division's part in any defence of Paris. French High Command had decided to hold the line of the rivers Somme and Aisne. The 51st Division was to remain under French command and hold the left flank of the

Somme, adjacent to the sea. The rail parties would be taken to Neufchâtel, 35 miles south-west of the Somme. The road parties would loop round Paris via Gisors, some 30 miles north-west of the city centre, and head north-east towards the Somme.

The next morning, 27 May, the Kensingtons moved again, at 0530 hours. The route to be taken from Sezanne to Gisors was via Montmirail, La Ferte, Meaux, Claye Souilly, Le Mesnil, Amelot, Survilliers, Luzarches, Beaumont, Meru, Chaumont en Vie and thus to Gisors. This route would take troops round the north of Paris. Although the original destination was Gisors, 15 miles away from it the column was diverted to Liancourt St Pierre. Here they halted overnight:

> The Divisional transport and the lorry borne troops travelled about 300 miles of French roads. The movement of soldiers is never a simple operation, and the Fifty First's march to the sea was made against time, in a country stupe-fied by sudden invasion, over roads that were roughly parallel to the German corridor and no more thaan thirty-odd miles away from it. From the Forest of Argonne, where men, wagons and guns had lain hidden among the trees, to the Haute Foret d'Eu, where they assembled for battle, was a three days' journey in drill order: over an indicated route, at an ordered speed, in a fixed density of so many vehicles to the mile. Supply points and staging areas had to be arranged. Advanced parties must be told off, road pickets detailed, motor-cyclists sent forward at such-and-such a time. The huge assortment of Vehicles – there were about three thousand of one sort or another – had to be marshalled according to their purpose and their kind: troop carriers and bren carriers, company vehicles an cooking trucks, blanket lorries in the transport echelon, water trucks, utility trucks and trucks mounting light machine guns for anti aircraft defence … the timetabled movement of Divisional trans-port through an invaded country; but the movement was completed speedily and witout appreciable loss. As far as Paris the roads were almost empty, but throughout the journey drivers were troubled by great clouds of dust, and despatch riders with inflamed eyes were temporarily blinded by it. Yet barely half a dozen vehicles were lost. Some idea of the problem of fuel supply may appear in the fact that during the final month of its existence the Division's average petrol consumption was sixteen thousand gallons a day.

> The train parties took a long route round the south of Paris. They too went to Vitry le Francois where, according to an officer of the 8th Argylls, 'the train stopped as a French ammunition train in the station had been hit by a German bomb about ten minutes before our arrival and was still in the proc-ess of exploding.' When the ammunition wagons had finished their feu de joie the troop trains went on and fetched a great circle by the Loire … then they turned north to Le Mans and Rouen, left the railway and took to the roads and the Norman woods. French buses bore them forward, buses that

were battered and bruised, fore and aft, by frequent collision, and pitted with numerous bullet holes. The drivers, French civilians, drove at a furious pace, and the column was directed by a French subaltern, with a megaphone, in a small Citroen that travelled more furiously still. This, providentially, was a day of heavy mist and pouring rain, the only bad weather the Division had till its last day came with a more wretched dawning. The long column, grouped far too closely on the open road, was protected from German bombers by cloud cover and the low sky: sixty miles were covered without mishap.

By cornfield and soaking pasture, by dripping orchard and dales that were full of mist, the Division advanced. Over the hedgerows loomed the spire of a village church, or the shadowy chancel of a ruined abbey. Above a river, pocked with the rain, stood the square keep of a fallen castle, and heavy trees disappeared in cloud over the low hills. Down the weeping roads, drenched and miserable, came refugees fleeing from the north.[40]

ARRIVAL AT FOUCARMONT: EVACUATION OF CIVILIANS BEGINS

The Kensingtons moved on 28 May from Liancourt to Foucarmont, a few miles south-west of Blangy on the Bresle River in the Forêt d'Eu. They were now close to the Channel coast and only about 20 miles from the front line along the Somme River. Now the battalion was held in the divisional reserve. Initially one company was kept at ten minutes' readiness and the company commander detached to 154 Brigade HQ as a consequence of the delayed arrival of the division's other machine-gun regiment, the 7th Royal Northumberland Fusiliers. The Fusiliers finally arrived in time for the Kensingtons to be stood down at 1800 hours on 29 May.

Lt Col Parker gave senior officers what information he could on the tactical situation:[41]

SECRET
DISTRIBUTION: List 'A'   28th May 1940

The following information is contained in 51 Div Operation Order No. 12

Yesterday the GERMANS secured the Bridgehead across the SOMME at ABBEVILLE.

An attack was carried out by Allied forces, including British Armoured Forces, to regain the Bridgehead but the final result is not yet known. On the left a British Force succeeded in driving the Germans back over the CANAL DE LA SOMME.

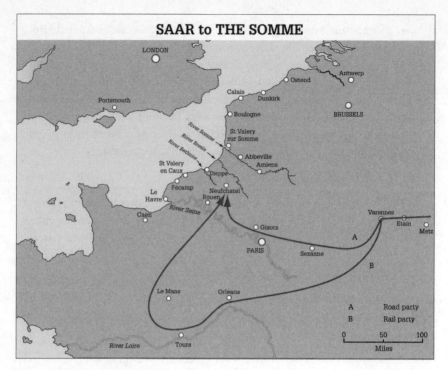

Saar to the Somme

The 51 Div has been allotted the role to hold the crossing over the R. BRESLE from incl SENARPONT to PONTS – ET – MARAIS with French Marines on the left. The Div. will be prepared to move forward when concentrated, to assist in securing and holding the Bridgehead over the R SOMME at ABBEVILLE.

The position will be held with:

153 Bde on Right
152 Bde in Centre
154 Bde on Left

O.C. Coys may send an officer to obtain boundaries from the I.O. if they wish to do so.

1 Kensingtons are at present in Div Reserve and have no role except to be prepared to undertake active operations at a moment's notice.

1/50,000 maps are being issued to Coys.

In summary, the Germans held two bridgeheads on the south side of the Somme at St Valery sur Somme and Abbeville. The British 1st Armoured Division had recently arrived in the area under French control. It was lacking its infantry brigade and one tank regiment. On 27 May, with French artillery and infantry, 1st Armoured Division launched an attack on both bridgeheads. The attack failed with serious losses. On 28 May the French tried again and failed. On 29 and 30 May the French made further attacks and were met with further failure. At the time of Lt Col Parker's briefing the 51st Division was to come under French command and take part in a further attempt on the bridgeheads.

On 30 May the evacuation of civilians continued using 30cwt trucks and a large French lorry complete with petrol that was pressed into service to assist the trucks. The evacuees were taken to the town of Neufchâtel. On a happy note, the battalion received its first post for a week, and large quantities of cigarettes and chocolate were salvaged from stores at Formerie and distributed to the troops. Companies continued to set up roadblocks on all entrances to the village. The next day, 31 May, the evacuation of civilians continued. In retrospect this was fortunate. A few days later, at dusk on 3 June, Foucarmont was bombed, causing great damage to buildings and resulting in numerous civilian casualties. The Kensingtons escaped with very few minor casualties and only slight damage to vehicles.

ENEMY AIRCRAFT AND PARACHUTISTS

At 1930 hours on 31 May a report came in from French troops on motorcycles that five German parachutists had been dropped 4 miles away in the vicinity of Blangy. A small air battle took place over Foucarmont and an incendiary machine-gun bullet fell near some trucks, setting the grass on fire. Lt Col Gordon Parker issued orders that all posts and sentries were to be warned immediately to keep a strict watch for the parachutists. All companies were to detail one officer to be on duty throughout the night, and a patrol of one NCO and three men were to visit posts and company areas continuously during the hours of darkness. All persons, whether civilians or soldiers of an Allied force, were to be carefully examined and any suspicious characters were to be escorted to Battalion HQ, where an officer would be continuously on duty.

At the same time orders were issued concerning the engagement of aircraft. At 1930 hours, the same time as the report of German parachutists came in, an aircraft bearing French markings had been fired on by the battalion's anti-aircraft machine guns. Lt Col Gordon Parker himself had personally stopped certain guns firing. NCOs in charge were not, in some cases, in possession of binoculars and obviously opened fire, although in doubt, because they heard other people do so. The greatest care was to be exercised by NCOs before they allowed their guns to open fire, and if in their opinion any doubt existed they were not to permit their guns to fire. There was in fact a standing order for the whole of the BEF prohibiting the firing of any anti-aircraft weapon during the day at aircraft flying between 1,000ft and 5,000ft that could not definitely be identified as enemy. It was considered 'much better to let an enemy plane escape than risk bringing down an allied one'. Company commanders were required to take immediate steps to acquaint Bren gun teams with these orders.

Lt Col Gordon Parker's concern about possible casualties from what would now be called 'friendly fire' was mirrored by directions issued by Gen. Fortune on 3 June and circulated (as below) by Lt Col Parker:

The Divisional Commander has found it necessary to draw attention once again to the importance of becoming air-minded. Strictest discipline will be exercised within the Battalion as regards taking cover when planes are signalled. It is most difficult to distinguish an enemy plane from a friendly one and the Bosche are reported to think nothing of flying the Allied colours. In these circumstances it is necessary to have an air alarm on the approach of any aircraft, and the all clear when the aircraft passes. The alarm – a series of medium blasts on the whistle – will be sounded by all A.A. and other sentries. On the alarm being sounded all ranks not on sentry duty will immediately take cover and remain under cover until the 'All clear' signal is sounded. This signal will be one long blast on the whistle. Experience has shown that except in an attack the Bosche is unlikely to bomb heavily any places unless there is quite definite evidence that there is someone there. On fine days Units and sub-units are NOT to risk sending out convoys of transport to the front line. If it is essential for certain vehicles to approach the forward villages or leave them, they must do so at long intervals and not at excessive speed, making a dust.

Bombing. The effect of enemy bombs is very local. It arrives with the noise of an express train and has a very excessive explosion. The Bosche employs this weapon to attack the nerves. In the event of enemy bombs dropping in the vicinity or localities occupied by sub units or men of this Battalion, the drill will be to assume the prone position with fingers in the ears. Deep slit trenches, preferably away from trees, should always be available for those not actually in the front line.

A.A. sentries. It must be firmly impressed on all ranks the A.A. sentries must not read books or recline in any way over A.A. weapons. All sentries must be properly posted and visited at irregular intervals. Any man found not doing his duty will be dealt with by Court Martial.

O.C. Companies will arrange to talk to the men sympathetically and intelligently about the effect of the enemy's bombs.

Operations on the Somme

51st Division placed under the command of French IX Corps and ordered to attack German bridgeheads – A and D Companies, Kensingtons, to support 1st Gordons and 4th Seaforths – Tuesday 4 June 1940, the attack fails – Wednesday 5 June 1940, Germans counter-attack in strength – Withdrawal to the Bresle River – The tactical situation after the withdrawal to the Bresle River – Withdrawal to Bethune River and the race for Le Havre. Germans reach Rouen – Ark Force formed – Recce troops of 7th Panzer Division get between 51st Division and Ark Force

51ST DIVISION PLACED UNDER THE COMMAND OF FRENCH IX CORPS AND ORDERED TO ATTACK GERMAN BRIDGEHEADS

Advanced Divisional HQ had been established on 28 May at St Leger in the Forêt d'Eu, south-west of the Bresle River. 'The Division was placed under the command of the French and ordered to hold the line of the Somme from Erondelle to the sea … with the Lothians and Border Horse taking over a position … on the extreme right from Erondelle to Tourbieres, a front of twenty miles or more.'[1]

The task was an impossible one and Gen. Fortune had prepared a contingency plan to fall back over 100 miles to the port of Le Havre if evacuation back to Britain by sea was decided on. Also in the area was another British force known as 'Beauforce'. This formation, subsequently renamed the Beauman Division, was an improvised force of miscellaneous units whose original role had been to guard British lines of communication between the BEF and its supply ports. When the BEF was cut off by the German advance these units were hastily formed into three brigades – A, B and C – under the command of Brig. (later Maj. Gen.)

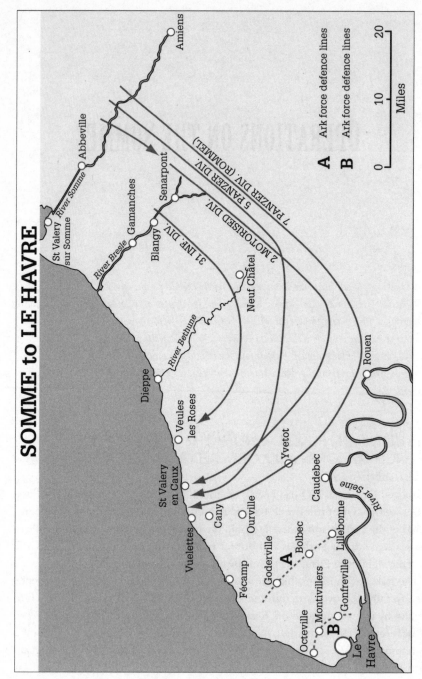

Somme to Le Havre

A.B. Beauman. Although the force became known as a division, its troops were neither trained as front-line infantry nor were they fully equipped as such. It included three anti-tank batteries and an obsolete field artillery battery but it lacked the full range of supporting arms that a regular infantry division had, most notably signallers. Despite its deficiencies, its units were to fight tenaciously and well.

The first day of June had found the Kensingtons still at Foucarmont; the evacuation of civilians continued for the next two days. Artillery thudded and rumbled in the distance on and off all day. The CO of the Kensingtons visited the 4th Black Watch at nearby Realcamp on 2 June since the plan at the time was for B Company Kensingtons to support 4th Black Watch in the defence of the Bresle River, the fallback stop line some 14 miles south-west of the Somme. This plan was to change abruptly when at 1515 hours a message was received ordering the CO and one company commander to report to 153 Brigade at 1600 hours. Brigade HQ was situated at Tours en Vimeu, 12 miles north-east of Foucarmont and only 7 miles from Abbeville and the front line. The CO had taken Maj. de Chimay, the OC of A Company, with him, and it is likely that it was at Tours en Vimeu that they were told that an attack was to be made on the German bridgehead across the Somme at Abbeville. After the conference 4th Black Watch left Realcamp immediately for Le Plouy where it was held in the divisional reserve. The CO and Maj. de Chimay reconnoitred potential forward positions. On his return de Chimay said that the aim of the attack was to force the Germans out of Abbeville and hold the Somme until the French had time to prepare positions on the Seine as far as Maginot.[2] There is no record of the response to this fantasy plan other than the decision by Reg Wood and his chums to dine out in style that night on the assumption that it would be the last opportunity to do so for some considerable time. They had 'an excellent dinner … with excellent wines'. The next day, 3 June, sub-units of the Kensingtons began to take up their positions. B Company moved to positions in defence of the Bresle River together with a battery of anti-tank guns and a company of Royal Engineers (REs). According to Ellis:

> 153 Brigade [was] in reserve on the Bresle between Senarpont and Blangy. The nine mile stretch of the Bresle on their right was held by an anti tank battery and a company of the Kensingtons' machine guns, with the Composite Regiment of the 1st Armoured Division behind them.[3]

A Company moved to Lambricourt. D Company moved to St Maxent. C Company remained at Foucarmont with Battalion HQ. With impeccable timing, thirty soldiers arrived at Battalion HQ as First-Line Reinforcements (FLRs).

The area over which the fighting was to take place in 1940 was quite separate from the area of the great battles of the Somme in the First World War, which had taken place about 50 miles away farther upstream to the north-east of Amiens. In 1940 the battle took place on the lower Somme, an agricultural landscape of small villages and farms. The enemy had already established two significant bridgeheads across the river, at St Valery sur Somme and Abbeville. Gen. Fortune was ordered to attack the bridgehead at Abbeville on 3 June. It was a strong position that had been held by the Germans for two weeks. They had had plenty of time to dig in and prepare their defences. The late arrival of French units made it necessary to put the start date back to 4 June.

A AND D COMPANIES, KENSINGTONS, TO SUPPORT 1ST GORDONS AND 4TH SEAFORTHS

The attack on the Abbeville bridgehead was to be spearheaded by the French 2nd Armoured Division and 31st Division, each coming under the command of 51st Division.

The Kensingtons' war diary contains a copy of the 51st Division's Operation Order dated 3 June 1940. It begins by setting out the situation regarding the enemy, who continued to hold bridgeheads south of Abbeville and at St Valery sur Somme. Elements of the German 57th Infantry Division had been identified in the Abbeville bridgehead and of the 1st Motorised MG battalion in the neighbourhood of St Valery sur Somme. An order of battle of the 2nd Motorised Infantry Division, found at Beheen, showed that this division had recently been in this district, but identifications had not been obtained. Reports from refugees and from members of the BEF who had crossed the Somme agreed on the fact that German troops north of the river were mostly members of motorised units.

The intention was that 51st Division, with the French 31st Infantry and 2nd Armoured Divisions attached, would attack and capture the Abbeville bridgehead. The general objective of the attack was to secure the high ground on the south bank of the Somme and to dominate the crossings of that river. Wood:

June 3rd. After an early lunch we left in my truck, taking with us our batmen, an orderly and rangetaker from each Platoon, to meet Chimay at Miannay. About a mile from Miannay we were warned by an M.P. that we were under observation from the enemy for about 200 yards so we went as fast as possible until we went down the dip into the town where Chimay was waiting for us at the cross-roads in his Humber Snipe. He said that our destination was Lambricourt, a small village about a mile to the west and we were to follow him carefully as a platoon of the R.H.Fs had taken the wrong road a day or two before and lost four trucks on the main road to Abbeville which had been shot up by an A/T gun. As we sped along the leafy country lane into Lambricourt there was a sudden whine and rush of wind and two shells dropped just behind us, shrapnel flew up on to the bonnet of the truck and without a word we all dashed from the truck into the ditch but fortunately no more came over. Evidently the enemy had observed us on the Route Nationale and only just misjudged the time it would take us to reach that section of the road. It was one of the closest shaves I had had from shelling and we all returned shaken to the truck and drove on into the village. Lambricourt was a small village lying in a dip, from the centre of which road ran back over the west to Lamantant and forward into the bois de Cambrai joining the Route Nationale outside Abbeville. Chimay showed us the empty and evacuated house which he had chosen for Coy H.Qs and having parked the trucks in an adjoining orchard we went up to the ridge in front of the village for a recce and observed the Grand Bois on our left through which the Gordons and Black Watch were to attack, the gap between that and the Bois de Cambrai to which it was thought the enemy would try to retreat to when the attack on the Grand Bois commenced. Nos 4 and 6 Platoons were to be practically side by side, 6 on the left of the road and mine on the right. Our task was to enfilade the Grand Bois just in front of the advancing Gordons, to cover the gap between the two woods and stop any nuisance fire from the Bois de Cambron. The position was not an enviable one, right on the top of the ridge, no cover and very hard ground making it very difficult to dig in during the few hours of darkness at our disposal and the necessity of maintaining absolute silence. Just on the left of my platoon was one of the 4th. Bn Black Watch, another on their left and another on the main road to Abbeville where we could see the trucks of the R.H.Fs which had been shot up as previously mentioned. In front of us were abandoned armoured cars and light tanks of the 1st Armoured Division. Mike and I proceeded to peg positions for our guns crawling about through the long grass to do so and chose places for our Pl H.Qs on the road back to the village where our trucks could also be harboured under cover of the trees. The Coy Cdr of the 4th, Black Watch was then told what time we should be coming into position and asked him to warn his respective platoons. On arrival back at the village we both stressed strongly the fact that better positions would be available on the hill behind, from which we could do overhead fire over our own troops in front and at the same time obtain good and uninterrupted observation. However Chimay said the Brigadier was adamant that we should be alongside the front infantry platoons. Mike was going back at 21.00hrs to lead Charles and the Coy in, who were due to arrive at 21.30hrs. Meanwhile we had time on our hands so explored the village. An old lady was discovered who refused to be evacuated and in the cellar of a house we found some barrels of what we hoped was Calvados but turned out to be extremely bitter cider. Throughout the afternoon desultory shelling went on, on both sides. At 18.30hrs Lloyd and the other batmen produced an excellent meal and we listened to the wireless and heard that the B.E.F. still left in France was holding the line of the river Somme with units of the French army whilst behind us another French army was being rapidly organised. At 21.30hrs the Coy arrived and our platoon trucks were soon in position under the trees whilst the rest of the Coy trucks and No 5, which was in reserve, were parked in orchards. When all the kit was unloaded and the platoons ready to move up, Chimay, Mike and myself went forward to see the Black Watch Coy Cdr and find out whether the area in front was clear of German patrols so that we could move into position [after which] we took our platoons up the road and into position. Previously the whole scheme had been explained to all the troops and above all the necessity of maintaining absolute silence. None the less they seemed to drop everything and make more noise than on training at home. However by 23.30hrs we were in position and everyone started to dig as quickly as possible but even so dawn found us with very shallow gun pits and an even shallower O.P. Thus we 'stood to' feeling none too happy or secure.[4]

TUESDAY 4 JUNE 1940, THE ATTACK FAILS

The attack was to start at 0330 hours on 4 June and was to be carried out in four parts.

Part 1 was an attack by 1st Gordons from the Cahon area to Cambron, supported by A Company Kensingtons and one troop from 51st Anti-Tank Regiment RA. The objective was to capture the spur overlooking Cambron by attacking from the north-west. Artillery support would be provided by 75th Field Regiment RA. The morning of 4 June dawned with the Somme River valley covered with a light mist. Harpur:

Half an hour before dawn on June 4th the divisional artillery fired salvo after salvo on to the enemy for nearly an hour. At times the woods in front were blotted out with flame and smoke, making it seem impossible that anyone could survive. When the barrage lifted, however, and 1st Gordons, supported by 1st Black Watch, attacked through the Bois de Cambron, enemy resistance was strong. Verey lights were fired to show the positions of the leading British troops, and the machine guns of A Coy fired belt after belt just ahead, switching their fire from time to time to the Grand Bois de Cambron from which enemy fire was being directed on to A Coy's position. As the Gordons neared the end of the wood heavy mortar fire fell on A Coy. causing several serious casualties, including Sgt. Bailey and Pte. Nesbitt, but the machine guns continued firing and the divisional artillery was requested to deal with the mortars. The enemy was now retreating across the gap from the Bois de Cambron to the Grand Bois, and afforded a magnificent target for the machine guns. As the Bois de Cambron had been cleared one of A Coy's platoons was sent there to support the Gordons in case the enemy counter attacked.[5]

This was the only attack of 4 June that was even moderately successful, although the Kensingtons did suffer several serious casualties. Reg Wood thought 'it was obvious that something had gone wrong' and recorded details in his diary:

Jun 4th. At 03.00hrs a terrific artillery bombardment of the two woods began, shell after shell went whistling over, landing with a terrific roar amidst dust, smoke and debris in the woods. In half an hour this crashing cascade of shells went over and it seemed impossible that anything could be left alive in those woods. At 03.30hrs a Very light went up on our left and the Gordons started their attack through the wood. Soon another light went up which meant we were to put down fire just in front of them as they advanced. We opened up and traversed along as the lights went up. We kept up this hail of lead for a quarter of an hour until the guns were red hot and by that time the very lights were only about 100 yards from the edge of the wood and the gap.

A red light went up then and we stopped firing. After an interval of 10 minutes a hail of M.G. bullets came whizzing over. We were directly exposed and I never felt so uncomfortable in all my life with only long grass in front of us and no protection at all. A Cpl of the Black Watch lying beside me was hit in the shoulder and an O.R. whose arm was touching mine was hit by a bullet there at the same time as he was shot in the heel. This fusillade continued for about ten minutes and then stopped as quickly as it had started. I crawled forward some distance to see if I could possibly pick out the enemy M.G. nests and thought I observed what might have been some camouflaged mounds about 300 yards in front of the Bois de Cambron. When I had crawled back to the platoon I found that [men] on the guns and personnel from Pl H.Qs had pulled the wounded back and were taking them down to the R.A.P. in the village. However our success was short-lived as a rain of heavy things shook the ground and we now found ourselves under intense mortar fire which I believe came from the road on our right. Sgt Bailey was hit in the back and Pte Nesbitt was badly wounded in the legs. The mortar fire was now getting almost unbearable and it was with great relief that we received a message to withdraw our guns from the ridge into the copse down the road but to have them ready to be rushed up again at a moments notice.

It was obvious that something had gone wrong with the attack as the Gordons and Black Watch should have crossed the gap to attack the Bois de Cambron. Recce planes were now very active and we kept well under cover as they 'hedge-hopped' over us. Of course we still had not yet seen our first R.A.F. plane in the air. Chimay came to see us and said that the main attack on Abbeville had failed due to the fact that the French tanks had all run out of petrol a mile from their objective thus causing, through their lack of support, the Seaforths to advance across open country swept by murderous M.G. and mortar fire. Moreover the R.A.F. had failed to turn up and bomb the Abbeville bridges. The Gordons had, therefore, stopped when they got to the end of the Grand Bois and were now consolidating their positions with the 1st. Black Watch and a reserve platoon had also been sent off. He added further that the Gordons casualties had been heavy. Whilst we were waiting in the ditches along the road M.G. bullets came whizzing over the crest but it mercifully stopped when a stew came up in containers from Coy H.Qs. Soon afterwards, Col Wright of the 1st. Gordons came round and congratulated us on the excellence of our support which had worked exactly as planned. I thanked god that I had worked out my safety angles alright. M.G. bullets continued to come over the crest and made life rather uncomfortable but otherwise the early afternoon was quiet.

At 15.00hrs Chimay came round with the news that the Gordons were evacuating the Grand Bois as intelligence reports stated that German tanks were massing and a large-scale counter attack was to be expected that night or tomorrow morning. The Gordons were to take over the positions of the 4th. Black Watch and one M.G. platoon was to stay and get in position with them along the ridge, the other to go back with Chimay over the ridge behind to Le Montant and the platoon with the Gordons in the Grand Bois was to stay with another Coy of the Gordons opposite the end of that wood. My platoon was to stay, so I again stated strongly that the ideal position was on the hill behind the village where we could get an uninterrupted view but as Brigadier Burney was not coming round until 18.00hrs nothing could be done at the moment. I therefore put my platoon into position again on the ridge and soon afterwards a large number of enemy bombers flew towards us so low that the faces of the crews could easily be discerned. To our relief they flew past us and then circled slowly around Marimay. Bombs glinting like large silver fishes in the sunlight came whistling down from underneath the planes, the ground all round us shook heavily and we kept as much under cover as possible until the bombers had flown past us again. After that everything was quiet again, the birds began singing, the sun shining, and it seemed difficult to realise that only a few hours previously this place had been an inferno of death, destruction and noise. The Gordons had now joined me and they were all very disheartened at having to withdraw from their conquests of the morning, particularly as it had been bought at a dear price, nearly half of every company involved being casualties.

Brigadier Burney came round and I pointed out to him very forcibly how wasted M.Gs were in this position and pointed to the better one on the hill behind. He told me to take him to it and on arrival there agreed that it offered a far better position. The range was about 3000 yards and there was no really difficult overhead problem. I immediately went back, loaded the kit and platoon onto the truck and moved up the hill behind to our new positions where I parked the trucks in a small copse and the troops immediately started digging in. I went down to the village and liaised with Capt Stanisfield, the Gordons Coy Cdr, and asked him to keep me informed of any orders for withdrawal. Johnny Rhodes was also there with his battle patrol which had done much stirling work on the Saar, and he had led the attack. Whilst we were talking bullets again came whistling down into the village from an enemy M.G nest sited on the Abbeville road. We rang through to the gunners to engage it. On arrival back at platoon H.Qs I found R.Q.M.S. Edgecombe waiting in a Battn H.Q. truck with mail and rations for the Coy. I told him that Coy H.Qs were at Le Montant but took off him our share of the rations and also mail which was especially welcome. Brackley soon had a good stew going and we ate a satisfying meal. The counter-attack was expected the following morning and I wondered with no A/T guns or tanks in our sector how we could possibly deal with the enemy tanks. The platoon was to 'stand to' in shifts during the night but everyone was to be ready for action from 02.00hrs onwards.[6]

There were three other attacks in the overall scheme.

Part 2 was an attack by one regiment of the French 31st Infantry Division, supported by one light tank battalion from the French 2nd Armoured Division. The final objective was the Somme canal west of Abbeville. This attack collapsed and incurred heavy casualties.

Part 3 was an attack by the French 2nd Armoured Division, supported by 4th Seaforths, a platoon of D Company Kensingtons and one troop from 51st Anti-Tank Regiment RA. The objective was to capture the twin ridges overlooking Abbeville, the Mont de Caubert spur and another ridge of high ground. The success of the whole operation greatly depended on this. Artillery support would be provided by the French 31st Divisional Artillery. The attack did not go according to plan. The French heavy tanks were late in arriving at the start line and lost the advantage of the ten-minute artillery barrage. Once they set off they ran into an undetected minefield and then fire from field and anti-tank guns. Casualties were severe but some reached the base of the Mont de Caubert and the Mesnil Trois Fetus and drove off the enemy. The light tanks which were supposed to support the 4th Seaforths were thirty-five minutes late in arriving, and when they did arrive were few in number. The Seaforths finally advanced to the left and right of the Bois de Villers, each accompanied by just three tanks and in the face of heavy machine-gun fire. Of the 100 men of B Company 4th Seaforths, eighty-three had been killed or wounded in the first minutes of the advance. C Company suffered equally.[7] The regimental history of the Kensingtons describes the attack:

The 4th Seaforths, supported by a platoon of D Company, Kensingtons, met with … misfortune. In the open country the tanks were speedily eliminated but despite this the Seaforths, supported by the Kensingtons' fire, went on against a stream of enemy machine gun fire and a hail of mortar bombs and shells. The casualties sustained were enormous, but without armour there was no hope of forcing the enemy from his positions and eventually, many companies having been practically annihilated, the attack was called off.[8]

Part 4 was an attack by 4th Camerons supported by D Company Kensingtons. The objective was Caubert and a nearby wood. Artillery support would be provided by 1 RHA (Royal Horse Artillery). The 126 men of the Camerons B Company moved off at zero hour and immediately came under heavy machine-gun fire after going only about 100 yards. One officer and forty other ranks survived. D Company also ran into heavy fire. Both companies encountered advancing German infantry at battalion strength. One platoon of D Company reached Caubert.[9]

The part played by D Company of the Kensingtons in supporting 4th Camerons is, somewhat sketchily, recorded in the Kensingtons' history:

When a company of 4th Camerons, supported by a section of D Company Kensingtons, advanced through the cornfields they were met by withering fire from well sited machine guns and mortars. Due to bitter hand to hand fighting it was not easy for the Kensingtons to lay down effective counter fire without hitting the Camerons, but whenever the opportunity occurred the Germans were given a great deal of their own medicine and this undoubtably helped lessen the severe casualties sustained. On the left another Company of Camerons, supported by a further machine gun section and French tanks, proceeded to attack Caubert and succeeded after fierce engagements in reaching the first objective, only to be met, as they advanced, by intense machine gun fire from a ridge dominating the countryside which was supposed to have been captured by the French tanks. Unfortunately many tanks were blown up by undetected mines or accurate anti tank gun fire, and those that did reach their objective ran out of fuel and so became casualties.[10]

In the Kensingtons' war diary on 4 June were written these terse words: 'An attack, to clear the Germans from the ground south of the Somme, started. The attack was not successful.' A Company had suffered two casualties from Allied artillery 'shorts'. One D Company platoon and one section had been in action and suffered six casualties. Two D Company platoons had remained in an orchard near Martainneville le Bus. B Company reported intense artillery fire and the presence of unidentified aircraft in front of the Blangy–Aumale sector.

WEDNESDAY 5 JUNE 1940, GERMANS COUNTER-ATTACK IN STRENGTH

The Germans had been preparing for a major assault against the Allies' hastily cobbled-together Somme front since the end of May. It was code-named 'Plan Red' (*Fall Rot*). The German C-in-C, Field Marshal von Brauchitsch, confidently expected to use his numerical superiority of two to one to break through the Allied line and penetrate rapidly and deeply behind it before the defenders could withdraw or organise new defensive positions. His confidence was well founded. There were 104 German divisions to take part in the attack. Against this the Allies could field just forty-nine French divisions plus the British 51st (Highland) Division and 1st Armoured Division.

153 Brigade was to the right of 154 Brigade and, in view of the seriousness of the situation, both it and 152 Brigade were ordered to withdraw. Sub-units of the Kensingtons were supporting troops in each of the three brigades and incurred several more casualties: Pte Tondeur was badly wounded in the back; Sgt Milnes, Pte West and Pte Paul were also wounded; and a section of Lt Lavington's platoon of D Company was overrun. Harpur:

> Enemy planes had been very active towards dusk on 4th June and Stukas dive bombed Miannay, completely blocking the important road junction there. On the morning of the 5th the bombing of Miannay caused the withdrawal of 153 Bde. to be carried out only with difficulty and under the close fire of the enemy, but A Company [Kensingtons] eventually reached its destination at Moyennevile. 153 Bde. were now along the line of Miannay–Hymmeville and A Company were soon called to their support. During a short action several casualties were sustained, including Pte. Tondeur, who was badly wounded in the back. Soon afterwards Sgt. Milnes, Pte. West and Pte. Paul were also wounded. On the right 152 Bde. were falling back to roughly the line Oisement–St. Maxent, covered by the Lothian and Border Horse and remnants of French 31 Division. Earlier on in this operation a section of Lt Lavington's platoon of D Company, Kensingtons, was overrun by the enemy ... throughout the day the enemy pressure was maintained, well supported by the Luftwaffe which dive bombed many units ... by now B and C Companies of the Kensingtons were in action endeavouring to hold a front larger than ever thought possible but nevertheless managing to prevent the enemy from completely splitting the Division into small pieces. It was now decided to try to hold the line of the River Bresle and a gradual withdrawal thereto would take place.[11]

The CO of 7th Argylls, Lt Col 'Copper' Buchanan, had already telephoned Brigade HQ for support and was told that the only reserve available was a single platoon of the Kensingtons. A heavy mortar barrage was opened against the Argylls' Battalion

HQ in the Franleu village school, which remained under small-arms and mortar fire all morning, with German troops actually probing into the environs of the village. Linklater:

> The German stream, by now, was driving the Division back along its whole front. As the incoming tide, advancing over flattish sand, comes in by sudden trickles or runnels – a channel here, a channel there – then, drowning the islets it has surrounded, goes on with never deviating purpose, though still by unexpected sallies, so the Germans found gaps and entry in the twenty miles of hill, hedgerow, village, wood and rolling field from Limeux to the sea. The front was too long, its defenders too few. It was a physical, a numerical impossibility to hold so long a line with only one division; but nowhere was it abandoned without fighting.[12]

Reg Wood wrote:

> **Jun 5th.** There was a very thick mist at dawn and it was impossible to see a hand in front of me. However at 04.00hrs it suddenly lifted. I sent a D.R. off to the Gordons Coy H.Qs in Lambricourt but he soon returned with the news that the place was deserted. As I thought the road behind us to Le Montant was probably cut by enemy forces I decided to go through Lambricourt and try to reach Miannay and then withdraw along the Route Nationale until I found someone. The trucks were hastily loaded and M.Gs mounted at the rear of each and with everyone grasping their small arms we shot into the village. About 50 yards away I saw out of the corner of my eye a German but we were out of sight round a bend before he realised what was happening, then as we passed the road leading up to our old position I saw a line of tanks halted at the A/T barrier which the Gordons had created. I thanked god for that, and again we were past before they could take any action. On reaching Miannay, the entire cross-roads were blocked by the massive craters caused by the bombing of yesterday afternoon, but as all the houses nearby were knocked flat it was a simple movement to drive over the rubble and back onto the road again.
>
> Soon afterwards I ran into Col Wright and he told me I should find de Chimay at a small village just off the main road about 5 miles back. As we drove along we found the ditches full of troops and we realised we were driving along the front line but there was nothing else to be done and soon we reached a cross-roads, turned left and went towards the village. There we met Chimay. He said that he and Coy H.Qs and No 6 Pl had only just got away from Le Montant in time and proudly pointed to a bullet in his truck. Apparently the enemy had broken through on our left flank at the junction of the British and French forces, towards Le Treport on the coast and it was

feared that some of 154 Bde had been cut off. Our sector had therefore had to fall back. No 6 Pl was in position in front of the village, No 5 had gone off to support the L. and B. Yeomanry at Oisemont and mine was to go over to a wood on the left about 1000 yards away where there was a Coy of Black Watch. I drove off and we harboured our trucks at the entrance of the wood. As the troops started to off load and I went forward to find the Black Watch we suddenly came under intense mortar fire from a hill 200 yards away supposed to be in the hands of another Coy of the 1st. Black Watch. Pte Tondeur was badly wounded in the back, Pte West likewise in the legs and Sgt Milnes (my Platoon Sgt) and Pte Paul were slightly wounded. We jumped on the trucks again and drove hell for leather deeper into the wood towards the Black Watch but we only came under rather wild rifle fire from the enemy who were where the Black Watch should have been. I decided that the only thing to do was to go back as quickly as possible to the village as we should be wiped out before we could have got the M.Gs off the trucks. On arrival there, the village was being evacuated and Chimay was relieved to see me as the Black Watch Coys had returned by a different route, having been driven out of their positions soon after I had left to join them.

We all retired to another village about three miles away and I left my wounded at the R.A.P. Chimay said that once again the enemy had appeared where he was not expected and I was to take up a position on the outskirts of the village with a Pl of the 1st. Gordons. The entire Battn, together with the 1st. B.W. under Col Honeyman were to hold a line along the village. Chimay established his Coy H.Qs in an orchard and suggested I put my Pl H.Qs there also as my platoon was only 100 yards away. Whilst seeing my sections into position and giving arcs of fire on the Route Nationale about 1000 yards away, an enemy truck appeared and was promptly engaged. No further sign of the enemy was obtained during the morning but a Coy of the 4th. Black Watch had been with us at Lambercourt earlier on came through having been badly shot up. An O.R. reported that their Coy Cdr had been badly wounded and whilst he and another were trying to help him along, they were overtaken by a German officer and troops. The German officer said it would be better to leave the wounded Coy Cdr with them as the movement would cause him great pain and he said he would take care of him and told the two O.Rs to go off back to rejoin their comrades. In the afternoon three enemy bombers came over and dropped a stick of bombs on the main road through the village. They scored a direct hit on a 30cwt truck close by us. Shelling was also active with many landing in our immediate vicinity. After tea Chimay went off to a Brigade conference and on his return said we were pulling out again that evening and withdrawing about 12 miles. He was leaving ahead and I was to follow the Gordons out who were bringing up the rear. As they would be marching, I foresaw a very uncomfortable night drive on a dusty road with overheated engines due to the low speed. I was to follow C Coy, 1st. Gordons out as soon as it was dusk, i.e. about 22.00hrs. In the break-through yesterday, he also said, the enemy had encircled two Coys of the Argylls, a section of Jack Lavington's platoon of D Coy and a Coy of the Camerons; the latter however had fought its way out. I went up and warned my platoon to have everything ready to move off at 21.30hrs and told them, meanwhile, to get as much rest as possible. After supper I lay down on some blankets on top of ammo boxes and with some petrol tins as pillows and although the shelling started again I was too tired to worry about the ammo or the petrol having had no sleep for 60 hours. At 22.00hrs C Coy of the Gordons marched out and I followed behind at a speed of about 2½ m.p.h. The night was as black as pitch and the road being dusty we were soon covered in layers of dust hurled up by the tramping feet. We hadn't been going for long when the engines of the trucks started getting overheated but there was nothing we could do except hope for the best. The drone of enemy planes was heard constantly overhead and they no doubt knew a withdrawal was in progress and the para-chute flares they kept on dropping were very disconcerting as they lit up the area all around for many minutes. Once again we sighed for our first sight of a British plane.[13]

At this point it may be useful to summarise the position in which the 51st (Highland) Division now found itself. The German armoured thrust west from Sedan, which had reached the Channel coast on 20 May, had cut the division off from the main body of the BEF. Including the Highland Division and the 1st Armoured Division there were more than 140,000 British troops cut off in the area to the south of the Somme. Many of these were lines of communication troops and base gar-risons. To the north the Dunkirk evacuation had ended on 4 June with a total of 338,226 British and French troops being landed in England. The attack on 4 June by the 51st Division and French units on the German bridgehead at Abbeville had failed. The German counter-attack on 5 June had inflicted heavy casualties on the division and left it severely weakened. Gen. Fortune consequently demanded and secured the agreement, albeit reluctant, of Gen. Altmayer, the commander of the French Tenth Army, of the 51st Division's withdrawal to the Bresle River, some 12 miles to the south-west. From this point onwards, rivers were to assume a very significant tactical importance. Linklater:

> Brigadier Stanley-Clarke, commanding 154th Brigade, had by six o'clock on 5th June withdrawn his headquarters to Dargnies [2 miles north-east of the Bresle], and the Brigade artillery had all gone back except for two troops of 17 Field Regiment caught at Ochancourt. Contact had been lost with 153rd Brigade on the right, and the enemy's forward elements were already

between Dargnies and the Bresle. Some of the bridges over the Bresle had already been blown. 152nd Brigade had fallen back to the railway line running north west from Oisement to the [Blangy–Abbeville] main road. Their numbers gravely diminished in the battle for the bridgehead, and now tired by a long day's rearguard action, the men were too exhausted to stop a serious attack.[14]

Back at the Kensingtons' Battalion HQ at Foucarmont on 5 June, C Company was moved to the Bois de Beaumont 'and remained on wheels' (i.e. was not deployed to static positions). B Company, from the Bresle, reported two enemy aircraft shot down by French fighters near Realcamp, and one German who came down by parachute captured by British troops. The Germans were advancing along practically the whole divisional front. There was considerable enemy air activity, including several dive-bombers, but no sign of Allied aircraft. Two bombs were dropped in an orchard about 200 yards from Battalion HQ. The two forward companies, A and D, were now pulling back towards the Bresle. On 5 June A Company withdrew their HQ and one platoon to Acheux, about 4 miles west of Huchenville and Limercourt and still 7 miles from the Bresle.

WITHDRAWAL TO THE BRESLE RIVER

At dawn on Thursday 6 June the division was spread on a line running north-west–south-east roughly 5 miles from the Bresle River, which was in front of and parallel to it. According to Linklater:

> There was no hope of holding this line. The division had orders to delay the German advance beyond it for a limited period only. Withdrawal across the Bresle was already decided, and the new front would run from Blangy to the sea. The pretence of holding, even for a day, an intermediate line between the Somme and the Bresle had to be abandoned. We had neither enough troops or sufficient fire power to meet the enemy's attack, the main stream of which was now flowing against our coastal flank. The Germans could no more be contained than water in a basket; our line, torn open on the left, was as full of holes as wattle, and there were no adequate reserves with which to close them. It had become perfectly clear that General Fortune could hope for nothing better than a rearguard action, by which he might punish and delay the German advance, maintain the cohesion of the division, and keep touch with the French formations that were falling back on his right.[15]

On 6 June a divisional operation order was issued, confirming a withdrawal that night with the intention of securing the line of the Bresle River between Senarpont, 5 miles south-east of Blangy, and Le Treport, at the mouth of the Bresle on the coast. Bridges were identified for use by different units and all bridges would be blown up by the REs when the last unit had crossed. Foucarmont, it should be appreciated, was situated 5 miles to the west of the Bresle on the disengaged or 'friendly' side.

At 1100 hours D Company Kensingtons moved to Biencourt, only 2 miles from the Bresle, but returned to Foucarmont late in the evening. During the day several German bombers had passed over the village and at 0445 hours two bombs had been dropped, one of which fell about 90 yards from Battalion HQ, doing slight damage. A British bomber had been brought down and crashed at Aubermesnil, 1 mile south of Foucarmont. The German advance had continued all day and a small enemy force actually crossed the Bresle and infiltrated woods south of Eu.

At 2030 hours on the evening of 6 June, Battalion HQ moved 5 miles north-west to Grandcourt. The second-in-command, the MO, B Echelon and HQ Company remained at Foucarmont. The next day at Grandcourt there was considerable air activity, both Allied and German, in the vicinity of Battalion HQ for much of the morning, but no bombs were dropped nearby. The following account from Reg Wood's diary of A Company's movements from 6 to 9 June shows the speed of events as the Kensingtons pulled back with the rest of the division:

Jun 6th. At last dusty and with red-rimmed eyes we reached a village at about 03.00hrs and here we were to stay until further information arrived. I fixed my platoon up in a barn and went into a farmhouse where I discovered a bed already made (evidently the owner had not much time to gather his things together before leaving) but just as I was about to flop on it, Hector Christie, the 1st. Gordons Adjutant, said another platoon of my Coy had arrived and I was to go off with them and join de Chimay. I got the men out of the barns and then followed No 6 Pl off along the dirty roads again and into the grounds of a large Chateau at Grandevilliers where 153 Bde H.Qs was situated and we parked our trucks in a long avenue of trees behind 5 Pl and Coy H.Qs. The time was just on 05.00hrs and we all immediately fell fast asleep. No one stirred until 09.30hrs when we were awakened for breakfast. Soon afterwards Chimay went off on a Brigade recce whilst the tired Coy carried out truck maintenance and gun cleaning. Enemy aircraft were extremely active and were bombing French troops moving up. Just after lunch Charles was called to Bde H.Qs and told to send my platoon off to assist the Black Watch at a village about 3 miles in front.

Half an hour later I left and after crossing a river was stopped by a French officer commanding an A/T battery and told I couldn't go on any further as the enemy were ahead. I told him the 1st. Black Watch were in the village across the fields but he shrugged his shoulders. However I had my orders so proceeded along the road across the fields. Half way across a hail of M.G. bullets skimmed the top of the truck from our left. We put on full speed and rushed down the hill into the village. As we entered the square I saw Germans lolling in the doorways of houses so I told Peach to drive in a circle and beckoned the other trucks to overtake us and speed on back up the hill. Fortunately all the drivers had also seen the enemy and they shot past us in a wide circle and when the last truck passed mine we followed them hell for leather up the hill. This whole operation took about a minute and we were nearly out of sight before the surprised Germans could take any action. As my truck disappeared over the next hill a few rifle shots followed us. Once again we ran the gauntlet of the enemy M.Gs. As we rushed along raising clouds of dust I prayed that the French A/T gunners would recognise us before shooting. Fortunately the officer did so although as we passed him his expression clearly said 'I told you so'. On arriving back at Coy H.Qs I reported to Charles and he went off and complained to Brigade. They said it was the first information they had had that the Germans were so close.

At 16.00hrs Chimay returned from his recce and said the whole Division and the French army were to withdraw across the river Bresle that night and take up positions in the foret d'Eu. For a change the French were to cover our withdrawal and were moving up a reserve Division for that purpose. Chimay said he was going off first to recce our new positions and told Charles to lead the Coy off at 18.00hrs for Millebosc. As we moved through the Foret d'Eu large numbers of scruffy French passed us moving up with even scruffier horse transport although it was noticeable that now the French were not giving the thumbs-up sign which they always gave when we were moving up and they were moving out! The road ahead of us was full of other divisional transport and as we crossed the river Bresle, fleets of enemy bombers roared over us and soon we saw bombs coming down just in front. A gunner convoy was hit which caused a stoppage of about 20 minutes and when we moved on we passed through a small town which had received the full weight of the bombs, burning trucks and guns, French soldiers and civilians lay dead and wounded amidst the ruins on the street and the burning houses. We skirted the craters and heard bombing again from further on and presently a car passed us on the way to the town, where there was an R.A.P., with a Brigadier wounded in the head inside. From now on our biggest worry was to dodge the panic stricken civilians fleeing into the woods.

Eventually we arrived at Millebosc and saw on the other side of the river Gamaches blazing merrily which the planes had bombed on their way back. In the village, besides ourselves, was a Coy of the 7th Norfolks, two batteries of medium and heavy guns, a 6 inch Howitzer battery and an A/T battery. Whilst we harboured in the orchard which Chimay had chosen for Coy H.Qs, some stragglers of another Coy of the Norfolks came through saying that the enemy had crossed the river and were in the wood on our left flank. Chimay at once sent No 6 Pl off to take up a position watching the road from the wood … My platoon was to go into position on a field on the outskirts of the village on the road leading down to the river Bresle and foret d'Eu in the direction of Gamaches. An A/T barrier was to be erected across this road and any civilians coming through were to be searched for arms in case they were fifth column-ists, and their trucks and wagons searched. As we started digging in rain began to fall and we were obviously in for a very wet and another sleepless night. A battery of 6 inch Howitzers was behind us and the battery Cdr told me that he was certain there was a lot of British infantry in the woods in front of us and on our left and that Chimay was flapping unnecessarily. Crowds of civilians came streaming through down the road from Gamaches. At dusk this stream of unhappy refugees, not knowing where they could or were to go, stopped and we settled down to an uncomfortable night.[16]

June 7th. At 03.30hrs No 6 Pl came down the road from the village and Mike said he was going off to join the Black Watch who were said to be in the wood about a mile in front. Breakfast came up in hot boxes from Brigade and soon afterwards Chimay came round to say he had been mistaken the previous night as the village had never been endangered and the 153 and 154 Brigades were in the foret d'Eu in front of us. No 5 Pl was being sent off to join the Black Watch too and my platoon was to stay in front of the vil-lage in case of counter penetration. 6 inch Howitzers and 25 pounders were concealed in the orchards close behind us and enemy recce planes were very active during the morning trying to spot them. Anything moving on the road from the village past my platoon to the foret d'Eu was machine-gunned by the enemy fighters and we kept well under cover whenever they were about.

At lunch-time I went back to Coy H.Qs and met Ray Milton who had just arrived on a motorbike to see if our transport was alright and had also brought some mail with him which was to prove the last we should get. I took the opportunity of giving him a field service postcard to send off for me when he arrived back at Battn H.Qs. My latest letter was Jun 4th. and was full of the success of the evacuation of Dunkerque. At 13.00hrs the wire-less announced that the British army on the Somme was still holding on tenaciously to its positions in face of insuperable odds – at that time we were about 30 miles behind the Somme! In the afternoon counter battery work was engaged in by both sides so we all kept our heads well down. At 18.00hrs I received a message to take one of my sections and report to the 1st. Gordons Battn H.Qs in the wood on our left in front. We waited until there were no enemy aircraft about and left at top speed, leaving Sgt Webb behind in charge of the other section. On arrival at Battn H.Qs in a chateau in the woods,

Col Wright informed me that we would not be required until the early hours of the morning when he would take me on a recce and show where he wanted my section. He invited me to dinner which I eagerly accepted and then went back and told my section to prepare themselves a meal and have a good rest whilst they had the chance. I had an excellent dinner with Col Wright, Major Hutchinson, the 2 I/C, and Hector Christie, the Adjutant, and then went back to my truck to get a few hours sleep.[17]

On Friday 7 June Capt. Holding, officer commanding B Company, sent a situation report to Battalion HQ:

> 7 Platoon area HODENG bombed 13.00 to 20.00. Nearest 25 yards. French troops in position near 9 Platoon ELLECOURT. Enemy aircraft active. No bombs yet. Outlook unsettled.

Later on 7 June, at 2355 hours, Battalion HQ moved again. Once more it was to the north-west, 5 miles to the Bois Ricard near Auquemesnil and only about 4 miles from the coast. There they were joined by HQ Company and D Company who arrived from Foucarmont at 0400 hours. The convoy had been bombed on the way and some damage had been done to vehicles. The MO was extremely busy assisting with casualties both civilian and from other units. Of the Kensingtons, two men suffered shell shock and three were reported missing. During the night news was received that Foucarmont had been heavily bombed causing considerable damage. L/Cpl Thompson (HQ Company) had manned a Bren gun and continued firing at enemy aircraft despite the very heavy bombardment. Wood continued:

> **June 8th.** I woke up at 02.00hrs feeling better having had a few hours sleep for the first time for six days, Having washed and shaved I waited for the first signs of dawn before going to report to Battn H.Qs. On arrival there I went off with Col Wright and my orderly in his car down the road through the wood towards the river. A very thick mist was about and he stopped the car just short of where the wood ended and we walked down towards the river. Col Wright said his C Coy was in position along the front of the wood overlooking the river and the hills behind and he thought the enemy were in strength on the hill and possibly had M.G. and mortar nests right down to the river. I prayed the mist would not rise as we were in open country and had a steep slope to negotiate before reaching the comparative shelter of the wood. After walking along the river for a bit we ran into a Gordons patrol and then went back to where we had left the car and struck along a path through the wood until we reached the Coy H.Qs of C Coy well dug in. Col Wright introduced me to Capt Culver, the Coy Cdr and then left. Culver took me round his platoon positions and showed me where he wanted my section.

Its primary task was a fixed line on the river where a bridge was blown in case the enemy should attempt (or had attempted under cover of night and morning mist) to rebuild it and was about 800 yards away; the secondary task was the road along the crest of the hill opposite which was at the moment shrouded in mist still. The positions which C Coy were occupying could not be called good ones being on a forward slope of the wood and amongst trees very closely planted together restricting considerably adequate vision of field of fire. Moreover the ground was extremely hard which would make digging in very difficult and laborious. I sent my orderly back to bring the section up and told him to bring the trucks right up to the Gordons Coy H.Qs in case we had to make a quick get-away, although it was doubtful if it would be very quick as the path through the woods was only just wide enough for the trucks to get through. I had decided to establish my Platoon H.Qs with the Coy H.Qs and had also left my D.R. behind at Battn H.Qs and requested Hector Christie to give him any orders for me which he might receive.

Whilst waiting for the section to arrive Culver said the Division was holding an 18 mile front! And if the enemy attacked in force there was no hope whatsoever of preventing a break-through. When the section arrived digging in was at once started, with the guns mounted just in front of where the pits were to be. About 06.30hrs the mist lifted. Soon afterwards an enemy plane flew down the river but we didn't engage it as we did not wish to give our position away. Shelling was also active but they mostly all fell about 800 yards behind us. Later on an enemy mortar opened up on an A/T troop sited behind some bushes about 100 yards in front and to our left. Most of the crew were hit and we managed to pull the wounded in but had to leave the dead behind. L/Cpl Essex crawled forward to the O.P. which had had a direct hit and brought back the only man left alive there, the Pl Cdr who was badly wounded. On his way back he stopped a large jagged fragment of H.E. from the mortar in the back of his head. Gordon stretcher-bearers took the wounded back to their Battn H.Qs and they were then taken to the R.A.P. at Millebosc in a truck. Meanwhile my section and the Gordons mortar had effectively engaged the enemy mortar. Towards lunch enemy planes were very active and to our surprise and astonishment several British fighters appeared and we saw an enemy plane hit and its pilot come down by parachute.

After lunch an order of the day came round from the French army commander saying there would be no withdrawal from the line of the river Bresle and every man would fight to the last man and last round. At 19.00hrs the French army commander issued orders to withdraw! Except for the bren gun carriers my section was to be the last out and I did not look forward to moving my trucks through the track in the wood in pitch darkness. The

Gordons were to start moving out at 23.00hrs and I was to withdraw at 03.00hrs and join my Coy at Dieppe on the line of the Bethune river.[18]

June 9th. The Gordons were late in getting out and I did not leave until 04.00hrs in broad daylight. Once we had left the foret d'Eu we put on all speed across the open road to Millebosc and in the far distance on a road parallel saw large numbers of German tanks moving. Near Arques-la-Bataille I ran into Johnny Padfield and C Coy who were halted and drawn up under some trees. They were making for Forges but had heard large numbers of enemy bombers about. However, I continued and just before entering Arques-la-Bataille a whole fleet was seen in the distance. We rapidly drove under some trees and they roared over us, the town received the full weight of the bombs and soon smoke and flame were pouring upwards. When they had departed we drove on into the town and saw some fearful carnage; horses, civilians and French troops all mixed up together and direct hits scored on the railway station. We approached Dieppe and saw columns of smoke arising and guessed that they had been bombed also. As we drove down the main road towards the harbour we saw Chimay standing outside a house which he was using as Coy H.Qs. He told me to put my trucks and men under cover in a nearby garage and then join him. He said as far as he knew Divisional H.Qs were being established in a wood outside Arc-la-Bataille and he was going later when all the aircraft had disappeared to find out what was going to happen to us next. Shortly afterwards large numbers of enemy planes appeared and we rushed down to the cellars of the house. Without any R.A.F. opposition the enemy proceeded to systematically bomb the town and a large R.A.S.C. depot close by was hit. A great deal of damage was done and several ships in the harbour had direct hits As soon as the raid was over Chimay said we would clear out so we left the town as quickly as possible. Half way towards Arques-la-Bataille more enemy air formations were seen but we were on an open road so could do nothing about [it] except stop and dive into the ditches. The planes roared over us but made no attempt to bomb or machine-gun us.

We resumed our journey and saw in the distance hundreds of enemy planes so rapidly pulled into a large orchard near Arques-la-Bataille where we found B Coy were too. The planes seemed to be about everywhere and thuds and clouds of smoke could be (heard and) seen in the distance. We stayed in the orchard all morning and had a meal after which Chimay went to Div and soon returned with the news that we were to join the Div H.Qs at Arc-la-Bataille and Nos 4 and 5 platoons were in Div reserve. No 6 Pl had withdrawn from the Brese with the Black Watch and were now in position along the Bethune river. We parked under an avenue of trees at Arques-la-Bataille and awaited further orders. Planes were active in the afternoon but otherwise we had no scares.

At 15.00hrs Major Walden turned up and said the French were really making
no effort to fortify the Seine and the Germans were driving hard towards it
in the centre, the situation was getting hopeless and the 51st Division was
going to retire on Le Havre and be taken off. Units had been formed of the
officers and troops of base details at Rouen and they were coming up to our
L. of C. B and C Coys who had had practically no action since we arrived
from the Saar were going back to Le Havre that night with Bn H.Qs and
154 Brigade to prepare defensive positions around Le Havre so that the rest
of the Division could withdraw through them. D Coy was to remain up with
the Division with the R.H.Fs and A Coy was to go back into Le Havre and
be in Battn reserve. So it was arranged that when No 6 Pl had rejoined us
we should leave for the wood where Battn H.Qs were, near La Chausee, and
spend the night there and leave for Le Havre at 07.00hrs the next morning.
As soon as No 6 Pl arrived, we left for La Chausee and reached there an hour
later. We were all soon bedded down and looked forward to our journey to
Le Havre the next morning.[19]

To strengthen the 51st Division and help it hold the Bresle, A Brigade of the
Beauman Division (formerly 'Beauforce') was sent to it. The brigade consisted of
4th Buffs, 1st/5th Foresters and 4th Border Regiment. Also with the 51st was part
of the 1st Armoured Division, the remainder of which was elsewhere under direct
French command. Harpur:

By midnight 6th/7th June most of the division was across the river, and
although all ranks would have longed for a good night's sleep it was essential
to dig in along the outskirts of the Bois Militaire running along the line of
the river. During the withdrawal, B Coy. [of the Kensingtons] commanded
by Capt. Holding, were left behind owing to non receipt of orders and found
themselves at dawn on the wrong side of the river, in the midst of the enemy.
However, as soon as the position was realised the company speedily cleared
out, cossed the river over a bridge not yet blown, and again took up their
place with the division right in the front line. Towards the coast the enemy was
already across the river but was eventually forced to withdraw after intensive
shelling and machine-gunning by the divisional artillery and the Kensingtons.
During the day many excellent targets were offered to the battalion by enemy
trucks bringing up fresh troops. The enemy air force was, however, very active,
and each brigade had its share of bombing and many cursed the absence of
the RAF. The wonderful feats of the British airmen over Dunkirk were, of
course, unknown, as everyone was far too tired by the constant fighting by
day and withdrawal by night to worry about what was happening elsewhere.
However during the afternoon of June 7th a few British planes were seen and
everyone cheered to see enemy planes being brought down.[20]

It had been a difficult withdrawal with the enemy in close contact:

> … most of the division had moved back towards the Bresle with the enemy closely following so that many times machine gun platoons of the Kensingtons were rushed hither and thither to lay down rapid defensive fire. As the hours went by the enemy never seemed to the tired British troops to relax his pressure, and it soon became apparent that the withdrawal over the River Bresle would have to be speeded up. Eventually orders were issued for the river to be crossed in the early evening if possible, and the new front would run from Blangy[21] to the sea, again a distance of over twenty miles.[22]

The Bresle front stretched from the coast inland to Gamaches. The 1st Black Watch held the line at Gamaches with the 1st Gordons to their left as far as the hamlet of Le Lieu Dieu on the opposite side of the river. The 5th Gordons were in reserve in woods near Millebosc. The 4th Black Watch held Incheville, the 4th Borders held the line to Eu and the 6th Royal Scots Fusiliers, a pioneer battalion which had been in the area before the arrival of the 51st Division, held from Eu to the sea. Behind the front line were what remained of the 7th and 8th Argylls, and also the tanks of the composite regiment of the 1st Armoured Division.

The 4th Black Watch had found Germans already at the Beauchamps river crossing but managed to force them to withdraw. At Ponts et Marais sappers blew the bridge while under mortar and machine-gun fire during which PSM O'Neil won the Military Medal. The Germans had already got other troops across the Bresle at Eu. These troops proved persistent and stubbornly resisted attempts by the 4th Borders and a company of the Foresters to winkle them out.

THE TACTICAL SITUATION AFTER THE WITHDRAWAL TO THE BRESLE RIVER

> Meanwhile the news from the right of the division was very disquieting: enemy armoured forces were reported to be closing on Rouen; if true it meant that [the division] would soon be cut off … A probing attack was made by the enemy … soon after dawn on the 8th but was beaten off with only a few casualties, of which A Company [Kensingtons] was fortunate in having only one. B and C Companies on the right were still holding an incredibly thin and long line and when it became known that enemy armour was breaking through in force towards Rouen it was obvious that, despite the French Army Commander's order that there would be no withdrawal from the River Bresle, something would have to be done if the French and British troops were not to be cut off.[23]

The Bresle, in common with several other rivers in the area including the Bethune River, flows from south-east to the north-west and into the English Channel. Some 40 miles to the south-west of the Bresle is the Seine River, flowing due west in a series of wide loops to join the sea at Le Havre. The Seine presented a huge barrier since it is wide downstream of Rouen and there were no bridges across it. The great danger to the British was the possibility of a rapid and outflanking German advance south-west of Rouen. If this happened the 51st Division would be surrounded by the enemy to the north-east and south-east and by the uncross-able Seine to the south. The next step would be another rapid German advance north to the Channel, cutting off any chance of reaching Le Havre and evacuation. Throughout 6 June there were reports that German armour had broken through on the right flank. Ellis and Linklater:

> Many of these [reports] were false or exaggerated, but in fact the German 5th and 7th Armoured Divisions had begun their thrust towards Rouen and their leading elements were already some miles south of the road between Poix and Rouen; their 2nd Motorised Division was to follow close behind; the 6th Infantry Division was coming up on their left and the 32nd Division on their right was only ten miles away. The German XV Corps Diary records: 'Avoiding woods, roads and adjoining villages and favoured by the gently undulating country practically free from ditches, the Corps advanced south-wards across country, deployed with tanks in front and infantry in vehicles in the rear.'[24]

> In the evening disastrous tidings came … The enemy's armoured divisions had broken through the French at Amiens, and were advancing on … Rouen. The French IX Corps was being torn apart … and the Fifty-First would be cut off from Rouen, which was its base of supply. Hurried arrangements were made to use Le Havre as an alternative source of fuel and ammunition. There was, however, no gun ammunition available at Le Havre, so a last train was loaded at Rouen, with shell and anti tank mines, and sent from there to be left en cas mobile in the neighbourhood of Foucart. But it never arrived. It was searched for and could not be found. The Germans must have inter-cepted and captured it somewhere between Cleres and Bolbec.[25]

On 7 June Gen. Maxime Weygand, the French supreme commander of land forces, had arrived at the headquarters of Gen. Altmayer's Tenth Army. He was described as being emotional and stressed. Asked by the British liaison officer what troops were guarding the line of the Seine River, Weygand's reply made it clear that there were now no French reserves available at all.

WITHDRAWAL TO BETHUNE RIVER AND THE RACE FOR LE HAVRE. GERMANS REACH ROUEN

During most of the day – the 8th June – our artillery was active, and so was the German Air Force. The enemy's mortars – ubiquitous, innumerably reinforced, magnificently handled – continued to do damage, and bren-carriers hunted his patrols in the Incheville woods … from the extreme right of the front came the news that inland the situation grew worse and worse, where the French, like the Stock Exchange at Budget time, were a prey to rumours. Not that rumours were necessary to create despondency: the truth was bad enough. Two panzer divisions, the 5th and 7th, were already at Buchy, fifteen miles north east of Rouen. With German tanks thirty miles behind [the division] there was no longer any hope of holding the line of the Bresle. There was no longer any purpose in fighting to deny the enemy every rood and furlong of the ground. There was no chance for the Fifty-First … of a retirement east of Rouen. The only way of continued retreat was over the Seine west of Rouen, where some motor barges had been collected and the regular ferries warned of what they might have to do. But the utmost speed would be necessary … the slow rearguard action must become a swift and decisive withdrawal.[26]

Orders were given for all units to withdraw to the line of the Bethune River. Divisional HQ and Battalion HQ of 1 Kensingtons were situated at La Chaussée and A and B Companies awaited orders in woods outside Dieppe, which were being heavily bombed and were ablaze in many parts. C Company was about to proceed to Forges when news was received that enemy armoured forces were already there:[27]

In the afternoon orders were issued that the division … would withdraw during the night to the line River Aisne–Bethune, running from Dieppe in the west to Neufchatel in the east. By this time all ranks were dog tired, having had no sleep for many nights, let alone a wash, and nerves and tempers were becoming frayed. In these circumstances it was amazing how determined everyone was not to be down hearted. That night's march was to prove the worst of any yet undertaken; the motorised units had to follow the infantry, which led to engines getting overheated; dust was everywhere and drivers fell asleep at the wheel through sheer exhaustion. To make matters worse enemy planes were constantly overhead dropping parachute flares to spot targets on which they dropped bombs. Dawn on June 9th found the division across the river with the exception of the divisional cavalry, the Lothian and Border Horse, who were covering the withdrawal and were still in touch with the enemy. It was obvious that Rouen would soon fall to the enemy and that the allied forces had no hope of crossing the Seine and withdrawing behind the line which General Weygand, the new French C.in C. was supposed to have established there.[28]

The division was to use all its available vehicles as troop carriers. But each round trip would be about twenty-eight miles and the roads were still crowded with human wreckage, with fugitives and burdened carts and broken motor cars. The arteries of France were choked and she was visibly dying … Withdrawal of the infantry from their forward positions was in some places a delicate process; but the Germans … did not interfere and from eleven at night till four in the morning the successive battalions were embussed and driven down the dark and crowded roads to their new lines. There had been no time to reconnoitre, and positions were not finally occupied till well after daybreak … The troops, tired though they were, set to work on defensive positions; but the Germans did not closely follow the withdrawal.[29]

The Kensingtons were clearly quite widely scattered at this stage. Sgt Tussler, for example, was commanding 9 Platoon of B Company during its withdrawal from Ellecourt on the Bresle to Neufchâtel, a distance of 15 miles. On reaching Neufchâtel it was discovered that one NCO and seven privates were missing. With two volunteers, Ptes Hunnigan and Lucas, Sgt Tussler returned to Ellecourt to search for them. This search, unfortunately unsuccessful, was carried out in ignorance of enemy movements and under repeated bombing.

The indefatigable Capt. Padfield, OC C Company Kensingtons, sent a somewhat disgruntled message to the adjutant on 8 June:

General situation today about the same. Scanty information indicates unknown quantity of troops from Borders & Buffs … in front from line running roughly from Eu to position in Foret d'Eu left of Incheville. Company Sherwood Foresters came in last evening and pushed forward into forest this morning. Contact with enemy established with, it is understood, favourable results. Brigadier's intention now split Company into Platoons attached to infantry battalions. Preliminary warning order move forward to St. Pierre attached unknown infantry battalion to assist repel Bosche counter attack. Moving approx 14.00 hours though no specific instructions to hand. Imagine similar roles other platoons if reported reinforcement rumours correct … will advise earliest moment. Have instructed platoon commanders they insist on feasibility of task. This village infested our artillery who fired the whole of last night. No information available as to effect. Bosche shelling forward rather weakly direction Eu with apparently little effect. Increasingly impertinent overhead despite our few fighters. Have stationed D.R. at Brigade

1 Charles Frost, at Pirbight soon after enlisting in March 1938.

2 Sgt Thompson instructing in gun drill, 1939.

3 Cpl Ted Simmons, 1939.

4 Lt Reg Wood.

5 No.1 Section, 8 Platoon, B Company Kensingtons. Reculver, August 1940.

6 1st Kensingtons, sergeants' mess, Hothfield Place, Ashford, September 1940.

7 Sgt Ted Simmons, 1940.

8 Sgt Ted Simmons, 1942.

9 Lt Reg Wood, VJ Day, 1945.

10 Charles Frost WO3 Platoon Commander.

HQ. Awaiting promised visit of M.O. and request water truck local supply having dried up. In view of splitting up of Company point out difficulty of unified command. Everybody fit.

On 8 June Weygand finally and belatedly ordered the French IX Corps and 51st Division to withdraw to Rouen and cross the Seine. It was far too late. German armour was already in the process of carrying out another spectacular advance, led by Rommel's 7th Panzer Division. They were only four hours from Rouen. On 6 June they had advanced a farther 12 miles south before turning south-east towards Rouen. By 9 June the city was in German hands. The 51st Division was now cut off. Gen. Fortune knew that now the only way in which he could reasonably expect to save his division was by evacuation from Le Havre. There was, however, still the matter of the time it would take the non-mechanised French IX Corps to get there.

With the German armour at Rouen, and the bridges there across the Seine blown, Gen. Fortune decided to make for Le Havre in four stages. It was 60 miles away and the French horse-drawn transport could only manage 15 miles a day. The plan was therefore to reach Le Havre on 13 June. Orders were given to withdraw from the Bresle towards the next river, the Bethune. From now on it was to be a race to get to Le Havre before the enemy got to the Channel coast and blocked the 51st Division's escape route.

ARK FORCE FORMED

By the morning of 9 June the division was dug in across the Bethune with four battalions holding defensive positions along the river from Dieppe to Martigny. They included the 2nd/7th Duke of Wellington's Regiment, a lines of communication unit which had been guarding Dieppe. Ellis:

> Fortunately the enemy were slow to follow up the withdrawal, perhaps because they were delayed at two of the Bresle crossings which were held by D Company of the 4th Border Regiment and A Company of the 1st/5th Sherwood Foresters. Orders for the withdrawal failed to reach these two companies and in default of orders to move they stood fast. For six days they held on, denying for that week the passage of the river which they had been ordered to guard. Not only did they beat off all the enemy's attacks and withstand his efforts to dislodge them, but they made prisoner of some of their attackers. Only on June 13th when the Germans had brought up artillery and mortars to reduce their position and when they learnt that all other fighting north of the Seine had ceased, did they at last yield. It was a soldierly performance in the best tradition.[30]

At this point Gen. Fortune must have realised that there was now a serious risk that the enemy would get round behind him and cut the route to Le Havre. At Arques la Bataille on the evening of 9 June he held a divisional conference to explain the situation to his brigade commanders. Le Havre was now the only suitable and accessible evacuation port. He had decided that it was essential to send a strong force ahead to secure and hold the approaches to Le Havre. This force was to be called 'Ark Force' and would consist of all of 154 Brigade, A Brigade, 6th Royal Scots Fusiliers, two artillery field regiments, an anti-tank battery and three companies of engineers. Most significantly for the Kensingtons, Battalion HQ together with B, C and HQ Companies were also to go with Ark Force, leaving A and D Companies with the main body of the division. It was a sound tactical move to take steps to secure the route ahead, but it was going to be a tight race, and the commander of Ark Force, Brig. Stanley-Clarke, was told categorically by Fortune that if the rest of the division was cut off Ark Force was to head on at full speed to Le Havre with the object of evacuation. With the situation as critical as it was there was no time to lose units; Ark Force began to move out immediately. The wisdom of this would be apparent the next day. The three companies of the Kensingtons left La Chaussée at 2130 hours. By 0630 hours on 10 June HQ and HQ Company were at Contremoulins, 6 miles south-east of Fécamp. B and C Companies arrived at 1030 hours. A and D Companies, in the words of the war diary, 'remained forward'.

In creating Ark Force and detaching it from the rest of the division Gen. Fortune had consciously broken a cardinal rule of military strategy: the injunction that a force should never be divided. One might wonder whether he had seen an opportunity to combine a tactically necessary and justifiable task of reconnaissance in force with the chance of giving a large proportion of his division at least some chance of escape through Le Havre. In his signal to the War Office he had made it clear that in the event of being cut off from Le Havre he would 'pivot on one of the northern ports' in the hope of evacuating 'a few' men. He must have known by 9 June that the chances of saving the division by doing that were then very slim, but Ark Force would at least give over 4,000 men some hope. We must, however, also take into account the urgent request for help received from Lt Col Butler, commander of the British garrison at Le Havre.[31]

At 1137 hours on 9 June, a prescient, not to say valedictory, message was sent by Gen. Fortune to the War Office:

> Ninth Corps including French divisions and two weak cavalry divisions moving west to Le Havre 51 Division on sea. Sending rearguard to reinforce French on line Fecamp–Lillebonne. My speed depends on French movement about 20 kilos a day. Tomorrow morning line should be Dieppe. Essential that air delay enemy movement especially A.F.V. to south on Saint Saens-Bolbec road also his infantry advance from east. Air support requested to prevent unrestrained bombing. Naval support along coast also of great moral support. If

enemy break through French or cut me off from Le Havre, will attempt pivot on one of northern ports ... in hope of evacuating a few men from behind bridgehead. My rearguard assisting French Fecamp–Lillebonne has orders to drive on Le Havre to attempt embarkation of as many men as possible.[32]

RECCE TROOPS OF 7TH PANZER DIVISION GET BETWEEN 51ST DIVISION AND ARK FORCE

The extreme danger of the 51st Division's position was demonstrated on Monday 10 June when reports came in of further probing advances by German armour:

To Divisional Headquarters at La Chaussee the early morning of the 10th had brought the news that German tanks were approaching Dieppe from the neighbourhood of Totes, which the French were believed to be holding. This report came in at half past five. An hour later it was confirmed by information that the tanks were then within six miles of La Chaussee. Two pounder anti tank guns were ordered to block the road, and at eight o'clock the tanks were temporarily halted after they had advanced another three miles. This was the altered situation which Major Johnston had to report to the commander of Ark Force ... and within a few hours of his leaving the apparent isolation of the Division had become a certainty. News came that enemy tanks had been seen west of the river Durdent, which empties itself into the Channel some five or six miles beyond St. Valery, and the hope of withdrawing to Le Havre had to be discarded.[33]

There was more bad news. At about 1100 hours on 10 June, a wireless lorry, sent after Ark Force to maintain radio contact, had run into reconnaissance troops of the 7th Panzer Division on the main road to Fécamp. The signaller, with great presence of mind, managed to get off a message before he was captured. Ark Force had just got out in time but the enemy were now between 51st Division and Le Havre. To find the enemy so close, in an area behind the division and thought to be secure, must have been shocking. In order to establish the Germans' strength and dispositions the Lothians and Border Yeomanry, as the divisional armoured reconnaissance regiment, were sent forward. They were accompanied by an anti-tank battery and Reg Wood's 4 Platoon of A Company Kensingtons:

As definite news of the enemy was very vague a mixed recce force was hastily gathered together at Divisional HQ consisting of the Lothian and Border Horse, commanded by Lt. Col. Lord Ansell, an anti-tank battery of 51 Anti Tank Regiment RA. commanded by Major Peacock, and a machine gun platoon of A Company Kensingtons, under the command of Lt. Wood. This force was to proceed along three parallel roads towards Fecamp and Le Havre in three bounds and report each bound clear to Divisional HQ, and deal if possible with any opposition. The division was to follow up gradually ready, for instant battle, with French IX Corps on the flank. The recce unit threaded its way towards Fecamp, and only on the left flank was serious opposition encountered and suitably dealt with. Nearing Fecamp it was obvious there were considerable forces between this town and Le Havre and there was no alternative but to prepare to defend St. Valery and trust in the Navy. A recce was thereupon made of this area and local opposition speedily eliminated.[34]

This account of the reconnaissance needs to be treated with some caution. The job of an armoured recce regiment is always, by its nature, dangerous, and in this case the Yeomanry in their thinly armoured light tanks, armed only with machine guns and their Bren gun carriers, were probing forward against reconnaissance units of Rommel's 7th Panzer Division. Crossings of the Durdent River at both Cany and Veulettes were found to be in enemy hands and the Yeomanry suffered casualties in the skirmishing there. Rommel had reached the Channel coast at Les Petits Dalles, 10 miles east of Fécamp, in the afternoon of 10 June. His orders that morning had been unambiguous. The 7th Panzer Division was to strike north to the sea as fast as possible with light reconnaissance vehicles and armoured cars pushing ahead of the armour. These, as already mentioned, ensured that their presence was known, thus spreading alarm and panic among the civilian population and clashing with British armoured recce troops in the area.

Wood describes 4 Platoon's experience with the recce force, which advanced as far west as Fécamp:

Jun 10th. At 06.00hrs Maj. de Chimay came and said the enemy had broken through and we were to go to the support of the 51st A/T Regt at a small village close by. We reached the H.Qs of the A/T Regt and each platoon was told off to a separate battery. Mine was about ½ mile away and guarding a cross-roads and a railway line to Le Havre. French troops were moving both ways obviously very fed up and with their morale completely gone. A few tanks were seen in the neighbourhood but they disappeared before the A/T guns could engage them. Soon after the inevitable stew had arrived from Coy H.Qs. At 13.00hrs I had a message to report back with the platoon to Coy H.Qs and there Chimay told me I was to report to Div H.Qs. As I drew near the village I saw a German bomber on the ground which a Bofors A/A gun had brought down. On arrival I was told to report to Lt Col Lord Anson, the C.O. of the Lothian and Border Horse, a tank unit, which was the 51 Div cavalry. He said that reconnaissance tank units of the Germans had been seen near Forges and Rouen, and convoys moving along the Route Nationale to Le Havre had been fired on by the enemy. A mopping-up party was therefore being formed of his own unit, 1 A/T battery and 1 M.G.

platoon (mine) and was to move in bounds to Le Havre reporting each found clear to Div which would then follow up. Opposition, if light, would be dealt with on the spot; if heavy, reserves would be called up and alternative routes worked out for the Division. One squadron of tanks was to take the main route to Le Havre along the Route Nationale, another with Battn H.Qs, my platoon and the A/T battery were to take a minor road in the centre and the other squadron the coast road and tracks. Wireless communication was to be maintained throughout, from squadron to Battn H.Qs and thence back to Division.

At 17.00hrs after a good meal we left and completed the first bound without anything of note happening. Soon afterwards, however, firing was heard on our left and that squadron reported German tanks in vicinity across their front and possibly spreading towards us. The column was stopped, the A/T gunners rushed their guns out and we mounted our Vickers alongside them. Heavy firing continued for some time until the message came through that the opposition had been liquidated. Soon after we had moved on a message came from the squadron on the coast road for a M/G. section as a number of enemy infantry were on a hill outside a village. This was sent off and when we heard that the obstacle had been overcome we moved on again and later reached the outskirts of Fecamp where an old gentleman rushed out of his house, gave me a bottle of Calvados, and before I could thank him had rushed back to his house again. Fecamp was blazing as its oil tanks had been bombed a few hours previously but there were several British merchant ships lying off the shore. Near the harbour we met some sailors who said they had orders to wait and see if anyone wanted to be evacuated. We explained the situation to them and asked for the town major but that individual was drunk as a lord and had barricaded himself in his office and refused to come out. A message now came through that the squadron on the Route Nationale had encountered heavy opposition and had seen large formations of enemy tanks approaching Fecamp. We therefore withdrew some distance, [advised] Division and harboured for the night in a small village near Veules-les-Roses and not far from St Valery en Caux. The village was put in a state of defence and whilst some rested, others watched and waited.[35]

As recounted, the so-called 'mopping up party' had found itself with more mopping to do than it had expected. The divisional cavalry unit, the Lothians and Border Horse Yeomanry, provided light armoured support with their Vickers Mk VI tanks and had been ordered to recce the Durdent River east of St Valery. They found the enemy in possession of the bridge at Cany, in considerable strength at Veulettes on the coast, and all of the intervening bridges blown. Two of the Yeomanry tanks were knocked out at Cany, and at Veulettes C Squadron was told to hold the village at all costs. Despite reinforcements being sent, the Yeomanry were forced back towards St Valery.

It now became clear to Gen. Fortune that escape from Le Havre was no longer an option. The last remaining hope now was St Valery en Caux. Orders were given to withdraw there. A signal was sent to the War Office: '… can I be assured that if I cannot bring my division to Havre I can count on your being able to embark personnel from north coast? Have only two days' rations.'[36] Wood:

Jun 11th. Early in the morning a message came through from Division that it was hoped to evacuate the Division and the French army that night from St Valery en Caux as it was impossible for us to get through to Le Havre. The C.O. of the Lothians was to make a recce for positions for forming a perimeter around the town. Accordingly he took the A/T Commander and myself in a bren-gun carrier and we made a circle of about 10 miles from the town and earmarked positions for a Brigade of supporting troops. Soon afterwards, however, General Fortune said he could only spare two Battns, the 1st. Black Watch and the 1st. Gordons together with the R.N.Fs and Lothians to hold the perimeter on the east flank and on the west would be the French of whose support he was very dubious as the Corps Commander had already tried to send a message of surrender to the Germans.

A and D Coys of the Kensingtons were to establish themselves on the cliffs west and east of St Valery respectively to prevent counter penetration by the enemy along the beaches and flanks and also if necessary to fire at any sign of the boats being rushed, this particularly referred to the French troops who were to embark on one part of the beach and harbour whilst we had the remainder.

When the main force had been evacuated the Lothians and R.N.Fs were to withdraw through us and be taken off and then we were to go and last of all the Gordons and Black Watch. Our chances and those of the Gordons and Black Watch of being taken off seemed very slight as we were not due to leave until 03.00hrs when it would be daylight, even assuming everything went according to plan. Just as we were about to split up and go to our various destinations, a large body of troops in the distance started firing on us. We immediately unleashed the tanks who went forward and it transpired that they were French troops mistaking us for the enemy. I then left with my platoon for St Valery but on a road leading to the village we were suddenly fired on so we rapidly reversed and went onto another road also leading into St Valery. As I passed through Cailleville I was amazed to see Div H.Qs there as they were supposed to be in St Valery. A minute later I saw de Chimay and he said the French had let the enemy through on the east and Div H.Qs had had to beat a hasty retreat to Cailleville. Meantime operations were in progress to clear the enemy out of St Valery and I was to stay with him. I was sent to put my guns in action on the road leading from Cailleville to St Valery and to stay there until dusk and move them into a position on the cliffs overlooking the town. No 6 Pl was away with an A/T battery and No 5 was with de Chimay still. At 14.00hrs the enemy patrols had been driven out and well away from St Valery and Div H.Qs had returned there.

Meanwhile enemy tanks had been seen in our rear coming from the Rouen direction and supported by infantry. 25 pounders of the 23rd. Field Regt were rushed up and fired point blank at a range of 500–800 yards at the tanks. Some horse-drawn French guns came galloping into Cailleville and we thought 'good, their help will make a lot of difference' but the French unhitched the horses from the guns and ammo limbers and galloped away as fast as they could on their horses. The enemy attack was soon dispersed but enemy planes were overhead the whole time and St Valery was the target of many attacks as well as any troops seen moving about. Several times Cailleville was machine-gunned from the air. At 16.00hrs another large bombing attack was made on St Valery which left it well ablaze.[37]

ST VALERY EN CAUX

UNSUITABILITY OF ST VALERY AS AN EVACUATION PORT

St Valery en Caux was dangerously unsuitable as an evacuation port. It is situated in a break in the 300ft-high chalk cliffs through which the railway and the main road ran. The harbour was very small, and dried out at low tide. Most dangerously of all, if the enemy could seize and secure the clifftops they would command both town and harbour, as well as the sea approaches.

On 10 June the Royal Navy had sent three destroyers, *Bulldog*, *Boadicea* and *Ambuscade*, with orders to investigate potential embarkation sites from Fécamp, west of St Valery, to Dieppe in the east. Near St Valery HMS *Ambuscade* was hit by shells from an artillery battery of the 7th Panzer Division. At Veulettes, HMS *Boadicea* was taking sixty troops off the beaches when she was heavily engaged by another battery. Linklater adds that the ships were off St Valery on the night of 10 June and that boats sent into the harbour found no troops there except for a number of wounded, which were taken off by the tug *Stalwart*. Early on 11 June the destroyer HMCS *Restigouche* went to Veules les Roses and took some troops off the beach.[1] After this incident further close inshore operations by warships in daylight were forbidden.

The War Office was still insistent that since the 51st Division was under the command of IX Corps no evacuation should take place until ordered by the French.

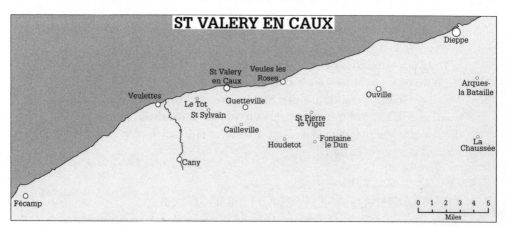

St Valery en Caux

By 11 June, however, French command and control arrangements had virtually collapsed. Authority to evacuate was finally given by the French Adm. Platon, commanding at Le Havre, late in the afternoon of 11 June. Fortunately, Adm. James, C-in-C Portsmouth, had not waited for the French and had already assembled a force of over 200 assorted vessels ready to evacuate the division and the remains of the French IX Corps from St Valery during the night of 11/12 June. At 0845 hours on Tuesday 11 June, Fortune signalled Adm. James, copied to the War Office:

> Intend to embark whole force tonight, Tuesday provided sufficient ships and boat transport are available. If embarkation cannot be completed tonight propose continuing a.m. tomorrow Wednesday. Consider air superiority is essential to neutralise shore batteries. Jumping Ladders and Nets are required to assist embarkation. Time of commencement and beaches to be used will be signalled. Embarkation tonight considered essential owing to probability of attack and shortage of rations, petrol and ammunition.[2]

DEPLOYMENT OF TROOPS IN A DEFENSIVE PERIMETER

Gen. Fortune's intention was to deploy the remaining infantry battalions and artillery in a semi-circular perimeter around St Valery, stretching from Le Tot in the west to Veules les Roses in the east.

On the western perimeter from north to south were the 2nd Seaforths at Le Tot and St Sylvain; the 7th Royal Norfolks and 1st Gordons at Ingouville and St Riquier les Plains; and the 4th Camerons at Neville. In support were 6 Platoon, Kensingtons.

On the eastern perimeter, starting from the coastal village of Veules les Roses, were a French artillery regiment, the 2nd/7th Duke of Wellington's, the 4th Seaforths at Yelon, the 5th Gordons around St Pierre Le Vigier and the 1st Black Watch at Houdetot.

On the southern perimeter were miscellaneous units of French troops supported by the tanks and carriers of the Lothians and Border Yeomanry.

The Kensingtons deployed all of D Company on the eastern perimeter, providing three platoons of four machine guns in support of the various infantry units. Major de Chimay's report[3] indicates that A Company had been placed in the divisional reserve and had spent the night of 9/10 June at Anneville, about 17 miles to the east of St Valery. It then moved to Cailleville, 2 miles south of St Valery, which it reached at 0600 on 11 June.

TRAFFIC CHAOS AND FRENCH INDISCIPLINE

Many accounts describe the chaotic situation that prevailed on the roads approaching St Valery. French transport of all kinds, both horse-drawn and motorised, ignored any attempt to enforce traffic control. The coast road had been reserved for British units but French troops, in panic at a rumour that the enemy were near, poured into it. Their transport was a mixed assortment of all types, badly disorganised and out of control. The coast road was jammed solid most of the night of 10/11 June. No attention was paid to British traffic control staff. Many units, including the Kensingtons, were delayed in reaching their positions, especially those on the eastern sector, where the congestion was greatest. These units also had the furthest to travel since they had come directly from front-line positions on the Bethune River. The 2nd Seaforths had been ordered to act as the advance guard and therefore to move first, at 2030 hours on Monday 10 June.

Divisional HQ was at Cailleville, just outside the village, but was considered too vulnerable there and reopened at St Valery. Two alternative locations in the town had already been hit by shellfire. At 1000 hrs on 11 June, Gen. Fortune issued the following directive to his troops:

> The navy will probably make an effort to take us off by boat, perhaps tonight, perhaps in two nights. I wish all ranks to realise that this can only be achieved by the full co operation of everyone, men may have to walk five or six miles. The utmost discipline must prevail. Men will board the boats with equipment and carrying arms. Vehicles will be rendered useless without giving away what is being done. Carriers should be retained as the final rearguard. Routes back to the nearest highway should be reconnoitred and officers detailed as guides. Finally, if the enemy should attack before the whole force is evacuated, all ranks must realise that it is up to them to defeat them. He may attack with tanks and we have quite a number of anti tank guns behind. If the infantry can stop the enemy's infantry that is all that is required, while anti tank guns and rifles inflict casualties on armoured fighting vehicles.[4]

Facing the weakened British division and its assortment of undisciplined French troops were a total of five German divisions and one motorised brigade. These were the 5th and 7th Panzer Divisions, 2nd Motor Division, 11 Motor Brigade, and 31st and 57th Infantry Divisions.

ATTACK ON THE PERIMETER

At 1400 hours on 11 June the 7th Panzer Division began the assault on the western perimeter. The 2nd Seaforths had concentrated their defence on the hamlets of Le Tot and St Sylvain. By 1430 hours ninety tanks were advancing on both positions. It was impossible for the defenders to hold off the tanks with anti-tank rifles, and the anti-tank platoon with its heavier weapons had become separated from the battalion and was on the eastern perimeter due to the traffic-choked roads. Some artillery support eliminated a number of tanks but the rest broke through, inflicting heavy casualties among the Seaforths and moving on towards the critically important western cliffs that overlooked the town, harbour and beaches. Soon German troops and armour were probing into the south-western outskirts of the town.

The next unit in the perimeter line was D Company of the 7th Royal Norfolks. The remaining companies of the battalion were back in the town setting up an inner defensive line. The Norfolks were a pioneer battalion, not first-line troops, but they had rifles and every man was wanted, even with rifles against panzers. When the attack went in against the Seaforths, the right flank of the tanks went straight over the Norfolks, who were dug into a cornfield in weapon pits. They were crushed, in many cases literally, by the tanks.

The 1st Gordons, in an orchard on the edge of Ingouville, were also in the path of the panzers. Their three supporting anti-tank guns were quickly knocked out and the German tanks passed Ingouville and carried on in the direction of St Valery.

The remaining battalion on the western perimeter was 4th Camerons. Luckily for them the German offensive had bypassed their positions and they were left intact.

On the eastern perimeter it was initially calm with no action until the late afternoon of Tuesday 11 June when at 1600 hours a co-ordinated attack began. British units were bombed and machine-gunned from the air, followed by an artillery barrage and an armoured assault. As on the western perimeter, tanks began advancing from the south-east. They were quickly engaged by the 25-pounders of 23rd Field Regiment RA. Some were destroyed, but most got through and attacked the positions held by the Duke of Wellington's, breaking through the perimeter and heading on west towards St Valery.

Following the attack by the tanks of 5th Panzer Division, the CO of 2nd/7th Duke of Wellingtons, Lt Col Taylor, had, at 2145 hours, ordered a withdrawal to the beach at Veules les Roses. It is an indication of both the confused nature of the situation and the lack of radio communication that he did not inform the adjacent 4th Seaforths of his decision to withdraw.

To the south, near St Pierre Le Vigier, 1st Black Watch had also been attacked in strength. The British positions were very vulnerable, especially since many of the troops had not had time to get properly dug in.

The southern part of the perimeter was defended by the light tanks and carriers of the Lothians and Border Yeomanry and by a French cavalry unit. No attack was launched on the defenders of the southern perimeter. French troops stationed slightly to the south were supposed to begin withdrawing at 2000 hours and the Yeomanry were to hold on as a rearguard until ordered to withdraw.

WITHDRAWAL OF PERIMETER UNITS TO ST VALERY

Orders for the Yeomanry finally arrived. They were to act as the division's rearguard, withdrawing at midnight to St Valery on foot after destroying all tanks and equipment and then holding the inner perimeter with 7th Norfolks while the rest of the division embarked. The Yeomanry marched off at midnight. From 4 miles away they could see their destination marked by two great pillars of red smoke rising far into the sky.[5]

It was obvious that, notwithstanding their courage and tenacity, the infantry battalions defending the western and eastern perimeters were unlikely to be able to do more than delay the two attacking German panzer divisions and supporting infantry. So it proved, and by the evening of Tuesday 11 June both perimeters had been penetrated by the weight of the German onslaught. Most units that could began to fall back to St Valery, which was now in flames and choked with men and vehicles.

It was around midnight, some two hours after the 2nd/7th Dukes had withdrawn to the beach at Veules les Roses, when it first became apparent to 4th Seaforths' CO that there were now no troops to his left. At 0200 orders were received to withdraw to St Valery for embarkation. The battalion marched off at 0300 hours and arrived without casualties.

INNER PERIMETER LINE CREATED

Once the western perimeter had been breached by tanks and infantry, Gen. Fortune was faced with a serious tactical problem. German tanks, artillery and machine guns now occupied positions on the western clifftops immediately overlooking the town, harbour and evacuation beaches. An inner perimeter defence line, with flanks on the eastern and western cliffs, had been set up on the edge of the town and was manned by the surviving four companies of 7th Norfolks. The defenders were to act as a rearguard as the rest of the division were evacuated. Those holding the line would be reinforced by one company from every unit as it withdrew through the line. French troops were supposed to guard the western cliffs in view of their strategic importance, but few had arrived and those that had quickly withdrew in the face of German armour. The western edge of the line was soon threatened by fifteen German tanks that had arrived on the clifftops. Linklater and Ellis:

The civil population had either fled or gone to ground in their cellars, and there was no more disorder in the town than the occasional stampede of two or three hundred army mules which had found precarious freedom in the streets. The only troops in St. Valery, except for a few men of the R.A.S.C. and Divisional Headquarters were the 51st Anti-Tank Regiment, most of the Norfolks, and a company of the Kensingtons, whose orders were to hold a narrow circle round the outskirts, and cover the final withdrawal of troops from the perimeter. But the possibility of such a withdrawal was menaced by the appearance, under a heavy smoke-screen, of German tanks and motor cyclists at the south-west corner of the town; and about five or six o'clock the streets were suddenly filled with the chatter and whine of machine-gun fire. The attack was beaten off, but patrols who went out … found clusters of tanks all round the town … waiting, sinister and still.[6]

A number of small but courageous parties tried to oust the enemy from houses near St. Sylvain and Le Tot, but in spite of all efforts the infiltration of St. Valery from this quarter was hard to prevent, as the German artillery and machine guns on the cliff tops maintained a continuous fire on the town and beaches. Small parties of the 1st Kensingtons and 7th Royal Northumberland Fusiliers (both machine gun battalions) and 7th Royal Norfolk (Pioneers) succeeded at last in pushing the enemy back to the wooded outskirts of the town, but the position of St Valery was now very grave. The enemy's capture of the western cliffs threatened the whole embarkation plan, for the cliffs were within the inner perimeter on which the final stand was intended and some of the planned embarkation points were now under close range enemy artillery and machine gun fire.[7]

With the enemy on the cliffs above and with their infantry probing the inner defences, and with much of the town blazing under a sustained artillery barrage, the prospects for evacuation of troops did not look promising. Nevertheless Gen. Fortune was still determined to proceed with the evacuation and at 2030 hours sent the following signal to both the navy and the War Office:

Consider tonight last possible chance of 51 Div. French authority given. Strength British 12,000 equal numbers French total 24,000.

At the same time a warning order was issued to all divisional troops that evacuation would commence at 2230 hours that night.

EVACUATION ATTEMPT AT ST VALERY

The first ships of the Royal Navy's rescue fleet had set sail from England during the evening of 9 June. The whole force consisted of sixty-seven merchant ships,

140 smaller vessels and warships. By 0600 hours on Tuesday 11 June an advance party of two destroyers and a transport were already tied up off the seafront. During the morning the ships on the seafront had come under artillery fire from a battery sited 3 miles away on the western cliffs, and had been ordered to sea immediately. By late afternoon the whole rescue force was spread out 7 miles north-west of St Valery. Of the civilian vessels only sixteen were equipped with radios. Linklater:

> Orders to evacuate came from the Admiralty but it was then too late. Fog had come down, delaying the return of the ships and obscuring from view all the coast. The tug *Fair Play* closed the beach about 12.30 a.m. on June 12th, slightly west of St. Valery, and landed beach parties. Heavy fire was opened on them at once and four boats were sunk. The cliffs and town were securely occupied by the enemy … The sloop *Hebe II* took off 80 soldiers from the beach close to St. Valery but she was sunk and lost with her commanding officer. On shore it was reported that a naval tow of four or five boats, trying to enter, had been sunk by gun-fire, and no other ships had come in. The latest news was that no ships were coming.[8]

Notwithstanding the failure of the evacuation attempt at St Valery, a very few troops did escape from the town. 2/Lt Walker and eighteen men of the 7th Norfolks commandeered a fishing boat on the western beach in the early hours of Wednesday 12 June and were eventually picked up by HMS *Harvester*.

EVACUATION OF TROOPS FROM VEULES LES ROSES

Veules les Roses is a small settlement on the coast some 4 miles east of St Valery. The first big ship to reach Veules on Wednesday 12 June began using her lifeboats to ferry soldiers from the beach back to the ship. She was joined by other merchant ships, the destroyers *Saladin* and *Codrington* and some smaller vessels. From 0230 hours until approximately 0900 hours on 12 June (reports of timings vary) a total of over 2,000 British and French troops were lifted from the Veules beaches. Then the ships and beaches came under air attack as well as a heavy artillery bombardment from both the east and the west, and the ships were forced to withdraw. Some troops used rifle slings and blankets knotted together to descend the 300ft cliffs and reach the beach with the intention of getting to Veules les Roses. Many fell and were killed in the attempt.

One unit to escape from Veules almost without loss was 385 Battery, 1st Royal Horse Artillery. They had been holding positions on the western perimeter until 0400 hours before withdrawing on foot into St Valery. The battery commander, Maj. Mullens, a territorial soldier, then led his men along the beach from St Valery to Veules. He was subsequently awarded the DSO.

Of all the British troops rescued from Veules les Roses, the largest single groups were the 500 men of the Duke of Wellington's Regiment (three-quarters of the battalion) and the 160 men of 385 Battery 1st RHA. The remainder were from a wide variety of other units, though relatively few were from the front-line units holding the perimeter. Two officers from the Lothians and Border Horse, Maj. Dallmeyer and Capt. Watson, got to the beach via a cross-country route along the clifftops. Watson remembered the naval beach parties as 'a lot of efficient burly sailors with revolvers at their side who gave any queue-bargers pretty short shrift'.

MOVEMENTS OF A COMPANY, KENSINGTONS

A Coy. Kensingtons [6 Platoon] were allotted the western [perimeter]. In the early morning the perimeter was fully manned. After a few probing attacks in the late morning the battle began in earnest in the afternoon. Owing to the short time for the reconnaissance and for digging in the perimeter was very thin in places and casualties, of which the Kensingtons had their share, were numerous. Eventually, after extremely bitter fighting in all sectors, the enemy broke through and captured, from the French, a hill overlooking the town, which was being steadily bombed and shelled … orders were issued for the evacuation to begin at 22.30 hours. Everything, including vehicles, was to be destroyed, and the troops manning the perimeter were to be withdrawn through a smaller perimeter round the town itself held by two infantry battalions and two platoons of the Kensingtons.[9]

The troops on the outer perimeter, after withdrawal, had orders to report at the railway station in the town, where they would get further instructions. However on arrival there, after a hazardous journey through the defile leading to the town, with the enemy not far away, they found no one there in authority. The streets, packed with soldiers of all units, were lit up by the blazing houses, and shells were landing from time to time. The inner perimeter was still managing to prevent the enemy penetrating into the town.[10]

After midnight a destroyer and two sloops were seen and a few troops managed to board the landing boats before the enemy appeared along the beach and forced the landing boats to withdraw. Hand to hand fighting now took place along the beach and in the caves, and as the first light of dawn appeared it was obvious that there was no hope of evacuation (at least until the following night), particularly as the three boats which had managed to come close to the shore had been sunk. During the last few hours of fighting Ptes. Farlander, Haslam, Paley and Summers had been killed.[11]

Fighting desperately on the beach in the dark and among the boulders and rubble at the bottom of the 300ft-high chalk cliffs, and in caves scoured out by the waves, must have been horrific. One of those killed during the day's fighting was 21-year-old Oliver Summers who had a widowed mother in Ramsgate. He is buried in the St Valery War Cemetery.[12]

In summary the dispositions given by various sources for A Company are as follows:

- Small parties of A Company and others pushed German infantry back to the outskirts of the town (Ellis, p.289)

- A Company (6 Platoon only) was thinly spread around the western perimeter. The attack on it began in the late afternoon of Tuesday 11 June. A Company incurred casualties. Troops manning the perimeter were withdrawn through a smaller perimeter round the town itself held by two infantry battalions and two platoons of the Kensingtons (Harpur, p.36)

- After midnight there was hand-to-hand fighting along the beach (Harpur, p.37)

- Troops withdrawn from the outer perimeter were told to report to the railway station (Harpur, p.36)

It is a measure of the utter chaos and confusion that must have prevailed that the above descriptions are not quite corroborated by Maj. de Chimay's report (see pp.114–8). He is quite clear that at 2300 hours on Tuesday 11 June he was at Cailleville, 2 miles outside the town, with two of his three platoons. The third platoon, No.6, was missing as it was in position west of St Valery. He then, as ordered, marched his two platoons to the railway station in St Valery, which, according to him, was reached at 0230 hours on Wednesday 12 June. Maj. de Chimay then became separated from A Company and it seems likely that from that point the two platoons left at the station were allocated to the defence of the inner perimeter. Lt Wood, however, states that the march to St Valery, led by de Chimay, left Cailleville at 2000 hours on 11 June.

If the timings set out in Maj. de Chimay's report are accepted as accurate, it follows that the only troops of A Company in St Valery until 0230 hours on Wednesday 12 June were those of 6 Platoon, and they had probably been on the outer western perimeter. Lt Wood's account is followed by Maj. de Chimay's official report:

Major de Chimay ordered Q.M.S. Minski to give everyone a tin of bully and a packet of biscuits which was all the food we had left and was to last until we reached England. At 20.00hrs [on 11 June] we left for St Valery, Chimay leading, myself next with 4 Pl, then 5 Pl and Charles [Mountford], and Coy H.Qs bringing up the rear. Chimay had previously stressed that if anything happened to him I was to lead the Coy on. On arrival at St Valery, still burning and with many ruins, I took my platoon up the cliffs and established positions and then went and reported to Chimay at Coy H.Qs which was at the railway station. The square was packed with troops and Chimay said there was obviously a first class mess up and that no evacuation seemed to be taking place. He was going down to the beaches to see what was happening as would also Div H.Qs. He again stressed to Charles and myself that if he did not return within a reasonable time, we were to take it that he had been hit and were to carry on ... I returned to my position and in the falling dusk an enemy attack was launched up the cliffs and along the beaches but after some tricky moments it petered out. Our main worry was ammunition as we only had enough for five minutes rapid fire. Shelling of the town now started spasmodically and mortars opened up on us. Grenades came flying from all directions and enemy patrols penetrated along the shore causing great damage. It was obvious that the French on our left and right had disappeared as mortars were established very close to us and A/T batteries were opening up on the beaches, firing by the light of flares which kept on going up. At midnight there seemed to be no sign of any evacuation so I went down to Coy H.Qs and found Charles very depressed. He said he had not seen Chimay since he left us and a naval officer had just landed and gone into Div H.Qs. I returned with a heavy heart to my platoon. Enemy flares were now lighting up the beaches and sea the whole time and I saw several M.T.Bs close into the shore manned by Royal Marines which were taking badly wounded cases on board.[13]

REPORT BY MAJOR DE CHIMAY

The Kensingtons' war diary, source of so much invaluable information, had accompanied Battalion HQ to Ark Force when the latter was created on 9 June. It consequently contains no detailed record of subsequent events in St Valery. It is some consolation to think that had half of the battalion not gone with Ark Force the war diary and all its information would most likely have been lost at St Valery. The odds would have been stacked heavily against Battalion HQ escaping and in those circumstances, as happened at Dunkirk, the war diary would have almost certainly been destroyed to prevent it falling into German hands.

Researchers can also console themselves with the knowledge that Maj. de Chimay, commanding A Company, later wrote a detailed report of events at St Valery, a copy of which was filed with the war diary. The report not only explains his very fortunate escape from Veules les Roses but provides a compelling picture of a steadily deteriorating tactical position, of constant withdrawal, and finally of the awful climax in the burning town as the evacuation failed.

Report on the Evacuation from St Valery (Veules les Roses)

On the evening of the 9th June A Coy was withdrawn from being under the command of 153 Bde and became divisional reserve spending the night of 9th/10th June at Anneville.

Early the next morning information regarding enemy tanks was received from G2 and the company was moved to the railway crossing west of La Chaussee. It was told to work in close association with the 51st Anti Tank Regiment R.A. and it continued to do so until the 12th, the guns covering the anti tank guns in the various positions they occupied.

Later that day Coy H.Q followed the 51st A/T. Regt. H.Q to a wood just south of Ouville, where Divisional H.Qrs. were then established. Movement was difficult owing to the amount of transport on the roads and also due to the French troops which appeared to be moving without method.

Whilst at Ouville some French civilians who had tried to get away returned with the news that when they reached Yvetot they had been met by German light motorised forces who had advised them to return. They reported the Germans as close as Yerville.

No orders were received until late in the afternoon when all spare kit was destroyed and at nightfall a move was begun to Cailleville which was to be the new divisional HQ.[14] This move was carried out with a good deal of confusion and the destination was only reached at about 6 a.m. the next day the 11th. Wrong orders were shouted out during the night and on one occasion the convoy had to turn round in a field as the track on which it had been put was so narrow.

No orders were received on the 11th until about 10.30 a.m. when it was said that the force was surrounded in the area St. Aubin, Luneray, Mautot, Cany, Corteville. It was said that the force would be evacuated at St. Valery and that the A/T Regt and the Coy would hold a narrower circle round St. Valery and cover the withdrawal of the remainder of the troops and I was to carry out a recce with the A/T Regt to decide on positions.

I first went to St. Valery with one of the battery commanders at about 1 p.m. The town was being shelled systematically with small calibre shells, the firing coming from the Fecamp direction. There was a large amount of French troops in the town who had suffered casualties and were in a panicky condition. As the afternoon went on the shelling increased and many fires were started.

We then carried out a recce west of St. Valery and it was whilst doing so that a heavy smoke screen was put down south west of the town and a tank attack supported by infantry took place. The tanks eventually reached St. Valery but were dislodged although some of their snipers remained and continued to fire during the night.

The engagement was a heavy one and when I returned to Cailleville to move out the platoons I found that Divisional Headquarters had moved [it had moved to St Valery during the morning] and I moved Coy H.Q. and the H.Q. of the 51 A/T Regt to an orchard at Guetteville and mounted guns at various positions to cover any open ground. About this time it was noticeable that firing was also coming from the Dieppe direction.

A platoon of D Company came through at great speed, going inland on the Angiens road. (Jack Lavington).

The French troops were now going through towards the interior in great numbers and very few of them had any arms. A neighbouring French artillery regiment sent in to say that the war was finished and that they intended surrendering and I thought it right to convey this information to Division. When I reached Cailleville I found that Divisional H.Q. had moved to St. Valery but I saw the Commanding Officer of the Lothian and Border Horse who told me that the French Corps Commander had given him similar information.

At about 11 p.m., the commander of the A/T. Regt came back from division and told me that an evacuation was to take place. I was to R.V. the Coy at the St. Valery station at 3 a.m. on the 12th where a guide would meet us. I was told that I could use transport but that it would have to be destroyed. I decided to destroy it immediately and march the Coy down. We took our guns but not the tripods. Meikle's platoon, no. 6, was missing as it was still in position west of St. Valery, but I was assured that it had already received instructions.

I aimed at arriving at the R.V. early and in fact got there at 2.30 a.m. We met considerable numbers of French troops moving inland and the road to St. Valery was littered with destroyed transport.

St.Valery was burning in several places when we arrived. The front part of the town was being systematically shelled and there was also signs of small arms fire in many parts of the town.

When we got to the station there was no sign of any guides and there were great numbers of troops practically crowded shoulder to shoulder. There was no shelling near the station and I therefore decided to leave the Company there and go forward to see if I could get any news regarding the evacuation. Before leaving I told Charles Mountford and Reg Wood to act independently of me if I did not return, and I also told the men that in any emergency they were to act for themselves if orders were not given.

The front of the town was now burning fiercely and was crowded with men of many units who were all crushing up the very narrow streets. Sniping was going on most of the time. I saw Johnny Dodge [D Company] who was with Colonel Barclay, the acting Commander of 152 Brigade. I also saw Meikle [6 Platoon] who told me that his platoon had suffered some casualties during the afternoon but that the bulk of it was there. As the shelling was heavy I decided to leave A Coy where it was and to get the men in the front part of the town into any shelters available. A number of them got into cellars and in a cinema which had a concrete roof.

I then went on to the jetty, where a large amount of men had congregated. It was then about 3 a.m. A machine gun was firing spasmodically from a cliff immediately west of St.Valery. There were a lot of wounded lying in stretchers at the Dieppe end of the jetty. I was told that wounded had been evacuated from there on the night of the 10th and that those I now saw were waiting their turn.

We could see no trace of any ships and we used various signals by lamp to attract their attention. There was no fog but the smoke from the burning buildings was going out to sea. There were no boats in the harbour but when I first got there two old dismasted fishing boats were being paddled out by some men [probably from the 7th Norfolks]. I understand that they were to make contact with any ships outside.

Colonel Barclay was very concerned about the men on the jetty and he thought that when daylight came heavy casualties would be incurred and the wounded would also be hit. He asked me to try and get some of the men away and I had considerable difficulty in doing so but eventually some 200 men followed me along the sea front, the tide having gone out slightly. It was difficult to get from the jetty to the shore which is a shingle one and three men had fallen and died.

About 500 yards down the shore we saw a small patrol boat about three miles out and Johnny Dodge decided to swim out to it. He had removed all his clothes and went out with a motor tyre inner tube. One man followed him but did not appear to be a good swimmer. In spite of lamp signals the boat shortly altered course and obviously did not see Johnny Dodge. When I last saw him he was some 500 yards out and the tide was taking him to the west. I believe that being a good swimmer he eventually reached the coast some-where west of St. Valery.

I then carried on along the shore and eventually we rounded a corner and saw the boats some four miles away at Veules les Roses. The cliff is about 300 feet most of the way between St. Valery and Veules les Roses and many of the men who tried to get down had been killed in so doing. I estimate the number at about 50. Some were tying rifle slings together in order to get down.

I saw many French troops at the base of the cliff. I do not know how they had got there as in every case they were alive though some were injured.

When I reached the boats there were a considerable number of French troops who were mobbing any small boat that came within reach, and at least one was beached as a result. I managed to wade out to a whaler and asked to see the Senior Naval Officer who I informed of the position at St. Valery and that considerable amount of men were there. I was then taken on the Duke of York, and shortly after reaching it shelling started and the fleet had to move out. It must then have been about 5 a.m.

Just before I reached the ships about ten German planes flew over the fleet and were engaged by the destroyers, and later individual bombers appeared but no damage was done, although my ship sustained seven hits from projec-tiles fired from guns sited on the shore.

When we moved out leaving some of the smaller boats vast numbers of men were running along the top of the cliff and descending by Veules-les-Roses.

On the *Duke of York* were 206 British troops with 11 officers, and 126 French troops with two officers. There were some 16 casualties which were looked after by Captain J K Sugden of the Duke of Wellington's Regiment. He had previously been a medical student and his services were invaluable. There was only one Kensington, Corporal Walley of B Coy, who told me that he had lost his company and had attached himself to an infantry battalion for the past few days.

I would emphasize that no mention of Veules les Roses was made in any order I received.

(signed) A. de Chimay, Major

Lt Roger Sandford (intelligence officer, 1st Black Watch) later wrote of descending the cliffs on a rope and reaching the beach where he met Maj. de Chimay:

... when I got to the crest the whole cliff top was alive with Frenchmen trying to get down the cliff. There was not a single break from St. Valery to Veules les Roses about 7 miles [to the north east] the average height was about 300 ft or a little more. When I eventually got down on car tow ropes tied together there were again about ninety Frenchmen to every ten English on the beach. There was a summer mist on the sea and no lifeboats had come in as they could not tell what was happening. The mist soon lifted and after signals they towed lifeboats in with naval pinnaces. As the lifeboats touched the beach all the French panicked and made a dive for the boats in front of the wounded. They broke up 3 and made them unseaworthy. A 2nd/Lt. in the Duke's Regiment who had quite a lot of men with him fixed bayonets and drove the French up the beach killing a Colonel and about fifty others. Major De Chimery [*sic*] from 1st Kensingtons of all people suddenly turned up. He was the MG Coy Comdr and we got grenades to hold the French off until all the wounded were shipped off, then the men, and finally we both swam and were hauled in the pinnace. We begged the Navy to hang on but about 6.15 to 6.30 they started shelling with A/T guns, three went slap through one boat and bounced across the water for about a mile before sinking. We then to our sorrow had to weigh anchor and get out while the going was still good. There is a hell of a lot I cannot write about, but I have told the whole story in detail to Col. Stephen.[15]

MOVEMENTS OF D COMPANY, KENSINGTONS

The movements at this time of A Company, Kensingtons, are known in detail as a result of Maj. de Chimay's lucky escape and his detailed report written after his return to England. If only there were a similar account of the fate of D Company on the eastern perimeter, but none has yet been found and nothing is known save what can be pieced together from scraps of information:

Meanwhile, a few miles to the east of St. Valery, part of 152 Brigade and attached troops of the Division had been in action during the night near a small port, Veules-les-Roses. To this port came some units of the Navy engaged in the embarkation and they succeeded, despite intense machine gun and shellfire, in taking off a number of troops, including Major de Chimay, commanding A Company, CSM Satchwell and twelve other ranks of D Company. Many of the Scots unable to get down the fire swept paths leading to the shore made improvised ropes of rifle slings and, thus outwitting the enemy, reached the beaches.[16]

We know that D Company had been deployed on the eastern perimeter and Harpur, above, tells us that thirteen Kensingtons (CSM Satchwell and twelve other ranks) managed to escape and were taken off the beach. This is subsequently confirmed by the entry in the war diary for 18 June recording their return to England. Tantalisingly, the war diary gives no names other than Mr Satchwell's, refers without explanation only to eight other ranks rather than Harpur's twelve and gives no further detail of the escape.

Harpur's account also refers specifically to Scottish soldiers using improvised ropes to descend the sheer cliffs. If the thirteen Kensingtons had also got to the beach by this method it would undoubtably have been recorded by Harpur. We have seen that at 2145 hours the CO of the 2nd/7th Duke of Wellington's Regiment had ordered a withdrawal to the beach at Veules. In this way the men of the Dukes reached the beach and it is not unreasonable to assume, although there is no direct evidence, that among them were the thirteen members of D Company, Kensingtons.

It follows from this that some units of D Company, possibly Company HQ, could well have been deployed with or near the Dukes at the end of the perimeter nearest the sea. Finally there is the fact that D Company's CSM, Mr Satchwell, was among the thirteen members of D Company who escaped. The logical place for the CSM to be is at Company HQ. Does this imply that all of them were from there?

Clearly very few of D Company escaped. In addition to those mentioned above two others returned to England. Pte Gratwood got back on 21 June having rowed back with seven other soldiers in a naval rowing boat. Pte Carty came back with two platoons of B Company who had found him in Cherbourg. With these sketchy facts and inferences about the fate of D Company we must, for the present, be content. Only one soldier of the Kensingtons, presumably of D Company, appears to be buried in the communal cemetery at Veules les Roses. He is Pte Alfred Cyril Parish, killed on 11 June. He was 22 and married to Kathleen.[17]

THE FINAL HOURS

Even as the evacuation ended at Veules les Roses, and as command and control began to fragment, the indefatigable divisional commander Maj. Gen. Victor Fortune was determined to do everything possible to hold on for a further day until nightfall to give the navy one final opportunity to come in and take off the remnants of his division. Unknown to Gen. Fortune, however, most of the vessels had already turned back, and those taking troops off at Veules les Roses would soon also be forced to withdraw. Even if it had been possible to hold out for another day the chances of ships being available and able to embark troops after dark were negligible. Fortune was not to know this, however, and set about planning the defence of the town. The success of this depended on retaking and holding the cliffs to the north-east and south-west, and thus preventing enemy artillery from commanding the beaches and harbour areas from which any evacuation that night would take place. It was a necessary but extremely ambitious proposal. Wood:

> **June 12th.** To add to our discomfort and misery, it now started raining. Towards 03.00hrs a message came through from Charles by a runner to say that he considered a mass evacuation was unlikely as the destroyers and cruisers out on the skyline dare not come any closer as enemy batteries were well established on the hills and cliffs which the French had deserted. When dawn broke it revealed two destroyers and a French destroyer coming towards the shore but still some distance away.

An enemy attack was launched again on the perimeter but it was beaten off chiefly due to the 25 pounders who fired their last rounds. Soon afterwards several bombers came over and the quay hospital and some M.T.Bs were hit. Meanwhile the French Corps Commander had twice hoisted the white flag on a chateau a mile away and both times it was shot down by the British troops. A conference took place at Division and the naval officer who had landed the night before, Lt Commander Elder, said there was a chance, if we could hold on for another day, of being evacuated that night. On the other hand it looked as if the warships on the horizon were steaming away as it was obvious that they had seen the town ablaze and thought we were finished. The three destroyers were probably coming in to pick up survivors. Unfortunately the code for use to the navy and to the War Office had been discarded after the fall of Dunkerque and although a Black Watch officer, Lt Davidson, had gone by sea to Le Havre to get the new one, he had had to return empty-handed and resisted the temptation to stay there and leave with the garrison troops there. It transpired later that some boats had managed to get in to Val de Roses, a fishing village about two miles away, and quite a number of troops had got away including most of the garrison force of Dieppe, and a Battn of the Duke of Wellington's Regt, whereas at St Valery we had only managed to evacuate some of the wounded and the Div I.O. with all the records etc. Unfortunately every unit left at St Valery had practically run out of ammunition, there was only enough for about ten minutes firing, there was no food and precious little water. The enemy were obviously massing for a large scale attack, there was no hope of holding them off with our depleted ammunition and we should be at the mercy of the bombers as the Bofors guns had no ammo at all. The French were either packing in everywhere or deserting and so in all these circumstances and to avoid unnecessary useless waste of life, General Fortune decided to surrender at 08.00hrs. Charles came and told me this at 06.00hrs. It was pouring with rain and we all felt very miserable when we heard it. He suggested that the non-essential personnel should be sent to the beaches in case, after all the wounded had been got away in the available boats, they might have a chance. I sent off my truck driver and D.Rs.

The destroyers were now about a mile off shore and were obviously coming no closer so at 07.00hrs I told the platoon (as no attack seemed to be developing now) it would be every man for himself at 08.00hrs. Soon afterwards, however, bombers flew over and one British and the French destroyer had direct hits. On the latter were Ptes Farlander, Haslam and Paley who were killed and Pte Green who managed to swim back to the shore.[18]

Enemy infantry were now in force along the beaches and as we had expended the last of our ammo we destroyed the guns and scattered the locks. I burnt all my papers and soon afterwards the order to cease further resistance came through and as we left to go back to Coy H.Qs we were overtaken by German tanks. An officer who spoke excellent English relieved me of my revolver. On reaching the town we were led into a large field and joined a large number of British troops including Salmon, Hammond and Lavington of D Coy who said Johnny Dodge was in the vicinity and thinking of risking the M.G. bullets and enemy batteries which were firing at anything moving out to sea. We sank down on the grass, wet, tired, miserable, dirty and hungry with little hope for the immediate future.[19]

As ever, there had been a problem with the French. On being briefed at around 0600 hours on 12 June about the British plan, Gen. Ihler, commanding the French IX Corps, which included the Highland Division, informed Gen. Fortune that he had decided to surrender. Fortune refused to accept this decision or to transmit Ihler's surrender telegram to the French commander-in-chief as requested, and left for a conference with his remaining brigade commanders and staff. The basic plan was for 5th Gordons and two companies of the Black Watch to secure the cliffs to the east of the town, for 4th Camerons to hold the southern fringe, and for 4th Seaforths to recapture the cliffs to the west. Three battalions that might otherwise have been available to support the attack were still in position on the outer perimeters, unable to withdraw to St Valery. The division as a whole had been weakened by the loss of a whole brigade and supporting troops, including three companies of the Kensingtons, when Ark Force was created. The situation on 12 June was highly confused. There was no radio contact between Divisional HQ and any of the battalions. Communication was reduced to runners, and it took time for the battalions to be contacted and given their orders. Troops were physically exhausted and virtually without food. Many weapons and vehicles had been destroyed as ordered the previous night and ammunition was running out. The units themselves were depleted after days of a fighting withdrawal. Most ominously the western heights, which the 4th Seaforths were expected to retake, were now held by the fresh troops and tanks of Rommel's 7th Panzer Division.

By 0800 hours the attacking troops were beginning to get into position, but soon a white flag appeared hanging from a church steeple. Infuriated, Gen. Fortune sent two staff officers to remove the flag and arrest whoever had hoisted it. They returned with a French major who said he was acting on the orders of Gen. Ihler who had ordered a surrender with effect from 0800 hours. Linklater:

There was indeed no reason, save honour, for fighting any longer. The Germans were in St. Valery. They had established their light field pieces, their heavy mortars and machine guns, about the harbour and in commanding positions overlooking the port. Through the rain over the Channel no one could see the promise of a white ensign. The hope of escape had vanished. But Victor Fortune had still to make his decision, and it was not easy. The hard core of the Fifty-First was fighting still, and would fight until its last platoon was overwhelmed. Was it possible to organise a counter attack on the German positions about the harbour and still maintain outward defence against the day's new pressure from east, west and south? Was there any hope, any chance at all, of regaining the town and holding it for another night? The men were weary to the very bone. Since the first week of May they had had no proper rest. There had been no chance to refurbish and reorganise the battalions after their fighting on the Saar. There had come instead the long march across France, and then the hurried advance to the Somme and the days of fighting before Abbeville. Then the contested retreat, with rearguard action by day and the dive bombers screaming from the sun, and by night the forced marches over roads that were a nightmare of lost souls and bewildered traffic. His Highlanders and their English companions-in-arms had left their dead in every Norman field from the Somme to the little Durdant, from the Cambron woods to the trees about the cemetery where the Black Watch were now at bay. Only a fragment of the Division remained, and those who survived were at the last pitch of their endurance. There was yet a stronger argument than human exhaustion. Not a round remained of gun ammunition; the Royal Artillery, which had fought throughout the retreat with dexterous gallantry and great accomplishment had fired their last shells before they took the breech blocks from their guns and left them to the enemy. The sappers had no stores: they had long been fighting as infantry, and on the Bresle a Field Company – the 26th – had been seen conducting itself with as much aptitude for battle as if it had been born, bred, taught and trained to be nothing else than infantry. But even the hardiest of infantry soldiers need more than a rifle and a clip of cartridges, and to lighten the load that was to have been embarked Fortune had given orders that all stores and vehicles and equipment should be destroyed, all gear cast away except what weapons a man could carry. But the Germans had their artillery, their abundance of mortars, their machine guns. To order a few companies of exhausted riflemen, with bren guns in support, to attack such a weight of metal would be little better than homicide. But the alternative was surrender, and the burden of such an act would rest on him. Fortune never shrank from making a decision. Now, facing the hardest question of all, he took the braver choice.[20]

The immediate problem now was to call off the infantry attack on the eastern and western heights. The 4th Seaforths had already begun to advance, but were stopped. The two companies of 1st Black Watch were under mortar fire and about to face a tank attack. The 5th Gordons had already lost D Company, which had been over-run by tanks that advanced behind French soldiers carrying white flags, and twelve tanks were advancing on two companies holding a sunken road. The 4th Camerons were not yet in contact with the enemy. Looking at it from the perspective of seventy years in the future, however, it seems obvious that to fight on would have achieved nothing more than a massacre and that in the unlikely event of the positions being held until dark there was now no prospect of a successful evacuation taking place.

In fact some units, including a section of the Kensingtons, did hold out for a while. Some troops were still holding positions on the perimeters, and elements of 1st Black Watch, 2nd Seaforths and 1st Gordons did not surrender until several hours after the rest of the division. Troops of the Black Watch at Houdetot, together with a machine gun of the Kensingtons and a troop of guns from 23rd Field Regiment, probably failed to receive the order to surrender since they stayed in position. Various accounts describe the emotions felt at the order to surrender. Many regarded it as an act of humiliation for the Highland Division. For all there was shock, and for many the shock was accompanied by disbelief. Some were in tears.

ARK FORCE ESCAPES VIA LE HAVRE

Composition of Ark Force and its objective – Kensingtons withdraw to Le Havre – Ark Force Operation Order No.2 – Enemy engaged near Fécamp and units prepare for withdrawal – Kensingtons, less two platoons, embark at Le Havre – Report of 8 and 9 Platoons' withdrawal

---

COMPOSITION OF ARK FORCE AND ITS OBJECTIVE

Le Havre is a large town and port on the Channel coast at the point where the Seine River joins the sea. In 1940 it was one of the main supply bases for the BEF, taking in stores, ordnance and motor transport as well as troops from Southampton. It had a small British garrison commanded by Col R.B. Butler. Le Havre is about 35 miles west of St Valery en Caux and the small port of Fécamp is situated on the coast road approximately halfway between the two. Once it was known that the Germans had taken Rouen, upstream on the Seine, it was realised by Gen. Fortune that if there were to be any chance of evacuation it could now only be from Le Havre, and Col Butler needed reinforcements if the port was to be defended. Meanwhile Ark Force, which had been created on 9 June from various units in the division,[1] was ordered to advance west, ahead of the rest of the division, to reconnoitre and secure the route to Le Havre, to which the division hoped to retire. In fact most units of Ark Force had reached Fécamp on the coast early on 10 June. The German 7th Panzer Division reached the Channel coast at Les Petits Dalles, 10 miles east of Fécamp, in the afternoon of 10 June, driving a wedge between Ark Force and the rest of the division.

Shortly after midday Maj. Johnston arrived with orders from Gen. Fortune. Fortune had been unambiguous in his orders to Brig. Stanley-Clarke:

Should it be apparent that enemy attack from the south or east [on 51 Division] has made any organised evacuation from Le Havre impossible you will withdraw [Ark Force] and evacuate at Havre as many of your force as you can, destroying all material and taking off such material as can be carried.[2]

Given the precise terms of these written orders from Gen. Fortune, and realising the threat posed by the enemy, Stanley-Clarke immediately ordered the majority of Ark Force to move west along the coast to positions 2 miles from Le Havre.

KENSINGTONS WITHDRAW TO LE HAVRE

Since the principal object of this work is to record the part played in the campaign by the Kensingtons it is appropriate from this point to follow the movements of Battalion HQ, HQ Company and B and C Companies as part of Ark Force in the withdrawal to Le Havre.[3] These units had reached Contremoulins near Fécamp on the morning of 10 June, the day after they had left La Chaussée. The conditions prevailing during the night move of 9/10 June were exceptionally difficult. Linklater wrote:

The night of the 9th was preternaturally dark. Oil refineries at Le Havre and along the river Seine had been bombed and set on fire, and a great ceiling of black smoke, greasy and impenetrable, was spreading to the north-east. Even when daylight came above the smoke, the country beneath it lay for hours in a dun twilight, and the monstrous cloud, stretching more thinly over the Channel, covered the sea with a sullen fog. At night the transport drivers on the coast road to Fecamp had to navigate a darkness so thick and evil smelling as almost to be palpable. The roads, as they were at all times, were clotted with refugees, and French batteries were also on the move. Ark Force fumbled its way between gross but invisible obstacles, and struggled through black confusion to its goal.[4]

Ark Force was about to occupy positions in a line at right angles to the coast from Fécamp to Lillebonne when it was reported that the enemy were already penetrating into Fécamp. The Kensingtons were ordered to move immediately to the Forêt de Montgeon at Le Havre. B Company was detached and remained behind, taking up defensive positions in the immediate vicinity. At Montivilliers, some 8 miles from Le Havre, the column was held up for forty-five minutes because the French had barricaded the road and were laying mines. Initially they refused to remove the mines to allow the column to proceed. The Kensingtons finally arrived at Le Havre at 1700 hours on 10 June. At 1800 hours C Company took up defensive positions. B Company was still in a forward position. There was intense enemy bombing activity during the night. Several bombs were dropped in the forest but no damage was done, although some vehicles were spattered with earth and stones and one bomb dropped within 30 yards of the HQ Company cooks. On the same afternoon that the Kensingtons had arrived at Le Havre Adm. Sir William James, C-in-C Portsmouth, also arrived at the port to assess for himself the likelihood of getting the whole of the 51st Division away from there. His conclusion was that, given the tactical position with Rommel now between Ark Force and the rest of the division, there was now no chance. He reported to the War Office:

> … from reports received of enemy mechanised forces and position of our line it appears highly possible that a large number of troops might have to be evacuated from coast in neighbourhood of St. Valery. I have moved small craft flotillas to St. Valery so as to be in a good central position if evacuation takes place from this coast and also transports to be assembled off this coast. I can control transport and small craft flotillas through the S.N.O. on the coast and they can be moved as required or withdrawn if not required. If General 51st Division will keep me informed of his intentions I will direct the evacuation forces to meet his requirements. Understand present intention is to fight back but if this proves impossible flotillas and transports will be ready on the coast.[5]

ARK FORCE OPERATION ORDER NO.2

Ark Force Operation Order No.2 was issued on 11 June. It began by stating that enemy forces had reached Fécamp the previous day but that there had been no information of enemy movement in the Lillebonne–Bolbec area to the southeast. French troops were holding positions from Lillebonne to Fécamp along the line of the railway. Once the decision had been made to abandon the proposed Fécamp–Lillebonne line it was decided to create two further defensive lines running north-west to south-east situated roughly north-east of Le Havre. These lines were to be held to the last man. Linklater:

> At nine o'clock on the 11th June Brigadier Stanley-Clarke gave orders that the Gonfreville–Montivilliers–Octeville line [line B] must be held to the last round and the last man. He knew then that the remaining Brigades of the Fifty-First were in desperate plight. He knew that Fortune meant to keep step with the French 31st Division which could march only eighteen kilometers a day, and he knew that before they could arrive he would have to fight to keep the port open. But he was still hopeful that Fortune and his tattered battalions would get through. Then the Navy reported that the other Brigades were completely cut off, and an attempt would be made to embark them at St. Valery. Thereupon arrangements were immediately made for the evacuation of Ark Force and the garrison of Le Havre. The Luftwaffe had been very active over Le Havre – three transports lying outside the harbour,

had been sunk on the 10th, and a transit camp intensively bombed – but the Royal Air Force had arranged to give support on the 12th.[6]

Operation Order No.2 sets out the detail. The forward line (line A) was roughly 10 miles from Le Havre and ran from Goderville through Breaute to Lillebonne. It was to be commanded by Brig. Green with headquarters at St Aubain (near St Romain de Colbosc) and manned by A Brigade from the Beauman Division, 17th Field Regiment RA, one troop from 75th Field Regiment RA and one company of the Kensingtons.[7]

The second line (line B) was much closer to Le Havre, about 3 miles away, and ran from the coast at Octeville curving round to Montivilliers and driving south to Gonfreville. It thus formed a defensive pocket round Le Havre. Line B was commanded by Lt Col Grant with headquarters at the Forêt de Montgeon at Le Havre, and was held by the remnants of 154 Brigade, 75th Field Regiment RA (less one troop on line A), 204 Anti-Tank Battery RA, two companies of the Le Havre garrison and one company of the Kensingtons.

The recipients of the operation orders were left in no doubt as to what was expected of them: 'Positions will be held until definite orders have been received. Under no circumstances will sub units withdraw until such orders are received. In the event of enemy attack it is the responsibility of every officer and man to hold his position at all costs and inflict the maximum loss on the enemy. This order will be impressed on all ranks.'

Administrative provisions were centred on Le Havre. The Forêt de Montgeon housed the main supply dump from which units could draw rations. The 154 Field Ambulance were also there with access to 11 General Hospital in the Palais des Régates. Petrol could also be drawn. Ominously, perhaps, there were no additional stocks of ammunition available. Presumably this was because although Le Havre was a BEF prescribed port for the import of general stores, troops and MT, ammunition came in via Fécamp, which had been in enemy hands since 10 June.[8] It should be appreciated that Le Havre was a big supply depot for the BEF, although by this time stocks had been deliberately allowed to run down by not replenishing them as they were used. Most of the ordnance stores had been cleared and MT reserves had been drawn on.[9]

The location of unit HQ and the total manpower strength of all units was to be reported forthwith to Ark Force HQ at 22 Rue Felix Faure since administrative arrangements had also been made for the evacuation of the force. With what must surely have been a sly sense of humour, the army's code word for the commencement of the evacuation was 'Whoopee'. How very appropriate that was for the soldiers who had endured so much for so long. Personnel were to be transported as far as the route Boulevard Foch–Place de Hotel de Ville–Boulevard de Strasbourg (where there would be traffic control points) and then marched to Quai d'Escale and Quai de la Floride. A possible alternative would be evacuation from the beach.

All vehicles were to be disposed of at Boulevarde Foch or Boulevarde de Strasbourg by being rammed together before final destruction by REs.

No lights were to be used and all personnel were to embark with one day's preserved and emergency rations. All light weapons, including Bren guns and mountings, full marching order equipment and petrol cookers were to be carried by troops to the point of embarkation. Any weapons left behind were to be rendered unserviceable.

ENEMY ENGAGED NEAR FÉCAMP AND UNITS PREPARE FOR WITHDRAWAL

Fighting took place in the forward line and was particularly heavy near Fécamp (approximately 5 miles from Goderville). Troops manning the forward line were ordered to withdraw and did so successfully, protected from enemy aircraft to some degree by the low cloud cover and rain. The town of Le Havre had been subjected to very heavy air raids during which several transport ships had been sunk and a transit camp had been gutted.

The inner defensive line was due to commence withdrawal at noon on 12 June but at the request of the French this was postponed for a further twelve hours to enable various scattered French units to reach Le Havre. During the afternoon a reconnaissance was carried out by officers of the Kensingtons, in the middle of another air raid, over the 2-mile route from the docks to the place where the vehicles were to be abandoned. Eventually the inner line withdrew. At this time Battalion HQ, with HQ and C Companies, was still in the Forêt de Montgeon at Le Havre and had been warned to be ready to evacuate at short notice, leaving MTs and all kit that could not be carried. There was considerable air activity, both enemy and Allied. Documents and maps were destroyed and a considerable amount of kit was either buried or destroyed. At 2130 hours on 11 June the battalion was warned that the evacuation would start that evening. The quartermaster dumped more kit and equipment, including ammunition and eleven jars of rum that he had carried from Armentières. He then set fire to the dump. At 2245 hours came the order to move. As the troops left, the forest was enveloped in a dense cloud of smoke and there were innumerable reports from the quartermaster's fire as ammunition exploded. As they left it started to rain, which was much appreciated as it hindered the operations of enemy aircraft. The battalion moved using surplus MT that had not been destroyed. It travelled from the forest down to the Place de L'Hôtel de Ville, Le Havre, in safety, although the town was burning brightly in many places and L/Cpl Graham, the provost corporal who was on traffic control duty, had been blown through a shop window by a bomb explosion. He was picked up by REs and put on board another boat. The trucks were parked and subsequently rammed together under the direction of the MTO where they were left for the REs to destroy. The battalion (less A, B and D Companies) marched with one file on either side of the street from there to the quay. All guns and MG equipment were carried through empty streets cluttered with debris and in the middle of a heavy air raid. Buildings everywhere were blazing and collapsing, making an eerie and frightening spectacle, but the docks were reached without loss.

KENSINGTONS, LESS TWO PLATOONS, EMBARK AT LE HAVRE

At 0215 hours on 12 June the Kensingtons embarked on the SS *Lady of Man*, where B Company HQ plus one platoon were discovered also to be on board. The other two platoons, 8 and 9, were missing and had still not arrived by the time the ship sailed at 0545 hours. They arrived, in the words of the war diary, 'after a peaceful though zig zag voyage, at 12.00 hours'. They had not arrived in England, however, but at Cherbourg, and disembarked to march three-quarters of a mile to a military camp where a meal was provided. The general expectation was that they and the other units of Ark Force were to be put back into the front line near Rouen. A considerable number of British troops were still in this area. They included the remnants of the 1st Armoured Division and two brigades of the Beauman Division.[10] To their undoubted relief, however, the Kensingtons were ordered to return to the ship and re-embark. The ship sailed that evening and they were at Southampton by 0830 hours on Thursday 13 June. Other units of Ark Force were also converging on the dock area of Le Havre to board ships at different quays, and by the morning of 13 June, 2,222 troops had been evacuated to England and 8,837 to Cherbourg as part of the Royal Navy's Operation Cycle.[11]

REPORT OF 8 AND 9 PLATOONS' WITHDRAWAL

When the *Lady of Man* sailed from Le Havre only one out of B Company's three platoons was on board. What happened to the missing two platoons is known thanks to a report compiled by 2/Lt Kent on 26 June 1940 and filed in the war diary. For their 'initiative and meritorious conduct', 2/Lt Kent of 8 Platoon and 2/Lt Shanks of 9 Platoon were each subsequently Mentioned in Despatches. Kent had joined the battalion on 9 May as a replacement for PSM Frost. He took over command of 8 Platoon while the battalion was at Foucarmont at the end of May. The following is 2/Lt Kent's report:[12]

Report On Withdrawal Of Nos. 8 & 9 Platoons 'B' Company, 1st Battalion Princess Louise's Kensington Regiment

On June 10th, whilst at Tourville near Fecamp, I had orders to report to the Commanding Officer of the Sherwood Foresters at St Jean de la Neuville. I led my platoon on my D.R.'s motor cycle through Annouville and intended striking the main road at Goderville. However, I was stopped by mined roads. I therefore proceeded west to Limpiville and took the following route: Epreville, Fauville, Yebleron, Roville and Bolbec to St Jean de la Neuville.

At Fauville I was informed that enemy A.F.Vs had just passed north towards Ourville and by all accounts I only missed these by minutes. This was confirmed by a French liaison officer at Bolbec. I met the acting C.O. Sherwood Foresters who took me around his positions which were situated in the front edge of a wood 200/250 yards behind a ridge which carried right across his front. I told him my fire would be useless in such a position. And he asked my views and I suggested moving battalion forward to a position 200 yards forward of said ridge. I was able to give cross fire across his front which was completely satisfactory.

At about 21.00 hours that night I was called to a hurried conference of Sherwood and attached officers. We were informed that the enemy were near to us and that we were to withdraw at once, M.Gs bringing up the rear. We proceeded in convoy and everything went well until we were stopped by darkness when we were told to wait for daylight.

The next order that came back was that we were surrounded and what could M.G. officer do. I said I would mount guns on truck, two guns facing either side of the road, and would at daylight proceed to head of the column and advance, neutralising the area as I went. This was met with approval and the guns were so mounted. During the course of the night rifle fire broke out in the following manner: the convoy was on right hand side of the road and some troops had got off and were on left hand side of road. A civilian car approaching the barrier at head of column switched on its headlights. An officer in rear gave order to open fire. Fortunately I was able to countermand this as many men of his own men were in line of fire which he did not realise in the darkness. Later rifle fire did break out and lasted some five minutes before it was stopped: the result was one officer killed, 2 officers wounded, and two O.Rs wounded. The cause of this outbreak I could not discover. Fortunately I had kept my men on trucks so they were safe from this.

At dawn we proceeded as arranged and met no enemy. We harboured in a wood an hour later on the other side of St. Romain [close to defensive line B]. At 07.00 hours we were ordered by the acting C.O. to return and take up our original positions again as there was a French line in front of these positions.

That night I visited my Coy Commander St. Aubin. At 21.30 hours he advised me to return immediately as he had heard of an imminent withdrawal. I got back to Bn HQ at 22.00 hours and a conference was held at at 22.10 hours. My orders were that M.Gs and artillery were to go to the Foret de Montgeon [at Le Havre]. As I withdrew with the infantry No. 9 platoon [commanded by 2/Lt Shanks] joined me enroute. I went to Montivilliers with the infantry and carried on from there independently to the wood. There I parked the trucks and made a reconnaissance of the wood. I found trucks marked 36 but no personnel. I went on my own initiative to the quayside and found the D.A.G.M.G. who told me not to delay but to get on board as soon as possible. I returned and brought the trucks down, loaded guns and ammunition on decks and, acting on orders, destroyed the trucks.

We were shipped from Le Havre to Cherbourg and arrived that evening (June 12th). I offloaded guns and ammunition and that night slept with them on the quayside. During course of night I made contact with Base Area Officer who said he would place M.P. on ammunition and have it sent to D.A.D.O.S. At 04.00 hours on June 13th we left with guns for a chateau at St. Pierre d'Eglise, where we slept in woods until June 15th, acting on orders from Base. During this period I submitted nominal rolls and list of deficiencies. At 14.00 hours June 15th we were ordered to march to a transit camp in Cherbourg. (8 miles). I managed to get transport for the guns but the men had to carry full equipment.

At the transit camp my loading party and guns had arrived and I met Pte Carty of D Coy there. On Sunday I was warned to get ready to leave from Quaie Normandie and arranged with the Major i/c for transport for the guns. An officer of another M.G. unit set out before me, leaving his guns and kit, saying there was doubt of transport arriving and he was getting his men away. I told him that I would destroy the guns if transport did not arrive.

The truck arrived for my guns but the driver in charge had no instructions about any other guns and was not prepared to take them. So I made up his deficiencies from this kit and rendered the remainder useless.

We embarked at 12.00 hours and set out to sea at 13.00 hours. Journey was uneventful except for bombing at Cherbourg. Arrived at Poole at 19.30 hours. We were dispersed to schools where we fed and clothed. I had two payments made to the men and managed to get some battle dress, side caps, boots etc. exchanged.

I heard from an N.C.O. on leave that some of the Battalion were at Mill Hill and as soon as I heard this wired my Coy Commander. On receipt of the Adjutant's telegram I saw the Major i/c Bournemouth B.E.F. but was told that Movement Control would take their own course.

On Friday (June 21st) I was told that guns might have to be left, so I had everything packed and labelled 'Mill Hill'. On Saturday (June 22nd) I had warning order to move on Monday June 24th and arranged transport for the guns. This was cancelled on Monday at 08.00 hours and I was told that the guns were to go to a dump at the Majestic Garage, Bournemouth. I had my inventory of guns, instruments etc. signed for by a Captain Alexander.

I enclose a list of gun kit, and Withdrawal Order (which the Sherwood Foresters handed to me).

Signed G Kent 2nd/Lt 26.6.40

Defending the Invasion Coast

JUNE 1940: THE BATTALION, LESS A AND D COMPANIES, RETURNS TO ENGLAND

B, C and HQ Companies of the Kensingtons, numbering approximately 350 men, disembarked at Southampton at 0815 hours on Thursday 13 June 1940; after two days in the transit camp there, they were moved by train on Saturday 15 June to the barracks of the MGTC of their parent unit the Middlesex Regiment at Mill Hill, London. The Kensingtons were accommodated at Mill Hill for three weeks and, according to the war diary, were shown great kindness by the CO of the centre, Col Browne MC, and his staff. Transport was waiting for them on their arrival at Mill Hill station, and accomodation and security passes were provided. On Sunday 16 June a short service was held by the padre, the Revd F.L.M. Bennett. On 17 June forty-eight hours' leave was granted to all ranks. On Friday 21 June ten second lieutenants arrived from the MGTC.

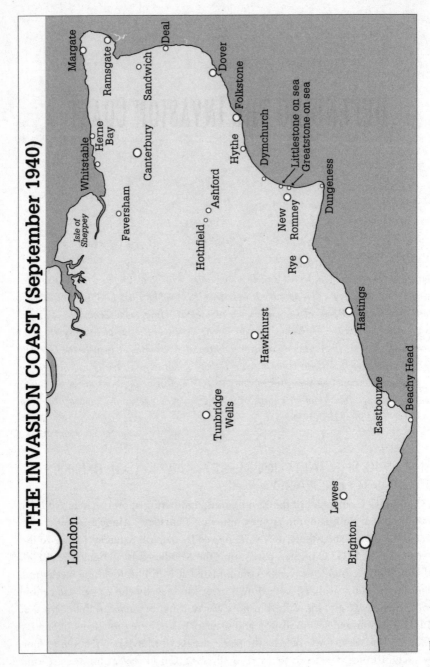

THE INVASION COAST (September 1940)

London

Margate
Ramsgate
Whitstable
Herne Bay
Sandwich
Deal
Isle of Sheppey
Faversham
Canterbury
Dover
Folkstone
Hythe
Dymchurch
Littlestone on sea
Greatstone on sea
Ashford
Hothfield
New Romney
Dungeness
Rye
Hawkhurst
Hastings
Tunbridge Wells
Eastbourne
Beachy Head
Lewes
Brighton

The invasion coast

THE FEW WHO ESCAPED FROM ST VALERY AND VEULES LES ROSES ARRIVE BACK

Slowly those few who had somehow managed to escape from France reported back.[1] L/Cpl Graham, injured by a bomb blast while on provost duty in Le Havre, and Pte Charlton (A Company) arrived on 13 June, Charlton having come from St Valery. Pte Holmes (A Company) was found on 15 June on the train from Southampton to Mill Hill. On Tuesday 18 June Maj. de Chimay arrived and on the same day CSM Satchwell and eight other ranks from D Company reported. Satchwell originally had twelve others with him. It is possible, perhaps likely, that Ted Simmons was with CSM Satchwell. He had found himself at Bournemouth and was anxious to tell his parents that he was safe, as mail had been disrupted for weeks. According to his younger brother the family had been told that Ted was formally reported missing.[2] His sister Vera worked in Marks and Spencer's new shop in West Ealing in London so Ted went into the Bournemouth branch and asked if they could telephone the London shop. This was duly done: Vera was given the good news and told to take the rest of the day off.[3] Meanwhile, the trickle of returnees continued. On 19 June 2/Lt Burton arrived from Cherbourg. On Thursday 20 June a boisterous telegram arrived from 2/Lt Kent in Bournemouth stating: 'Hear you are safe. Congratulations. Have 68 B and 1 D Coy here plus all gun kit.' On Friday 21 June Pte Gratwood from D Company arrived from Aldershot. According to the war diary he had crossed to the UK from St Valery en Caux to Ramsgate in a naval rowing boat with seven soldiers, and rowed in turns six at a time. The journey took two days and nights. Others arrived from elsewhere: Cpl Thompson, D Company (wounded at Foucarmont) reported, and Sgt Chapman reported on 23 June (no details given). On 24 June 2/Lt Kent and his sixty-nine troops returned.

The names of all those in the battalion who escaped from St Valery or Veules, and also of Pte Ford who escaped from the POW marching column, are listed in Table 1 (Appendix I).[4]

THE FIRST-LINE REINFORCEMENTS: APRIL–JUNE 1940

Part of the battalion, but not on its fighting strength and usually held in reserve, were the First-Line Reinforcements (FLRs). They were used to replace casualties.[5] The unit was commanded by Capt. Williamson, who maintained a war diary for the months April to June. A copy was filed with the battalion's main diary and it is from that copy that the following details have been taken. On 13 April 1940 the FLRs, comprising four officers and sixty other ranks, accompanied the rest of the battalion to Southampton, Le Havre and Yvetot. Here the main part of the battalion went on to Blangy while the FLRs went to Rouen, arriving at Rouvrey Camp, in the words of the war diary 'unheralded and unwanted'. Somebody evidently took pity on them because they were eventually taken on to the strength of 6 Company, 1 Infantry Base Depot. Practically no training had been done but despite that on

5 May one officer and forty-eight other ranks were sent to the battalion, which by then was in action on the Saar front. The officer was 2/Lt G. Kent, who was later to do well when commanding 8 Platoon of B Company. He was Mentioned in Despatches for extricating the platoon from behind enemy lines.[6] The arrival of the reinforcements at Battalion HQ at Bibiche on 9 May brought the battalion up to its revised war establishment, giving one extra man per machine gun (of which there were forty-eight in the four companies), resulting in gun crews of three.

The German attack on the west had started on 10 May and on the 12th a draft of twenty-four other ranks arrived from the MGTC at Mill Hill. At the same time one officer and twenty-nine other ranks were to have set out for the Saar but no train was available. The diary is silent until 21 May, by which time the battalion was at St Marie aux Chenes, making its way to the Somme with the rest of the division. For a reason that is not given, the remaining FLRs appear to have been ordered to move, and marched 24km to Evreux where they entrained for Le Mans. From there they marched another 10km to Mulsanne Camp where they waited for nine days. A general withdrawal seems to have been in progress as 5 Infantry Base Depot left for England on 29 May, but at the same time two officers and thirty-six other ranks arrived from Mill Hill. On 2 June thirty other ranks were sent to the battalion, which was then at Foucarmont, close to the Bresle. They arrived on 3 June, the very eve of the Allied attack on the Somme that was to fail and cause so many casualties.

The remainder of the FLRs appear to have left things very late since it was not until 15 June that they left Mulsanne Camp, heading fast by road for St Malo 'on any available vehicle'. A Belgian ship, SS *Princesse Marie-Jose*, took them to Southampton. From there they travelled by train to London and joined the rest of the battalion at Mill Hill.

REORGANISATION AND MOVE TO ASHFORD

Reinforcements began to arrive in an irregular flow (the details are set out in Appendix I). Nevertheless it was not until August that the Kensingtons were brought up to full strength again. It is tempting to speculate whether the Vickers guns so painstakingly brought back from France by 2/Lt Kent really did end up being dumped at the Majestic Garage, Bournemouth. On 25 June a warning order instructed the battalion to prepare to move to the Elstree and Boreham wood area. Two days later the order came to take over from the Welsh Guards at Elstree, but this was subsequently postponed indefinitely. In the final two days of the month, an officer and thirty-four other ranks arrived from 5 Infantry Base Depot and 147 other ranks arrived from 341 MGTC. A and D Companies, lost at St Valery, were re-formed. It is easy to detect the sense of urgency abroad. It was, after all, June 1940. Britain's land defences were weak and a German invasion was thought to be imminent. In Churchill's words: 'The Battle of France is over; the Battle of Britain is about to begin.'

It seems highly unlikely that the reconstituted A and D Companies would consist entirely of untrained reinforcements. It is probable that a number of seasoned troops from HQ, B and C Companies were transferred to A and D Companies. On 2 July at 1900 hours, a warning order to stand by for a move came from Movement Control, London Area. At 1415 hours the next day Maj. F. Walden, second-in-command, left with an advance party of sixteen for Ashford, Kent. He was followed on 5 July by the rest of the battalion, which left Mill Hill in two trains at 1400 hours and 1430 hours. The two trains reached Ashford at 1700 hours and 1740 hours, and the battalions marched from the station to Hothfield Place, 4 miles outside Ashford. This was to be a permanent home to Battalion HQ, HQ Company and to any of the other companies that were not occupying forward positions or on duty in the mobile reserve. Accommodation was satisfactory and, according to the war diary, after a while a regular programme of evening entertainments was organised, featuring films in the library and concerts by the Ashford Players and the Entertainments National Service Association (ENSA).

JULY 1940: COMPANIES DEPLOYED ON THE INVASION COAST

The vital sector from Sheppey to Rye was manned by the 1st London Division, with 23 field guns towards an establishment of 72, no anti tank guns, no armoured cars, no armoured fighting vehicles, no medium machine guns, and about a sixth of the anti tank rifles to which it was entitled.[7]

The Kensingtons were to take up a two-company front with the remaining two companies acting as part of the divisional mobile reserve. B and C Companies were to be the first to take up positions along the coast and on 6 July company commanders were out all day on recce.

For some people there is a certain magical beauty about the north Kent coast even now. The positions to be occupied by the Kensingtons stretched from the Isle of Sheppey to the Isle of Thanet and round the North Foreland to Sandwich and Pegwell Bay. In winter it can be bitterly cold, facing, as most of it does, due north. In a particularly bad winter the sea will freeze. Yet there is beauty in the winter landscape, on the ice-covered sheets of floodwater, and in the sweet-smelling smoke from the log fire of the remote marshland pub. In summer it can be like a land forgotten by time for anyone who wishes to lie watching the clouds above the Chislet marshes where the drainage ditches mark out the banks of the now dry Wantsum Channel, which used to cut the Isle of Thanet off from the mainland. Here the reeds and bullrushes sway against the blue sky with a soft rustle to accompany the song of the marsh birds. Head north and you can walk along the sea wall to Reculver with the salt marshes and drainage dykes on your left and the sea on your right. Ahead of you lies the tiny hamlet with its clifftop crumbling medieval church and its ruined

Roman fort. The fort was built to guard the Saxon shore in the third century, just as the same shore was guarded from the same enemy in 1940. In Roman times the fort dominated the entrance to the Wantsum Channel, preventing incursions from hostile German pirates. A few miles east of Reculver lie Herne Bay, Whitstable and the Isle of Sheppey. Herne Bay is a charming example of a late-Regency seaside town. Whitstable is a small port famous for its oysters. Sheppey is a low-lying island in the Thames estuary, which was reached in 1940 by a swing bridge joining the island to the mainland 4 miles north of Sittingbourne. The island is divided from the mainland by the Medway River to the east and the Swale River to the south. The main town is Sheerness with the naval dockyard that was operational in 1940 but is now closed. There was also an RAF Coastal Command airfield at Eastchurch.

On 7 August, 10 Platoon of C Company moved to Minster in Sheppey to act as part of the mobile reserve on the island. B Company HQ followed on 9 August, setting up shop in Minster Abbey (754822).[8] On 15 August, 10 Platoon HQ with one section moved to Warden Bay (467901), the second section moving to Leysdown (475891). A major reorganisation of troops in Sheppey then took place.

On 8 July B and C Companies moved into their new positions. Two platoons were to be stationed about 20 miles from Hothfield Place, close to Romney Marsh and Dungeness. 10 Platoon was at Greatstone on Sea and 12 Platoon was at New Romney. They had two operational tasks in support of 7th Somerset Light Infantry: first, to provide defensive fire across the beaches adjacent to the east face of the Dungeness salient, and second, penetration of the enemy's left flank in the area of Littlestone on Sea. Both platoons were attached to 135 Brigade but the attachment turned out to be temporary and on 10 July, 10 and 12 Platoons were moved back from Greatstone and New Romney to the area of Whitstable. The vacated positions were taken over by 7th Devons.

There now began what appears to be a frenetic scramble to occupy designated positions along the north Kent coast, from the North Foreland in the east to Whitstable and Sheppey beyond in the west.[9] At Hampton and nearby Swalecliffe, just east of the sleepy seaside resort of Herne Bay was 7 Platoon, while 8 Platoon moved to the low, wooded cliffs at Bishopstone just west of Herne Bay. A further section was in the salt marshes behind the remains of the Roman-Saxon shore fort, the coastguard cottages and ruined medieval church of Reculver. Inland at Sarre, with a section at sandy Minnis Bay on the coast, was 9 Platoon.

On 9 July 11 Platoon was ordered to Horton Park, just off the Ashford to Folkestone road and some 7 miles inland from Folkestone. The platoon remained 'on wheels' as part of 2 London Infantry Brigade's mobile reserve. Thirty-six new Vickers guns were delivered and promotions were announced: 2/Lt Shanks became captain and adjutant and Capt. Padfield MBE was promoted major. Lt Milton, 2/Lt Batty and 2/Lt Canfield Kerney were all promoted to captain.

B Company HQ was moved from Hothfield Place to Broadoak in order to be closer to platoon areas. More reshuffling was to take place. C Company HQ had established itself, perhaps comfortably, at the 'Rose Marie Café' at Whitstable (telephone 3319), while 7 Platoon from Hampton and Swalecliffe were moved to Herne Bay pier and the east end of the promenade. The vacated positions were taken over by 10 Platoon, and 12 Platoon took up positions on the jetty of Whitstable harbour and just south of Lower Island. The next day, 12 July, B Company HQ moved again, this time to Herne Bay, where they occupied Parsonage House, Parsonage Road. It may be that these moves had raised some concerns in official minds, since the war diary records on 12 July that: 'Lt. Col. Parker started a detailed recce. of the Divisional coastal front with a view to finding the best positions suitable for M.M.Gs.'[10]

The 1 London Infantry Brigade issued Home Defence Instructions on 10 July 1940. The Kensingtons' dispositions were as follows:

> B.Coy under the command of 8th Royal Fusiliers with sections at Reculver 668873, 654874, 625866 and 615864.
> C.Coy under the command of 1 Lon. Inf. Bde. with sections at 595860, 573856, Whitstable Harbour, 542841

As well as setting down the procedures to be followed in the event of an air raid, the instructions reminded recipients that it was 'very important that when pillboxes have been disguised as haystacks it should not be possible to set fire to the hay'.

It was not long before the Kensingtons experienced an air attack, the first of many over the next weeks. At 0100 hours on 15 July, C Company (presumably from the Rose Marie Café) reported bombs falling just outside Whitstable harbour and one just missing a section of 12 Platoon on the jetty. There were no casualties, although Pte Morrison had a lucky escape when a bomb fragment sliced through his coat. Later that day the movement of sub-units continued: 9 Platoon HQ and one section moved from Sarre to West Cliff and the second section moved from Minnis Bay to the club house. They were replaced at Minnis Bay by a section of 8 Platoon from Bishopstone. Meanwhile, the MTO took delivery of thirty new motorcycles and three 3-ton lorries.

DIVISIONAL ANTI-INVASION EXERCISE

A divisional anti-invasion exercise, including A and D Companies as part of the Divisional Reserve, was just getting under way and a bogus message had already been identified. On 19 July a genuine message from the division ordered A Company to rendezvous at the cross roads at Smeeth (6 miles south-west of Ashford) under the command of 2 London Infantry Brigade. A Company's role in the exercise was to assist in the recapture of ground 'taken by the enemy' in the area of the military canal and Postling Green. D Company was stood down, and Capt. Milton collected five more motorcycles.

On 21 July 2nd/5th Queen's Regiment were expecting the order to come from 1st London Division to move to the Ashford area as part of the exercise. It is instructive to study the planning for this given that there was a good chance that the real thing would kick off at any time. There were four tasks allotted to the battalion:

1. Protection of HQ 1 London Div at Eastwell Park.

2. Closure of roads through Kennington and Ashford.

3. Destruction of any enemy making an airborne landing. For this task a troop of artillery and two companies of the Kensingtons may be allocated by Division.

4. Provision of a Mobile Divisional Reserve.

A Company 2nd/5th Queen's Regiment was to take primary responsibility for protection of Division HQ. HQ Company was to recce and be prepared to occupy positions in Kennington. D Company was to do the same in Ashford. B and C Companies were to be in reserve at Wye racecourse and were to be ready to take offensive action against parachutists or airborne troops landing. Roadblocks were to be constructed by the REs and manned by HQ and D Companies. Thirty-six 3-ton lorries and a variety of other transport would be made available to the battalion. It was stressed that all transport was to be used in constant practice of operational roles, including embussing, debussing and loading of vehicles.

Instructions for intercommunications are simple and reveal alarming weaknesses, which have been commented on before. They state simply that intercommunications will be by:

(a) Despatch Rider   (b) Bicycle   (c) Runner   (d) Civil telephone

Companies were reminded to maintain close touch with the Home Guard in their areas and ensure that the best use was made of their services, particularly in the construction of Molotov bottles, of which they had made a close study. Here we have it: an infantry battalion faces invasion without a single radio but has a good supply of milk bottles full of petrol. Transport was limited too, although some vehicles were provided by the Royal Army Service Corps (RASC) in addition to vehicles that belonged to the battalion. B Company, for example, had six 3-ton lorries belonging to the RASC and one belonging to the battalion. A rifle company in an infantry battalion comprised three platoons plus Company HQ, an approximate total of 150 men plus personal kit and operational stores such as ammunition and grenades.

2 LONDON INFANTRY BRIGADE: OPERATIONAL PLAN FOR COUNTERING INVASION

Some positions occupied by the Kensingtons were within the operational area of 2 London Infantry Brigade, and their operational plan dated 10 July is of interest since its objective was to outline the procedures intended to counter an invasion. Before landing, the enemy was expected to attempt to create confusion by extensive bombing and dive bombing, gas attacks, dropping small groups of parachutists, obstructing military movement by causing uncontrolled civilian traffic, and generally disorganising the defence. To counter these actions the plan directed rigorous gas discipline, reduction of signal traffic to a minimum, ruthless control of civilian traffic, manning of key points of defence and ensuring that all troops were ready to move at thirty minutes' notice.

Non-brigade troops in support of 2 Infantry Brigade were 5 Troop Carrying Company RASC, detachments of 6 Buffs (at the Black Horse Inn 650598, and at Hawkinge airfield) and a platoon of the Kensingtons. The defence of Hawkinge fighter airfield would be carried out by one company each of 6 Buffs and 1 London Rifle Brigade (LRB) together with the 1 LRB Mobile Column. The 1 LRB was to carry out a co-ordinated counter-attack supported by artillery if necessary. The only beach in the brigade area was St Margaret's Bay, 4 miles north of Dover, which was to be held by a platoon of 1 LRB supported by a machine-gun section. In non-military language that means thirty-seven men and two machine guns were expected to hold the beach against several hundred German *vorausabteilung*[11] supported by ship-to-shore gunfire.

The plan stresses that despite obstructions there were many suitable landing places for troop-carrying planes, and parachutists could land anywhere. They were to be 'hit as fast and hard as possible', primarily by battalion mobile columns. Each battalion was required to organise a mobile column, which would consist of an infantry company in vehicles with sections from the company motorcycle and carrier platoons. In this case the primary task of the column was the reinforcement or relief of airfields. The secondary task was to act as a mobile reserve, ready to move in any direction. 'The value of these columns will entirely depend upon their ability to get off the mark very quickly. Frequent rehearsal "turn outs" will therefore be held.'[12] A brigade anti-tank company and battalion tank-hunting platoons were also formed. The tasks of each were suicidal, namely: 'to locate, harass, ambush and shadow enemy A.F.Vs. on the move and in harbour.' The plan also noted that: 'Pl H.Q. will carry dynamite and anti tank mines. Personnel will ride pedal cycles.' Here is an indication of how desperate things were. If the enemy had ever got ashore, pedal cycles and dynamite were to be pitched against Mk IV panzers. The plan ends with the following enjoinder: 'the enemy has been found to be particularly vulnerable to immediate counter-attacks. Full advantage will be taken of this weakness and there will be no hesitation in going for him.'

On 22 July B Company HQ moved from Herne Bay to Upstreet in order to be more centrally situated, taking over St Mary's school. In the meantime, the divisional exercise ground on, with another bogus message being received and identified as such by Battalion HQ.

On 29 July Pte Cresswell was killed in a motorcycle accident on the Ashford to Canterbury Road.

COMPARATIVE STRENGTHS OF BRITISH AND GERMAN FORCES

It will probably be helpful at this point to consider the comparative strengths of the German and British forces at this period.

We know now that by the end of August the logistical difficulties of organising and protecting the sea crossing for a large force had made changes necessary. The original plan had been amended to reduce the first wave from thirteen divisions to nine. The second wave was reduced to two infantry, four armoured and two motorised divisions with an extra two motorised regiments. The third wave comprised six infantry divisions. The total invasion force numbered twenty-three divisions with more in reserve, including a parachute division for use near Folkestone.[13]

In response to the threat, Britain could field twenty-nine divisions throughout the kingdom. The invasion threat reached a crisis in the first half of September and by then British forces, though stronger than in the summer, were still weak. Only four of the twenty-seven infantry divisions were fully equipped, and only eight more could be regarded as fairly well equipped. There were 348 medium and cruiser tanks in service.[14] Everything depended on whether the Germans could cross the Channel.

OPERATION SEALION

Documents confirm that the final German plan was to land the first wave of nine divisions on beaches from Folkestone to New Romney and Rye to Brighton with a parachute drop north-west of Folkestone. It was a formidable threat: in support of the invasion forces were 250 amphibian tanks, 38 anti-aircraft ferries which could also engage surface targets and 72 rocket projectors. The second and third waves would follow. In the east Dover was to be taken and the advance was to continue to a line from Canterbury–Ashford–Hawkhurst. In the west the high ground of the downs west of Lewes was to be held. Once the second and third waves had landed, the advance was to continue towards London with mobile formations pushing to the west of the capital with the aim of cutting it off.[15] Two infantry divisions were held ready to cross from Cherbourg to Lyme Bay, Dorset.

Had German assault troops landed and succeeded in establishing a bridgehead on a front from Folkestone to New Romney, the defenders would quickly have been in contact with them. Defending troops were to stop at all costs the enemy punching a hole in the beach defences that would lead to breakout, and would have incurred considerable losses in the attempt. It is probable, though speculative, since there is nothing to support the suggestion, that the Kensingtons would have been rushed down to the invasion area to help in preventing a breakout. Much has been written about Operation Sealion and there has been considerable speculation about how successful it would have been had it been launched. Many British sources disclose a widespread fear of enemy paratroops jumping from Ju 52 transport aircraft to seize objectives. This fear was fuelled by what had happened in Holland and Belgium, where forts, bridges and other key points had been seized and held in lightning strikes by airborne troops. In Britain rumours of sightings of *Fallschirmjäger* (paratroopers) were frequent throughout the summer.

Around the end of May and in early June the home defence forces were particularly weak. Divisions earmarked for the BEF had always been given priority over Home Forces in both troops and equipment, and on 11 May two more divisions, 1st Armoured and the 52nd, with elements of the 1st Canadian Division, had been ordered to France. With 1st Armoured Division went the bulk of Britain's armoured force.[16] By the time the Kensingtons arrived on the coast in July three divisions were stationed in the extreme south-east. The 1st (London) Division held the tip of Kent from Rye to Margate and along the north Kent coast to the Medway. The 45th Division held the adjacent coastline from Rye, west to Bognor, and north to the Thames. The 15th Division held Essex, while 43rd Division was in reserve north of London. Abandoned in France was much vital equipment: 600 tanks, more than 1,500 field and anti-aircraft guns, and some 850 anti-tank guns. By mid-September the New Zealand Division was also in Kent and forces at brigade strength were deployed along the coast in the Worthing and Brighton areas.

Any commander charged with determining the strategy to be employed in driving back an invasion force is always initially required to make a crucial tactical decision on the deployment of his defending troops. Should he spread the majority of his troops along the coast ready to strike immediately at any place where the enemy attempts a landing and, as he is landing, when he is at his most vulnerable? The initial attacking wave would also be fewer in number and more lightly equipped than successive waves. Armour and soft-skinned vehicles would come across with the second wave ready for the breakout from the beachhead and the thrust deep into the English countryside. Alternatively, should he hold the coast only lightly and concentrate his main strength well back in reserve behind defensive lines, but ready to counter-attack as the enemy's intentions become clear? The former option is perhaps the natural romantic emotional response based on the premise that not a single yard of English soil will be conceded to the king's enemies. There was, however, a very long coastline to defend and a large number of potential landing places to be covered. The second option had to risk the enemy achieving a breakout before British forces could concentrate their efforts. In May the chiefs of staff had chillingly admitted that: 'should the Germans succeed in establishing a force with its vehicles in this country, our army forces have not got the power to drive it out.'[17] At that time, before Dunkirk:

... the vulnerable stretch of coast from the Wash to Sussex was only relatively well guarded. In Eastern Command, whose troops would take the first shock of a seaborne landing ... there were six infantry divisions with less than half their approved establishment of field guns and only a handful of anti tank guns.[18]

The defence plan finally formulated by Gen. Sir Edmund Ironside, C-in-C Home Forces, was based on the second of the two options described above and was reliant on defence in depth. A series of stop lines and a major defensive line, the 'GHQ line', were constructed. In the event of a German landing, these defences, together with formations in front of them, would delay the enemy advance until mobile reserve forces could arrive. This would take time, though, and there were no local reserves and precious few anti-tank guns to support the defence lines. Collier wrote:

> The garrisoning of so widespread a system of static lines ... left too few troops available for counter attacks and threatened to direct attention too exclusively to purely defensive measures. Divisional commanders, finding that the manning of the stop lines would consume most of their manpower, and knowing that ... reinforcements could not reach them in less than twelve hours, were worried by the smallness of their local reserves and their consequent inability to take offensive action. The plan was widely criticised. The Vice Chiefs of Staff maintained that to make no major attempt to halt the enemy until a great part of the country had been overrun was a suicidal policy. The Chiefs of Staff ... agreed that the balance of the defence leant too far on the side of a thinly held crust on the coast with insufficient mobile reserves in immediate proximity to where penetration must be expected.[19]

Ironside was succeeded by Gen. Sir Alan Brooke on 20 July. Brooke favoured a much more offensive stance. Local mobile reserves were created and positioned close to expected landing places. At the same time divisions in the GHQ mobile reserve were moved forward into Cambridgeshire, Hertfordshire and Surrey, much closer to the coast. Anti-tank guns and field artillery were brought forward and sited within range of the beaches. To avoid the congestion seen in France caused by civilian refugees, some 207,000 people were moved from coastal towns in Kent and East Anglia in an attempt to keep roads clear for military traffic.[20]

The 1st London Division had issued an operational instruction on 25 July, which seems to reflect the change of policy. The following is an extract from the Kensingtons' copy:

> Home Defence emphasises the importance of attack to recover beaches and to dislocate the plans of enemy landed from the air. Area Defence is one of our problems; great mobility is necessary, and readiness to attack in any direction. Commanders will ensure that all units under their command are able

to concentrate and be ready to move at short notice. This concentration will take place on receipt of the code word (b) or on news of the enemy attempting a landing. Mobile Columns – early contact with the enemy landed from the air or who may have broken through the beach defences is essential. In Sub Areas 4 (Shorncliffe), 5 (Dover), 6 (Deal), 7 (Thanet), 8 (Sheppey) mobility in defence must be provided for. A defence which relies on occupying a series of defensive posts and has no provision for a mobile reserve is taking grave risks. An element of landward defence of the above areas should be well organised observation on the landward side with mobile detachments to move out and engage the enemy promptly. If contact with the Division is broken area commanders will not hesitate to act. The maxim of Nelson still holds good … no Captain will be wrong who lays his ship alongside an enemy's ship and engages her.[21]

The situation was still very difficult and it is fair to say that given the weakness of the land forces a great deal depended on the Royal Navy and the RAF.

AUGUST 1940: DEFENCE POSITIONS IN THE ISLE OF SHEPPEY

August began on a sombre note with the burial on the 1st of Pte Cresswell. He was interred with full military honours in the graveyard of St Mary's, Hothfield, the historic church being symbolic of the England for which he gave his life.

On 2 August 1940, Brig. Portman, commander of 2 London Infantry Brigade, sent a minute to HQ, 1st London Division:

The Commander XIX Corps visited this HQ on 23rd July and gave instructions that a recce of a position N. of DOVER should be made. This line will be held by troops from DEAL should the enemy overrun that area and should prevent further advance to DOVER. Depth to the line will be afforded by the Garrison of the Siege Battery situated at ST. MARGARETS AT CLIFFE, and searchlight and bofors batteries in that Area.

A postscript addressed to a brigade staff officer added: 'will you arrange for Kensingtons to send a Coy Cmdr to recce with 2 Bde or my sites on this line.'

Evidently Maj. de Chimay was saddled with this task since a copy of the report is attached to the war diary, initialled A.C. and dated 11 August:

Proposed M.M.G. positions
      St Margaret at Cliffe

I have marked the proposed positions on the map together with their arcs of fire.

I discussed these with Brigadier Portman this morning and later went over the ground with the BM [brigade major] who agreed that the position at Hog's bush was an exceptionally good one and thought that it could be incorporated in the defence scheme. He however considered that the position N. of Langdon Cross was too far forward of the general line which was to be held.

Both positions are being forwarded to Division for their consideration.

A.C.
11.8.40

At the same time there may have been some concerns about the state of the defences in the Isle of Sheppey. Maj. Padfield, OC C Company, reported to the adjutant, Battalion HQ, Kensingtons:

I visited Sheppey on 2-8-40 and contacted with Col. Bolton, commanding 2/6th Queen's Royal Regiment, in 35th Brigade. Col. Bolton is in charge of the defences of Sheppey and holds it with the skeleton force of his own battalion and some R.A.F. training personnel who are stationed at Eastchurch aerodrome.

The defence scheme differs materially from that in practice on the mainland and consists of the centralisation of troops at the various small towns on the island, who are always standing by in readiness to recapture points taken by enemy parachutists. There is a fixed impression that this will be the only method of attack and they are greatly concerned as to their ability, at present constituted, to do the job. In consequence they are particularly delighted at the prospect of Machine Gun help. Col. Bolton is of the opinion that our role for his purpose should be a mobile one, either by sections or as a platoon for the purpose of shaking up Jerry on any of the points of arrival on the island. I explained to him that we were most willing to fall in with his ideas providing we always had the overrider as to the suitability of the task for the MMG, and pointed out that the whole of coast defence from the M.G. angle was the subject of investigation by Col. Parker on behalf of the Divisional Commander. Col. Bolton professed to be an old machine gunner.

No 10 Platoon, commanded by 2/Lt. W. E. Walker proceeds to Sheppey on 7.8.40 and should take up position at about 12.00 hours under instructions from Col. Bolton. Early opportunity will be taken to contact him and a further report submitted in connection with his task.

Whilst at Sheppey it was ascertained that the Air Force at Eastchurch, under command of Squadron Leader Eades, DFC, had (or would shortly have) 8 Vickers guns for use solely in defence of the aerodrome to repel possible landings. I have written to Squadron Leader Eades. In an endeavour to establish the real position because I understand that none of the Air Force personnel are capable of firing the gun.

C.J.C.Padfield Major

SECRET

1ST LONDON DIVISION OPERATION INSTRUCTION NO.13

Date 15 Aug 40.
COMMAND OF TROOPS IN SHEPPEY

The command of the forces in SHEPPEY will be assumed by Comd 35 Inf Bde from 12.00 hrs 15 Aug 40, from which time Sub-area A.8 will cease to exist and Sheppey will become part of Sub-area A.3.

Comd 35 Inf Bde will have an office in SHEPPEY where a Staff Officer will be resident.

In order to provide for the possibility of communications between SHEPPEY and the mainland being severed, or other circumstances arising to prevent Comd 35 Inf Bde controlling the operations on SHEPPEY local cmds are appointed who will carry on.

SHEPPEY will be divided into two sectors each commanded by the officers nominated below. These officers will command all troops who may be in their sector or come into their sector:

Sector	SHEERNESS	Cmd. – OC Fixed Defences Thames & Medway
Sector	SHEPPEY	Cmd. – OC 2/6 Queens

Inter-sector boundary incl to
SHEERNESS – BARTON'S POINT
383933 – QUEENBOROUGH Lines
Canal (Not marked on 1" map). – Pier
344914

Signed at 12.42 hrs

for Colonel
General Staff
1st London Division

Advanced H.Q.
1 Lon. Div.
HOME FORCES

On 6 August movement of other sub-units had continued. The 7 Platoon HQ
and one section moved to Minnis Bay (730877) and the second section moved to
Westgate (776886). One section of 8 Platoon moved to Reculver (667875), and 11
Platoon and one section moved to Herne Bay (614866), the second section in position at the east end of the promenade (636866). The next day 12 Platoon HQ, with
one section, moved to Hampton, with the second section situated at Swalecliffe
(575856). Meanwhile, air activity was greatly increasing.

On 8 August the first information about prisoners of war was received when a
list containing the names of forty-two officers and men of A and D Companies
arrived from the Old Comrades Association. Another batch of ten names arrived
over the next few days. On 10 August the CO and Maj. de Chimay reconnoitred
suitable positions for machine guns along a line from White Fall (816636) to Inn
(775620), and on 12 August 120 other ranks arrived, having been posted to the
battalion from MGTC. The CO inspected the new arrivals. Later, after seeing the
Divisional CRA (Commander Royal Artillery) the CO went round posts with a
view to fixing their precise co-ordinates prior to the building of concrete machine-
gun pillboxes.

On Saturday 17 August A Company relieved C Company, the latter returning
to Hothfield. One platoon of C Company had been stationed on Sheppey and
after it had been relieved the new platoon commander submitted a report to
his company commander (Maj. de Chimay), who immediately forwarded it to
Battalion HQ:

SECRET
REPORT ON GUN POSITIONS of ISLE OF SHEPPEY
No. 1 Section
467901 40 yds south of lake. Fixed line & Safety. 5 degrees East of hd.

No. 2 Section
476901 Just north of HALT. Fixed line and Safety 464906

Pln H.Q
100 yards N.W. of Lake

<u>Telephone</u>   <u>Sheerness Military</u>

    Fletcher battery. Warden Point.

<u>Billets</u>

    2 extra rooms handed over by R.A.

<u>Task</u>

    We can fire on boats but as they require high tide to land we can not fire on landed troops for reasons of safety.

No 2 section position is bad.

I do not think task can be properly carried out, but I should like the Commanding Officer to see the four sites if that could be arranged.

<u>Infantry</u>

    1 Pln and 2 Plns of gunners guard our flanks. There are 3 four inch guns here, and a searchlight.

(signed) J. MACLEOD PRATT 2/LT.   17/8/40

Some days before 16 August (the order is undated) Battalion HQ issued 1st Kensingtons Relief Order No.1. This began as usual by setting out existing positions: C Company, less 1 platoon, was under the command of 1 London Infantry Brigade; 1 Platoon of C Company was on Sheppey under the command of 35 Infantry Brigade; four additional machine-gun sections were under operational command of C Company; and C Company also manned one beach light at Swalecliffe. A Company was ordered to relieve C Company on Saturday 17 August. One NCO per section was to be sent by A Company to each position twenty-four hours in advance. The main body was to report to OC A Company at 0930 hours on 17 August before moving to C Company positions. Transport used to move A Company personnel would also be used to take C Company troops back to Battalion HQ. All stores, ammunition, grenades and hard rations held by C Company were to be handed over to A Company. One NCO was detailed to instruct A Company in regard to the Swalecliffe beach light.

On 17 August an enemy aircraft was shot down just west of Whitstable harbour by a Spitfire that crashed near Seasalter. All the crew were killed but the Spitfire pilot was unharmed. On the same day a further list of eleven POW names was received.

DEFENSIVE POSITIONS IN THE SANDWICH AREA

On Monday 19 August D Company relieved B Company, which returned to Hothfield. The positions that D Company was to take over were within the area held by 198 Infantry Brigade, which commanded any sub-units of the Kensingtons deployed in that area. A machine-gun company comprised three platoons each broken down into two sections of two guns, giving one company the capability to occupy six section positions or more with half sections. These positions were sited at Sandwich, Pegwell, Minnis Bay and Westbrook. It is difficult to be precise because occasionally the entries in the war diary are, as in this case, devoid of grid references, unclear or otherwise incomplete. Once in position the relieving company followed the usual procedure and reported shortcomings:

To:- O.C. 1 Kensingtons   From:- O.C. D. Coy.

On taking over our positions from B. Coy. I have at present the following observations to make.

1. No.6 section. 15 Pl. at Sandwich firing in the direction of Pegwell. The beach between this position and Royal Marines M.G. position at 805752 is not protected except by occasional wire. Would suggest that the section of 8th Kings at Cliffsend, at present doing a bren gun task, be moved to Sandwich position to fire south.

2. A considerable amount of Dannat wire is required and have indented on 198 Inf Bde.

3. Beach Lights have been allotted as follows:
      2 lights to sec. of 8th Kings at Cliffsend , 2 lights to 5 sec. 15 pln at Pegwell

      These have been sited 100–150 yds to the right of gun position. These were tested on 21st August and the lights give adequate illumination at about 600 yds range.

4. No. 3 sec. 14 Pl. MINNIS BAY have arranged that A/T rifle of 6th Borders should be sited near M.G.s and covering similar arc as this had been firing into our position. No. 14 Pl. A/T rifle situated at Westbrook.

5. 8 Pl. Thanet Bn. Home Guard placed by Bde under command of D. Coy. Kensingtons with a view to defence of MINSTER.

6. There is insufficient ammunition with guns in event of active operations. At the moment we have 8,000 rds. with each gun. This will last half hour rapid and 1 hour normal fire.

(signed) C.K. Williamson Capt

FIELD 23.8.40   O.C. D Coy

<u>Information re Own Troops</u>

<u>Sandwich</u>   20.8.40

Lt. Foulkes. Phone. Sandwich 17.

On our right

16 Pl. D. Coy, 11th Royal Marine Battalion.
Section positions at Sandilands and Sandown Castle

<u>Sandilands</u> 3 Vickers. firing from pill box (1 gun)
and from house (2 guns) in S. direction along beach.
Fixed lines ranges 1400, 1700 & 1900 yds. 15,000
rounds Mk. vii & Mk.viii mixed per gun.

A/Tank rifle firing N. along beach
4 doz H.R.grenades
20,000 rounds for riflemen
Molotov and A.W.bottles

Have near R.E./S.L. detachment of 8 men and 1 Lewis
gun with 50 rounds per rifle.
<u>Sandown Castle</u>. 2 Vickers fixed lines N. along beach.

<u>A.Coy Royal Marines (Rifle)</u> HQ Mill Hill, Deal.
2 Pls in marsh and in 2 pill boxes on beach between
Sandilands and Sandown
1 Pl. at Chequers Inn in marsh.

<u>B.Coy Royal Marines (Rifle)</u> HQ at Worth
1 Pl at Worth, 2 Pls in the marsh.

<u>C.Coy Royal Marines (Rifle)</u> in Deal. HQ at R.M.Depot.
R.A.P. at Barton House, Worth

8th (Irish) Bn. Kings Regt. Bn. HQ St.Lawrence College Ramsgate
B Coy HQ Stonar lodge, Sandwich.

10a Pl. Sandown Lodge, Sandown Road, Sandwich (near small bridge on
road to Golf Club). Commanded by 2/Lt Ebbs.
12 Pl. Sandwich Bridge

11 Pl. Dorman Long & Cottels premises at Bloody Point. HQ N.A.A.F.I.
stove hut.

10 Pl. will shortly be moving up to a position on the train ferry berth. This is
below the water tower on which our guns lay their fixed lines.

MINES There is a double and in some places a treble bank of contact mines
laid along the crest of the beach between the Grosvenor Hotel (nr. Sandilands)
and Deal. These are mushroom type and are half buried in the shingle. They
are connected by galvanised wire and primed. They contain 45 lbs of Amatol.

INCREASING INTENSITY OF AIR ATTACKS

On 20 August the Kensingtons' popular MO, Capt. John Smith, died of wounds
sustained on 18 August in an air raid on Croydon. He was the son of Frederick
and Elsie Smith of Braunton, Devon. He was cremated at the Golders Green
Crematorium, North London.[22] He was replaced by Lt R.W. Brown RAMC.

The following days brought a significant increase in enemy air attacks: a main
road was blocked by bombing; an enemy plane crashed in Leysdown, another in
the sea off Reculver; three Dorniers crashed into the sea near Sheerness; four parachutists were in the sea off Reculver; a German pilot was fished out of the sea off
Seasalter and handed over to the London Irish Rifles, while a British pilot was
picked up by motor boat from Herne Bay; Minster (in Thanet) and Manston were
each bombed; Sandwich was bombed; Minster railway station was hit, damaging
electric mains; Ramsgate, and Manston airfield were each bombed; enemy aircraft were down at St Nicholas, Reculver and Herne Bay; an enemy plane was in
flames off Herne Bay, the pilot was handed over to Brigade Intelligence; bombs
fell near houses occupied by A Company in 4 Northwood Road and 8 Tower
Parade, Tankerton, near Herne Bay, windows shattered but nobody was hurt; a
British pilot made a bad landing after baling out and was picked up and taken to
204 Field Ambulance.

In the midst of the chaos 198 Brigade ordered a 100 per cent 'Stand to' at
0012 hours on 27 August. Stand down was only ordered nearly an hour and a
half later. The reason for the alarm was given as 'the presence of unnatural fog in
the Channel'.

Three more names of POWs were received, bringing the total for August to sixty-six. To end the month, on 31 August D Company reported that a section of their 15 Platoon had shot down a Dornier 17 from a position 'club house' at grid 796772. Of the crew two were detained at Deal Hospital and the other two handed over to the division.

The war diary for August ends with these words:

Air activity has been consistently intense since 13th August. The companies on detachment round the coast reporting numerous plane crashes and several high altitude and dive bombing attacks No days goes by without at least 4 air raids and large aerial combats have become an everyday occurrence.

SEPTEMBER 1940: CODE WORD CROMWELL, INVASION IMMINENT

September began and the intense aerial activity of the previous month continued. On 1 September a detachment from B Company was sent to guard the remains of a British plane at Elvy Farm. The next day D Company reported the crash of two twin-engined planes near Elmstone, another in the sea 4 miles north-east of Reculver and an unidentified plane which crashed 7 miles north-west of Reculver. On 3 September another German plane was in the sea off Reculver with the pilot picked up by lifeboat, and on 5 September D Company reported a German twin-engined aircraft in flames in the sea off Hook Beacon. The next day B Company captured a 21-year-old German pilot, Lt Christinnecke, whose aircraft had crashed just off the main Ashford to Maidstone road at grid 415665. Although slightly wounded, he had managed to set fire to the aircraft. A Hurricane was shot down and crashed nearby at grid 404652, and the next day A Company reported that an unidentified aircraft had crashed south of Herne Bay.

On 6 September 1 Section of the 1st Line Reserve under Sgt Steel relieved the 8th King's at Little Cliffsend (790821), the men of the King's returning to their unit. The next day 1 Platoon of 1st Line Reserve under 2/Lt Humphreys relieved 4 Platoon on Sheppey. After this, 4 Platoon returned to the Whitstable area where they relieved the two sections of 8th and 9th Royal Fusiliers, these two sections returning to their units.

More troops missing in France were reported as POWs. During the month of September the names of sixty-nine men were passed on to the battalion. When added to the sixty-six names passed on in August it gave a total of 135 men accounted for.

This was the critical period when an invasion was thought to be likely, and at the beginning of the month air photographs and other sources disclosed a sudden and striking increase in the numbers of barges at French ports (the number at Ostend alone increased from eighteen on 31 August to 270 on 7 September).

These were barges, which, full of troops, were to be towed across the Channel to the invasion beaches. Many more vessels of all types and sizes were moving westwards and massing in the French Channel ports. The RAF was not going to allow such preparations to continue unmolested and on the night of 5 September Bomber Command sent almost the entire Blenheim medium bomber force to strike at the concentration of barges. The next night the Blenheims were joined by twenty-six Hampdens and eleven Battles. Subsequently the entire bomber force was in use against shipping and barges and by 19 September over 200 ships had been sunk. Ships of the Royal Navy continued at night to poke their bows into harbours along the entire north coast of France and Belgium and bombard any vessels found there.

Four Germans caught landing in England from a rowing boat confessed that they were spies sent to report troop movements of British reserves. Other intelligence reports and favourable conditions of moon and tide led the Joint Intelligence Committee to inform the chiefs of staff on 7 September that an invasion might be imminent.[23] At 0115 hours on 8 September, code word B – Cromwell – was issued. Units took up action stations. D Company Kensingtons was ordered '100% stand to' until further notice. Leave was stopped but those actually on leave were not at this stage recalled. Despite the excitement, the rumours, the reports of parachutists and the ringing of church bells, the night passed peacefully. No Germans were seen. The defenders stood down, but the battleships *Hood* and *Nelson* were ordered to move from Scapa to Rosyth, closer to the Channel, and *Revenge* was already at Plymouth.

After the excitement of the invasion scare things appear to have been quiet for a few days. The war diary records on 9 September 'very quiet, little air activity' and that D Company reported that the Stour River had been blocked by two ships. The respite was not destined to last. On 11 September a Me 110 crashed 3 miles west of Charing and large numbers of British bombers were reported flying south. D Company observed cross-Channel shelling of Sandwich in the area of the Guildford Hotel between 1800 and 2130 hours. A message arrived from division advising that 4 and 5 Independent Companies would shortly be arriving in the area. Approximately 100 incendiary bombs were dropped in the vicinity of Hothfield station, and on 14 September the battalion anti-aircraft weapons fired at a large enemy bomber, which was flying low. On being engaged by ground fire the aircraft sheered off and disappeared into low clouds.

BATTLE OF BRITAIN DAY

Sunday 15 September was destined to be known as Battle of Britain Day, but in north Kent things were quiet at first. The first event of the day recorded by the war diary occurred at 1445 hours when a Me 110 crashed at Rippers

Cross (383624). The pilot, Lt Helmut Muller, aged 27, was killed. The air gunner, Sgt Andreas Hoffman, aged 25, was badly wounded in the back and was sent by Capt. H.W. Evasley-Jones RAMC to Chartham Hospital where he later died. The aircraft's flare pistol had been fixed by a tube to the fuel tank and was loaded ready to fire. The rear gun was in perfect condition and was removed with such articles as pieces of the dashboard, parachutes, rubber boat and clothing and taken to Hothfield Place. RAF Hawkinge and division were informed, and the pilot's body was taken to the mortuary at Hothfield Hospital. A Company reported a German bomber down in the sea 1 mile off Swalecliffe and a twin-engined plane shot down in the sea off Leysdown. D Company reported that bombs had been dropped and that the Belle Vue Hotel at Pegwell had been demolished. So ended the first Battle of Britain day.

On 26 September 2/Lt B.V.C. Harpur (later to be a co-author of the regimental history *The Kensingtons*) and 2/Lt H.J. Scannall ceased to be attached officers and were now formally posted to the battalion. On the following day 2/Lts Pennington, Gray and Stanes arrived from MGTC. On 25 September Battalion HQ had been informed by division that a new machine-gun battalion would arrive within the next few days and would take up positions presently held by the Kensingtons. It was confirmed the next day that the new battalion would be the 4th Battalion, Cheshire Regiment. Their advance party arrived at Minster on 28 September. On the arrival of the main body of the Cheshires a general reorganisation took place. B Company HQ moved to 'Fairlawn', Beltinge Road, Herne Bay (632864), and D Company HQ, with 15 Platoon and the Cliffsend section of 1st Line Reserve, returned to Hothfield Place after handing over their positions to the Cheshires. After handing over to 6 Platoon, 13 Platoon and the Sheppey platoon of 1st Line Reserve also returned to Hothfield Place. The Hampton section of 5 Platoon moved to a new position east of Whitstable at grid 556855 and 9 Platoon took over the old positions at Herne Bay pier and Hampton, while 8 Platoon moved into posts vacated by D Company at Reculver, and 7 Platoon moved into the old section post at 100 steps (643867), which then became a platoon post. On 30 September 14 Platoon returned to Hothfield Place after handing over to 4th Cheshires.

The weather had been bad on 16 and 17 September and the only enemy activity recorded in the war diary involved an enemy bomber circling low over Hothfield Place at about 2,000ft on 16 September, and reports by D Company on the 17th of a barrage balloon floating in the sea off Reculver and bombs being dropped on Ramsgate. On 18 September A Company reported twelve bombs dropped on Tankerton. No further enemy activity is recorded in the war diary during the rest of September. Historians know now that although daylight raids on London and on aircraft factories were to continue when weather permitted, on 17 September Hitler had ordered that Operation Sealion was to be postponed.[24]

As September drew to a close the total number of confirmations that members of the battalion were safe and had been taken prisoner grew to 135. A large number of Kensingtons were still missing and unaccounted for, however, and it is to this issue of casualties and prisoners of war that we must now turn.

PRISONERS OF WAR, CASUALTIES AND CONCLUSIONS

The journey to the prison camps – Escapes – Estimates of casualties – The sacrifice theory – Morale – The future

The period in 1940 described by this book was one during which the British Army was engaged in a war different from any other it had yet fought. The start of the German assault on 10 May saw the BEF forced to conduct a fighting withdrawal ending in the success of the Dunkirk evacuation. For the Kensingtons it also meant a fighting withdrawal, but one which ended in in the catastrophe of St Valery. The end of September saw the Kensingtons re-formed, the Germans defeated in the air and plans for the invasion of the United Kingdom postponed indefinitely.

For most of the men of the Kensingtons it had been their first time abroad as well as their first time on active service. For a few it must have brought back memories of the first war, some of which they might have preferred to forget. Some of the accommodation requisitioned from French civilians was very poor, such as dilapidated barns full of filthy straw. Some of the military accommodation taken over from the French Army, such as the dugouts during the Saar campaign, was little better. The fighting was generally in a defensive role and the French soon proved disorganised, demoralised and defeatist. The story of the disaster that overtook the Kensingtons has been set out above and needs no repetition, save this: despite losing two companies, morale remained high and the remnants of the battalion returned home ready to regroup and play their part in defending their country.

The part that the Kensingtons were required to play was, inevitably, a defensive one. They were to join 1st London Division in the defence of the east coast of Kent from the Isle of Sheppey and Whitstable in the west to the North Foreland in the east, then south to Dover, Folkestone and New Romney. It is the garden of England, a landscape of castles, oast houses, apple orchards and village inns. Unlike the battalion's time in France, there was no ally and therefore no Gallic misunderstandings, tantrums, tears or breakdowns, just a clear understanding of what had to be done and a resolve to do it. If Jerry came he would be thrown back into the sea. So, a 20-year-old platoon commander takes his machine-gun sections and sites them in the trenches next to the Share and Coulter Inn, or in the pillboxes at the end of the pier, or on the cliffs overlooking the estuary, and he sits back and he waits, staring out at the dark sea. Is that darker shadow a boat? Is that noise the sound of engines? Was that a flicker of light? Waiting is something the battalion did a great deal of during the months when they and others guarded the invasion coast. The crisis came in September but by the end of the month the immediate threat had weakened. The weather began to deteriorate, the daylight air attacks declined and the invasion risk dwindled until the next spring. Those Kensingtons still deployed on the coast were relieved by other units and returned to join the rest of the battalion at Hothfield Place.

THE JOURNEY TO THE PRISON CAMPS

So much for those who were lucky enough to get back. Many had not been lucky. The majority of the troops of the 51st Division who ended up as prisoners were captured at St Valery or Veules les Roses and were then marched by their captors 220 miles on foot from there to Holland. From Holland they were taken by barge to Germany and thence to prison camps. The following extracts from Lt Reg Wood's diary cover the period from 12 June to 10 July:

12th Jun. Marched to large field outside St Valery. Rain stops and sun breaks through. Order to march off over hills escorted by large line of tanks. Go past French battery all dead. Three R.A.F. bombers fly over the long column of British and French prisoners, engaged by combined A/A and A/T German guns. Very hot and dusty, marched for hours no rest, food or water. Picked up bottle of wine in a deserted village, ate half of emergency ration. At 14.00hrs arrived at small town, marched into farmyard and given a rest of 1 hour, pulled off boots from aching feet and had first sleep for many days. Off again, marched over hills, through villages and practically dead after 38 kilometer march. Arrive at village of Manneville and put in deserted farm, no food or water given, sleep under trees. Rain at night but past caring.

13th June. Awoke at 06.00hrs, very stiff. Shaved in water from greasy stagnant pool, first time for three days. No food. Taken off in trucks through charred remains of burning villages and smell of burning flesh. Amiens mass of ruins in centre of town. Arrived Formerie, blackened shell, dreadful stench. Taken into large field surrounded by heavy M.Gs. Lot of French and British prisoners already there including Brig Burney. Charles, Jack, Ham and myself shared a tin of herrings which, with tin of bulley, was all we had on us when captured. Went to sleep. Given cup-full of weak pea soup at 14.00hrs. Johnny Dodge arrived clothed only in trousers and greatcoat, said he had tried to swim out to get boats to come in closer but had returned to shore and found all his clothes gone. Slept in open field, very rainy night. R.A.F. bombed Formerie aerodrome.

14th Jun. Cup of ersatz coffee for breakfast. 12.00hrs cup of weak pea soup. Left field at 13.00hrs. Very few houses in town occupied. Obtained water on march from few houses that were still occupied, also scrounged small bowl. Villages on route all bombed, large bomb craters beside road, smell of burning flesh and decaying bodies. Arrived at Joillay tired out at 19.00hrs, led into field where cattle sheds with just roof and four pillars were. Given cup of ersatz coffee, small chunk of very stale bread, piece of horsemeat. Bathed feet in water in steel helmet. Rain.

15th Jun. Cup of ersatz coffee for breakfast. Got separated from rest when trucks arrived to take us off. Taken in truck to field 20 miles from Amiens near Liguiere. Previous trucks had gone on. Large numbers of Ps.O.W. already in field and some British but none of my party. Made a bed of loose straw gathered in fields with Padre Charles King of 7th. Norfolks who I had first met on the Saar. Johnny Dodge arrived with next truck to end. Cupful of weak soya bean soup at 12.00hrs, same again at 19.00hrs. Had wash in stream.

16th Jun. Weak coffee for breakfast, pouring rain. British officers allowed into empty houses by road, found a towel and Padre King made some cakes out of flour he had found in house. 12.00hrs Soya bean soup. Trucks arrive to take us on to Domart, 50 in small truck, towns burnt out, many bomb craters and abandoned and destroyed vehicles. Amiens mass of ruins. Driven into large field outside Domart, masses of British and French prisoners. Met Mike and Salmon. No food issued as French had queued up twice and taken our small share. Washed and shaved in muddy stream. Being Sunday night a prayer meeting was held.

17th Jun. Issued with ½ packet of British biscuits, small piece of cheese and cup of ersatz coffee. Marched off to Doullens 21 miles away, uphill, very hot. Managed to eat raw mangels and Swedes and ears of corn from the fields on the way. Many signs of ravages of recent war. Saw burnt out R.A.F. bomber with two shrivelled up skeletons inside it. Reached Doullens in late afternoon, many houses bombed. Marched into old monastery with tents in the grounds. French at once seized all the tents so we let them down and in the end we had half and they half. Made a stew of the turnips and Swedes we had collected on the way. At 17.00hrs ½ loaf of bread and cup-full of soup issued. Washed and shaved. Gave field service postcard to sentry in hopes that it might get home.

18th Jun. Issued with cup of ersatz coffee and ⅕ loaf of bread and marched off at 06.30hrs to St Pol, 16 ½ miles away. Reaching area of France that was inhabited again. Bought small pieces of bread for exorbitant prices and ½ loaf for 100 francs (11s/4d). French officers rushed into shops to get food. Old lady gave me two raw eggs which I sucked. Led into troops camp outside St Pol, knives, lighters, cigarette cases etc taken away. Issued with cup full of bean soup, small piece of meat and ½ packet of British ration biscuits. Then marched on a further two miles to St Pol racecourse where tents had been erected. Wrote down name, number and rank, civil German officer gave me a cigarette. Washed self and clothes which soon dried in hot sun. People from St Pol sold food at main gate, got bread, butter and cigarettes. Find a store of B.R. biscuits behind grandstand and have good feed for first time since capture. At 20.00hrs coffee issued and Reiney-Dougal D.A.Q.M.G. of 51st. Div made speech saying tomorrow would be issued with ½ packet of biscuits and a cup of coffee and that sick officers would go by truck but the rest would march 18 ½ miles to Bethune. He himself was going by truck (he wasn't sick!!) and Lt Col Swinborne, the G.I. of the 51st. Div would be in charge of the party marching.

19th Jun. Issued with ½ packet of B.R. biscuits and cup of ersatz coffee. Inhabitants en route very generous, particularly the women. Gave us coffee, wine, bread, chocolate and cigarettes in small quantities. In centre of mining district, outside Davion, led into a large field and women came in loaded with baskets and gave us sandwiches, lettuce, bread and butter, jam and coffee, sardines, cigarettes. Gave names and addresses to local Red Cross representative. Half an hour later resumed the march and in other towns and villages as we marched by people gave us strawberries, chocolate, beer etc and one dear lady gave me a bottle of champagne. Despite the good cheer it was very tiring, all the roads were cobbled and dirty and it was extremely hot. Bethune comprehensively bombed and shelled. Marched into sports stadium, filthy condition, masses of French there already also party that went by truck. Placed in grandstand, very draughty. Issued with bowl of soup and ⅓ loaf of bread. No washing facilities, latrines putrid. Settled down to cold night on stone floor of stand.

20th Jun. Only issued with cup of ersatz coffee before march of 21 miles to Seclin. Posters up in Bethune saying how British had deserted the French etc and French were fighting Britain's war. Received gifts of food on way from French population. Buy two tins of sardines for 20 francs at Busay. Marched into school at Seclin, French officers seized all accommodation inside so we had to sleep outside on concrete playground. Washing facilities and latrines dreadful. French girl whom I spoke to over wall got me some bread.

21st Jun. Issued with cup of ersatz coffee and then marched off to Tournai, 17 ½ miles away. German sentry said 'nothings in the stomach, I was P.O.W. in last war-in Liverpool and I-learnt-English-there'. After 3 hours march with no rest in boiling sun on dusty cobbles reached Sin. Local population streamed up to give us food. Crossed Belgium frontier. Atmosphere quite different, no signs of anyone willing to give us food or even water. Marched into jail at Tournai, cells with doors left open for four officers apiece and plenty of straw on the floors. Cold shower. At 14.00hrs given some bean soup and ⅙ loaf of bread. Buy through gates of jail butter, chocolate, gringoire, gingerbread, sardines and beer. At 18.00hrs some rice, a herring (raw) and ⅙ loaf issued. Heard we were to stay here another day and very pleased as after all we had been through this seemed like heaven.

22nd Jun. Bought cherries, chocolate and butter, raisins and beer. Washed clothes. Issued at 12.00hrs with ⅙ loaf of bread and cup of soup. At 18.00hrs the same.

23rd Jun. March to Renaix (Ronse) 15 ½ miles away. Belgian population now more friendly and generous. Germans objected to our songs whilst marching. Led into dirty unused factory. Given ¼ loaf of bread and not possible to buy any food. Gave cheque to Belgian Red Cross official with message to my people on back with hope it might get cashed. At 18.00hrs a cupful of potato soup issued.

24th Jun. Given cup of ersatz coffee and marched off to Ninove, 22 miles away. Very fatigued, hilly and dusty and hot. Marched into silk factory there and issued at 15.00hrs with ¼ loaf of bread and 2 ozs sausage. Buy food over garden wall of house adjoining factory; jam, cheese and cherries. At 20.00hrs issued with soup and ⅙ loaf of bread.

25th Jun. Stay at Ninove for further day. Issued with cup of ersatz coffee at 07.30hrs. Bought more butter, cherries, jam and gringoire over garden wall. ¼ loaf of bread issued at lunch time and cup of soup and same at 18.00hrs. Washed clothes.

26th Jun. Issued with cup of ersatz coffee at 05.30hrs and left for Aalst, 9 ½ miles away. Shortest march yet. Bought some chocolate and cigarettes outside gate, Half way received soup from Belgian Red Cross and gave a further cheque to Red Cross official. Led into barracks at Aalst. Bullying guards. Managed to buy some chocolate from a man who came in. At 18.00hrs issued with ¼ loaf of bread, 2 ozs sausage and ersatz coffee and then locked in barrack rooms, 200 in room meant for 40.

27th Jun. Issued with cup of ersatz coffee and slice of bread. Marched 20 miles to St Niklaas, bridges in this neighbourhood all blown up. Boy on bike gets cheese, 20 tins of sardines and half loaf of bread. Very fine cathedral in square at St Niklaas. Population give us beer and chocolate. Marched into barracks at 15.00hrs and register our names etc. Straw on barrack floor. Shop open in barracks and able to buy custard pies, cakes, chocolate and lemonade. Barbers shop also open. Issued at 18.00hrs with ⅓ loaf, lard and cup of ersatz coffee.

28th Jun. Stay in barracks for further day and very glad of rest as absolutely worn out. Washed clothes and had a hair cut. Bought sardines, cigarettes and 2 origano. Soup issued at midday and in evening, ⅓ loaf and small portion of butter.

29th Jun. Issued with cup of coffee and ⅓ loaf and set off at 06.30hrs for Holland where barges were to take us down the Scholdt into Germany. Passed through very beautiful forests with attractive cafes in them. Passed over Dutch-Belgian frontier, quite different. Everything very neat and clean and fields cultivated up to last inch of ground. Factory girls rushed out and gave us each a sandwich, Reached Huilst at 10.15hrs. Red Cross officials gave us 2 sandwiches each. Put in train, 70 in compartment for 40, very hot. Dutch threw food in to us. 11.30hrs arrived at Walsoorden, given extremely stale loaf, 3 potatoes and soup which was our rations for journey on barge. Taken to the river Scheldt and allowed to bathe. Boarded barge 'Queen Emma' at 17.00hrs. French seized all accommodation down below but left us the deck, we were thus really far better off. Sailed off at 18.00hrs. Went through locks and mass of waterways connecting Dutch islands. Girls in national costume. Tied up for night at Emmeircht, hoardes of French kept coming up from below and told what they could do.

30th Jun. Went into river Maas, concrete pill-boxes on banks of river, bridges blown up. Delightful scenery; Dutch men and women in canoes seemed oblivious there was a war on. At 11 o/c stopped at Dortrecht and a meat sandwich a head given us by inhabitants, also small quantity of honey. Speech by German officer from boat in perfect English saying how fortunate we were in coming into Germany and he hoped when we returned home we would take back many happy memories with us. Sun boiling hot; envied girls in bathing costumes. Arrive at German-Dutch frontier, forts blown up. At 19.00hrs tie up at Wesel and see our first German civilians; very apathetic and show little interest. Flags flying from all buildings to celebrate victory over France. German Luftwaffe soldiers and N.C.Os talk down to us. Boat pulls away and anchored midstream for night.

1st Jul. Boat ties up against wharf again. Steel helmets taken away (contrary to Geneva convention). Marched off boat, civilians stare, shops empty. Marched into large park and given ⅓ loaf, cheese and ersatz coffee. Wash and shave at taps in park. Women instructors teaching P.T. to small children. At 16.00hrs issued with ration for train of ⅓ loaf of bread, cheese. Marched off to station and put into 3rd Class carriages. Very delightful scenery at first, people working in fields think we are a troop train and wave. Enter Ruhr district, town after town smoke, noise etc. Bochum, Sterkrade. Go to sleep sitting up. Air raid alarm goes, searchlights in sky and A/A heard very close. Sentry says raid on Cologne. At 02.00hrs arrive at Heimar station, Marched to barracks partially built in side of stone quarry.

2nd Jul. Many Polish prisoners there. Barracks unfinished and unfurnished. Sleep in rooms on stone floors covered with straw but inside washroom and lavatories working. Each barrack wired off and only 20 yards exercise space. No view at all. At 07.00hrs gate opened to allow us to go into central compound to get ersatz coffee from cookhouse. Jack, Ham and Charles in neighbouring barrack, talk to them through wire. At 11.00hrs go to cookhouse to get potato soup, Polish cooks give us double portions on learning we are British. At 18.00hrs 1/5 loaf and small piece of cheese issued. Air raid warning during night.

3rd Jul. 07.00hrs ersatz coffee. Walk up and down the 20 yards stretch. 11.00hrs potato soup. Sleep until 15.30hrs. 16.00hrs issue of ⅕ loaf and ersatz treacle. Read terms of French armistice in old German newspaper. Air raid during night; heard bombs dropping.

4th Jul. 07.00hrs ersatz coffee. 11.00hrs tomato soup. 16.00hrs ⅕ loaf and bacon fat. Started to wash clothes outside but Senegalese took them off me and insisted on doing them.

5th Jul. 07.00hrs ersatz coffee, 11.00hrs potato soup, 16.00hrs ⅕ loaf and 2 ozs sausage. Very bored now nothing to do, nothing to read, nowhere to walk. Hope we get sent on to proper camp soon.

6th Jul. Usual issues of food. Up to now we had managed to augment the meagre rations by a tin of sardines a day which we had bought on the march. Heard we were to leave at 15.00hrs for final destination. Only train ration would be the usual evening ration of ⅓ loaf and 2 ozs sausagemeat. Doors locked of train, beautiful scenery, forests, villages etc. Ate ½ our ration and kept our other ½ for tomorrow.

7th Jul. Ate other half of our ration. Very hungry by midday and wooden seats of compartment getting very hard. Rumour we would reach Munich at 15.00hrs and be fed there but unfortunately passed through without stopping. Train very hot and very, very hungry. No water, Arrived at Nuremberg at 17.00hrs and saw people eating and drinking in station restaurant; made us even more ravenous. Typical Bavarian scenery, mosques, domes etc, Passed through Letmanthe, Altenhunden, Kreuztal, Regensberg, Muhldorf; very hilly. Frantic with hunger and thirst. Reach Laufen station at 21.00hrs.

8th Jul. Arrive at Schloss Caserne after ¼ hours walk from station at 01.00hrs. Used to be bishops palace, then barracks and now P.O.W camp formerly occupied by Poles but now by British officers. Marched into large garage, given 1/5 loaf and slept on straw. Issued at 07.00hrs with ersatz coffee and ½ loaf to last two days, bowl, mug, knife and spoon. Chair and table brought into garage and interrogation and particulars taken. All heads shaved. Issued at 11.00hrs with ½ litre soup and 3 potatoes and at 16.30hrs with ½ litre of soup and 3 potatoes. Interrogation didn't reach us so had to spend another night in garage. Place swept up by orderlies in red trousers who were part of International Brigade on way back from Finland and caught in Norway.

In the following March Reg Wood heard that they were to be moved by train to a camp in Poland. Weak and tired, they arrived at the station at last and prayed that the march on the other end would not be far. Gen. Fortune was on the platform and said he was coming with them. The train was very cold. Thin soup was dished out to anyone feeling weak. Fortune purchased ersatz coffee for everybody at a cost of 60 marks. After two days on the train they marched off with the general at the head. Luggage was getting very heavy; many people dropped and left it. At last after 4 miles of a staggering, weary march they arrived at an underground fort surrounded by an empty moat and barbed wire, and marched over the drawbridge and into a long underground tunnel. A proclamation was read out by an interpreter stating that owing to the fact that German POWs in Canada were kept in Fort Henry with not a shrub or patch of shade and in bad conditions, British prisoners had, in retaliation, been moved to this 'Fort 8' until conditions in Canada had been improved. All rooms were underground with eight- and twelve-tier beds, fleas and lice. Prisoners were locked in rooms at night with a blanket. Ablutions were old and primitive with some seats nailed down to give the exact number they had in Fort 8. The only exercise place was an area of about 100 yards in the moat, very narrow and with an excreta stream running through it. Fortune sent a telegram to the American Embassy. He himself was in a room with eleven others. No hot showers were available and water was supplied by pump only. All reading matter had been confiscated on arrival.[1] Fortune was 56 years old and throughout his imprisonment endured rigours that were taxing enough for men more than thirty years younger. Yet, as this extract shows, he always retained a concern for the welfare of his men.

ESCAPES

A surprising number of soldiers from all units of the division made the dangerous decision to attempt to escape from the marching column. Some were shot as they ran for cover and some were recaptured later, but a surprising number managed to get back to England after months of evading the Germans and the Vichy French. Linklater:

> When the captive-column of the Fifty-First had a little recovered from the exhaustion of the first few days – when men marched as if in a fearful dream of weariness and starvation – then some of the stronger and more daring found opportunity to elude their guards and go to cover in a roadside wood. Every day a few more escaped from the long column, and waiting for the night would turn on their tracks and begin a tedious long march to the coast, or farther still to the Spanish frontier. Then it was that the people of France showed their courage and abiding friendship, for in lonely farms or in villages under the very nose of the German conqueror these desperate fugitives found sustenance and willing help.[2]

Among the fugitives was Pte F. Ford of the Kensingtons. Ford's account of his escape records that his unit was in position at St Valery and surrendered with the rest of the division on 12 June. The prisoners were then marched approximately due north in the direction of Doullens. On 17 June, near Doullens, Ford managed to get out of the column and, with the help of a small compass, which he had hidden in his boot, made his way to Paris by way of Amiens, Beauvais and Pontoise. From Paris he made for Orleans, crossed the line of demarcation into unoccupied France and headed for Mont Lucon, Vichy, Roanne, Valence, Avignon, Arles and thence to Marseilles. Wherever he passed the inhabitants were very good to him, providing him with food, shelter and, in many cases, with maps. At Mont Lucon a French officer stopped him but made no attempt to have him interned. At Marseilles Ford managed to steal a motor boat, but only got as far as Port du Bac before the engine failed. He got back to the beach and, by jumping on a train, got to Port Vendres where he found a rowing boat and went well out to sea and down the Spanish coast, landing near Figueras. Here he was arrested and taken to prison. Later he was transferred to Cervera and then to Miranda del Ibro, from where he was eventually released and taken to Gibraltar. Ford left Gibraltar on 19 November and arrived in Liverpool on 4 December. On 6 December he was interviewed by officers of MI9. Ford's escape demonstrated qualities of courage, determination and self-reliance, and very properly he was subsequently Mentioned in Despatches.[3]

Interestingly, Harpur refers to other escapees from the column.[4] Pte R. Bailey also escaped at the same time and place as Pte Ford, but separately. They each hid in a wood, obtained civilian clothes from friendly locals, individually crossed into unoccupied France and got to Marseilles and then Spain after five months. They must surely have met each other at some stage but there is no record that they did. On their return each was awarded a Commander-in-Chief's Certificate of Gallantry. Unlike Ford, however, there is no record of Bailey being Mentioned in Despatches. It is a sad irony that each was subsequently killed in 1944, Bailey on 3 January with the 1st Battalion in Italy and Ford on 28 June with the 2nd Battalion in Normandy. Other Kensington POWs apparently also escaped but were recaptured. Johnny Dodge made several more unsuccessful attempts. Frederick Davis Ford was 25, the son of William and Grace Ford and was married to Gladys Ford of Tottenham, London. He is buried at Tilly sur Seulles War Cemetery. Raymond Bailey was 24, the son of William and Margaret Bailey and husband of Cynthia Bailey of Dorchester. He is buried at the Sangro River War Cemetery.[5]

ESTIMATES OF CASUALTIES

It is recorded in chapter six that in England during August and September the Kensingtons received official news that some members of A and D Companies were now prisoners of war, and the Old Comrades Association began to organise the sending of cigarettes and parcels. It took until March 1941 before almost all personnel were accounted for and even then some were still missing.

The fatal casualty figures are another matter. There are no precise numbers of those Kensingtons killed during the 1940 campaign, in addition to 274 reported missing (A and D Companies). The strength of the three companies from Ark Force (B, C and HQ plus Battalion HQ) was 350 on their arrival back in England from Le Havre on 13 June. All 119 names on the roll of honour have been checked against the Commonwealth War Graves Commission database to identify all those who were killed during April to June 1940. There are eight who were. Their personal details (age, date of death, place of burial and sometimes family details) have been extracted from the database and included in the narrative out of respect for the sacrifice they made. Eight deaths out of an establishment of 730 represents a casualty rate of 1.1 per cent. It is a separate issue, but in all the circumstances this figure does seem remarkably low.

The number of deaths, when added to other figures, has been used to estimate the numbers who were taken prisoner. It will be remembered that two entire companies, A and D, were taken prisoner at St Valery and that at full strength a company numbered about 140 men. Table 2 (Appendix I) is an attempt to break down such figures as there are and from them to extrapolate the number of prisoners. It is based on figures assumed to be correct, such as the battalion overall establishment figure and the number of those in Ark Force who returned from Le Havre. Put simply, the total number of men, other than prisoners, but including those killed and those who escaped, is added together and the total subtracted from the battalion's establishment of 730. What remains is the approximate number taken prisoner.

There are problems in compiling accurate figures for deaths and prisoners. The regimental war diary should have been one source of information but in the case of the Kensingtons the diary went with Battalion HQ and Ark Force. It consequently contains nothing about St Valery or Veules les Roses other than what is contained in Maj. de Chimay's report. Harpur records four deaths among members of A Company on the final night at St Valery, but it seems possible, or even likely, that there were more. Some information was later compiled by units in response to a request from the War Office for accurate casualty returns, and the replies could be shocking in the extent of the losses. Many units, like the Kensingtons, were able to provide the numbers who returned to England, but it was not known how many of those who failed to return were fatalities and how many were prisoners of war. In September the first lists of confirmed dead of the BEF were received by the British government from the French Red Cross. For the Kensingtons it took until March 1941, a further six months, before almost every man had been accounted for.

THE SACRIFICE THEORY

'The activities of the 51st (Highland) Division ceased' were the words later written by Lt Col Harry Swinburn at the end of his history of the campaign. So many men of the division had been killed and so many taken prisoner, and for what gain? The effect on the small highland communities from which many of the Scottish soldiers came was severe. It is therefore perhaps not surprising that a view has grown up that the division was deliberately sacrificed by Churchill in a failed attempt to bolster French morale and to encourage them not to capitulate.

On the face of it the sacrifice theory may seem an easy one to support. From 10 May there was a series of major failures of French command and morale at the highest levels, which led Churchill to believe that their capitulation was imminent. As early as 15 May, for example, when German armour broke out from the bridgeheads on the Meuse, the French premier Paul Reynaud had woken Churchill with a 7.30 a.m. telephone call to tell him that France was beaten and the war lost. A fortnight later Generals Weygand and Petain were conspiring together to sue for peace if the planned Somme attack failed. Churchill initially showed signs of susceptibility to this kind of pressure and could border on the reckless in his attempts to support the French. He was, for example, certainly prepared to consider sympathetically French requests for substantial numbers of additional fighter aircraft – on one occasion a request for as many as ten squadrons, or 120 aircraft, to be sent. These requests prompted the C-in-C of Fighter Command to write his famous memorandum warning of 'the final, complete and irremediable defeat' of Britain if the home defence was drained away. There was, however, a limit beyond which Churchill was not prepared to go. As early as 19 May that limit was reached when he issued a minute stating categorically that no more squadrons would leave Britain whatever the need in France. Whatever his earlier hopes about keeping France in the war, by 19 May Churchill was not prepared to sacrifice the RAF to do so. The French were not to receive massive British air support. Two weeks later over 190,000 British troops had been evacuated from Dunkirk. No more aircraft, and with the return of the second BEF, no more soldiers either. Is it really likely in these circumstances that Churchill believed that the sacrifice of one infantry division would stop the French from surrendering?

On its arrival in the Somme area from Lorraine at the end of May, the Highland Division had been placed under the command of the French IX Corps. The following fortnight was to begin badly and end in disaster, with a series of misfortunes in between, particularly the slow pace of the withdrawal towards Le Havre due to French horse-drawn transport. The fortnight began with the failed attack on the Somme bridgeheads on 4 June. It ended on 12 June with the surrender at St Valery en Caux of both the 51st Division and IX Corps.

On 8 June a formal recommendation that the division be removed from French command had been sent to the War Office by Lt Gen. Marshall-Cornwall, British liaison officer with the French Tenth Army. He feared that the 51st Division was in imminent danger of being cut off and he had completely lost faith in the French ability to resist. The proposal was, of course, far too sensitive for the War Office to contemplate but there is no doubt that the underlying and fundamental cause of almost all of the 51st Division's difficulties clearly stems from it being under a highly ineffectual French command. French morale finally collapsed when the German breakout came at Sedan. Given that it was by then impossible for the division to rejoin the BEF, it can perhaps be argued that there was one realistic alternative: instead of being directed to the Somme it could have been sent immediately to the major British base at Rouen. There it could have joined with the Beauman Division, the garrison forces and the 1st Armoured Division to create what would have been in effect a small British corps of two infantry divisions (one mechanised) and one reduced armoured division. Rested and replenished, this force could have co-operated with the French IX Corps to hold the line of the Seine pending the planned arrival at Cherbourg of the second BEF in early June and its concentration around Le Mans. In fact, in early June, immediately after the conclusion of the Dunkirk evacuation, Lt Gen. Sir John Dill, chief of the Imperial General Staff, told

Lt Gen. Alan Brooke that the 51st Division would join the second BEF as soon as it arrived in France. It was in Britain's best interests that if a second BEF had to be formed it was immediately reinforced on arrival by the addition of a battle-experienced and substantially stronger than normal division.

All of this employs a substantial amount of hindsight. Churchill was not to know that Britain could survive a French capitulation, nor that the Battle of Britain would be won and that, thanks to the RAF and Royal Navy, there would be no invasion. In May and June 1940 it was believed to be vital to keep France in the war and actions had to be taken in support of that aim. None of this supports the claim that a British division was knowingly and deliberately sacrificed in further-ance of that aim. What does seem to be the case is that the division was placed and then kept in a very difficult position. It was kept under the command of an ally whose morale had been broken and whose capacity to fight was at best severely impaired or, at worst, non-existent. That ally had become, as Adm. Jacky Fisher once described outdated British warships, 'too weak to fight, too slow to run away'. Yet there was no move made to redress the situation. A paralysis seemed to grip the War Office that verged on ambivalence at best, negligence at worst. It is perhaps these charges, not one of deliberate sacrifice, which can most properly be laid at the door of the British government.

MORALE

A dictionary definition of the noun 'morale' is given as 'discipline and spirit'. In other words, morale is a characteristic that embodies these qualities. It is difficult to prove a negative, but among all the records and accounts of the Kensingtons there is no record of any failure of either discipline or spirit. After their return to England in mid-June 1940 the Kensingtons had been posted straight back on to front-line operations, to be deployed in July as part of the anti-invasion defences in Kent. In the unlikely event that the enemy had somehow managed to evade the Royal Navy and get his assault troops ashore on the Folkestone sector, the Kensingtons would have been among the first defending troops that the *Vorausabteilung* would have encountered. The German advance might have been delayed but it is likely that the defenders would in the end have been overrun. Prisoners would not have been taken: they are a nuisance and require guards and rations. The front-line defending companies were stoical in their acceptance of a role that clearly demanded a high level of morale and personal courage.

By the end of September the Royal Air Force had defeated the attempt by the German air force to achieve air superiority over England, the Royal Navy con-tinued to make the English Channel an exclusion zone for the German navy and the immediate danger of invasion was judged to have passed. The Kensingtons had endured a difficult time in France and had lost two entire companies at St Valery. The 1st Battalion had by September been in almost continuous action for five months, and in due course gained three new battle honours to be added to its colours: Saar, Somme, St Valery en Caux. Battle honours come at a price, and by the end of June 1940 almost one-third of the battalion were prisoners, dead or missing. At least eight had been killed in France and another two, the MO and Pte Cresswell, were killed later in England. Many more had been wounded. The battalion had fought well in very difficult circumstances, had received the thanks of those units it had supported, and one of its members had been awarded the Distinguished Conduct Medal for gallantry. The CO, Lt Col Parker, later wrote of those months:

> I shall always look back with pride at the privilege of commanding such a magnificent body of officers, warrant officers, non-commissioned officers and men. During the difficult and anxious times in France, all ranks were ever cheerful and confident and always ready for any call that was made upon them. At home ... by your loyal efforts and hard work the battalion won the reputation of being one of the finest and best disciplined units in the army. Your exemplary behaviour whilst stationed at Ashford ... won the respect and admiration of the civil authorities and the inhabitants alike.[6]

On the continent a spirit of a different kind was demonstrated by a number of Kensingtons who were prisoners. It is difficult to understand how men forced to march very long distances each day on starvation rations, ill-treated and wearing broken boots, had any spirit left at all. Yet soldiers of the Kensingtons attempted to escape and at least one such attempt, by Pte Ford, was successful; Ford got home in December 1940.

Of the morale within the 51st (Highland) Division as a whole, Linklater wrote:

> The Hard Core of Discipline: It is, on the whole, against a background of rout and the sickness of despair that the performance of the Fifty-First must be assessed and the fact that signally emerges is that throughout its rearguard action and retreat the Division retained coherence. It remained a Division and discipline ruled until the very end. It had shown, both on the Saar and on the Somme, a finely aggressive spirit and a great stubbornness in defeat. It had discovered a remarkable unwillingness, incapacity is perhaps the better word, to admit defeat though the odds against it were always heavy ... what conclusively proves that the Division was a good Division is its continuing discipline. There is no sterner test of discipline than a long rearguard action ... the Fifty First survived those tests, and the Division was a Division till the end ... its spirit was unbroken and discipline was last in the field.[7]

Major L.F. Ellis expresses a similar view:

Withdrawal is a valid operation of war; ability to withdraw when occasion warrants is often a necessary prelude to eventual victory. But a long fighting withdrawal is also one of the most difficult operations of war, for it taxes severely the moral and physical strength of the troops and the skill and steady courage of their commanders.[8]

THE FUTURE

This account of 1st Battalion Princess Louise's Kensington Regiment covers the period of six months from April to September 1940, but at the end of the story it seems appropriate to devote a few lines to the movements of the battalion from 1940 until the end of the war and beyond. The 1st Battalion remained on home service until May 1943 when it sailed to Algiers. It subsequently took part in the Sicilian campaign, followed by the invasion of Italy. Soon after the war ended both the 1st and 2nd Battalions were disbanded and for a short time Princess Louise's Kensington Regiment ceased to exist. Perhaps the phrase 'was in suspended animation' is a better one for, on 1 May 1947, the TA was re-formed with the Kensingtons resurrected as a regiment within the Royal Signals. The formal title was eventually settled in 1949 as Army Phantom Signal Regiment (Princess Louise's Kensington Regiment). In 1967 the Kensingtons and the Middlesex Yeomanry were amalgamated and became 31st (Greater London) Signal Regiment (V).

It is now more than forty years since the Kensington Regiment lost its individual identity and during those years there have been many more, some would say too many, reorganisations of the TA. In some ways the Kensingtons have been fortunate since they have survived as a squadron of the Royal Signals. Their current title is 41st (Princess Louise's Kensington) Squadron (Volunteers) Coulsdon, and they operate from a drill hall in Coulsdon, Surrey. 41 Squadron is part of the 38th (Sheffield) Signals Regiment TA, which has three other squadrons based in Derby, Sheffield and Nottingham, and Blackburn and Manchester.

Let the end of the story be that of Maj. Ellis, referring to the 1940 campaign:

Our grievous losses do not give the whole picture. More important in the long run than the losses which the Services had sustained were their gains in experience and in confidence. The men of the British Expeditionary Force came back with a conviction that on reasonably equal terms they could defeat the enemy ... The three fighting services had together defeated the enemy's intention to destroy the British Expeditionary Force, and the Services and the Nation behind them faced the future with unshaken courage with a will to fight on which had been toughened and tempered in the fires of adversity.[9]

Sic Transit Gloria
Quid Nobis Ardui

TABLES

Table 1

Known escapees from St Valery and Veules les Roses

Name	Date of Escape	Company	Escaped From	Escape Method	Source	Date in UK	Notes
Pte Charlton		A	St Valery	Boat	war diary	13 June	
Pte Holmes		A	Not known	Not known	war diary	15 June	Found on train at Mill Hill
Cpl Walley	12 June	B	Veules les Roses	Boat	Maj. de Chimay's account		Separated from B Company
CSM Satchwell & 8 other ranks	12 June	D	Veules les Roses	Boat	war diary	18 June	
Major de Chimay	12 June	A	Veules les Roses		war diary	18 June	
Pte Gratwood	14 June	D	Doullens	Rowing boat	war diary	21 June	
Pte Ford		Not Known		Escaped from POW Column	National Archives WO/ 373/60	4 Dec	On foot via Marseilles

Table 2
Analysis of battalion strength on 30 June 1940, based on an establishment of 740 and excluding reinforcements

Date	Event	Numbers	Source
Various	Miscellaneous escapees arrived back from St Valery and Veules	16	war diary
May	PSM Frost (B Company) and Sgt Wilmott (D Company) killed (Saar)	2	war diary
11 June	Pte Parish (D Company?) killed near Veules les Roses	1	War Graves Commission
12 June	A and D Companies captured at St Valery	285 est.	war diary
12 June	A Company, four killed at St Valery: Ptes Summers, Farlander, Haslam, Paley	4	War Graves Commission
13 June	Battalion HQ, B, C and HQ Companies arrive back at Southampton	350	
19 June	2/Lt Burton returns from Cherbourg	1	war diary
24 June	2/Lt Kent and two platoons of B Company return from Cherbourg	70	war diary
Between 19 May & 23 June	Pte Piggott killed (place, unit and dates not known)	1	War Graves Commission
	TOTAL	730	Establishment approx. 740 all ranks (Ellis)

Table 3
Reinforcements sent to battalion in England from 17 June to August 1940

Date	Name	From	Number	Source
17 June	49 First-Line Reinforcements	St Malo	49	war diary
21 June	10 Second Lieutenants	MGTC	10	war diary
22 June	1 First-Line Reinforcement	Not known	1	war diary
27 June	2/Lt and 5 other ranks	6 IBD	6	war diary
29 June	1 officer and 34 other ranks	5 IBD	35	war diary
30 June	147 other ranks	MGTC	147	war diary
August	6 officers and 120 other ranks	MGTC	126	war diary
		TOTAL	374	

MGTC: Machine Gun Training Centre   IBD: Infantry Base Depot

Table 4
Officers and Warrant Officers 1st Princess Louise's Kensington Regiment (May–June 1940)

Commanding Officer	Lieutenant Colonel F. Gordon Parker
2 i/c	Major F. Walden
Adjutant	Captain A.L. Bryar
Intelligence Officer	2/Lt E.P. Shanks
Quartermaster	Captain E.D. Knight
Medical Officer	Captain J.W. Smith RAMC
Chaplain	A/Captain Revd V. Bennett
RSM	Mr A. Hill
RQMS	Mr R. Edgecombe
OC A Company	Major A. de Chimay
2 i/c	Captain H.R. Mountford
CSM	Mr Darling
Platoon Commander 6 Platoon	2/Lt A.R. Meikle
Platoon Commander 5 Platoon	PSM Thompson
Platoon Commander 4 Platoon	2/Lt B.R. Wood
OC B Company	Captain E.W. Holding
2 i/c	
CSM	Mr Hibberd
Platoon Commander 8 Platoon	2/Lt G Kent (previously WO3 Frost: killed in action)
Platoon Commander	2/Lt P.F. Smythe
Platoon Commander	2/Lt S. Caulfield-Kerney
OC C Company	Captain C.J. Padfield
2 i/c	Captain P. Beevor
CSM	Mr Skinner
Platoon Commander	2/Lt W.E. Walker
Platoon Commander	2/Lt H.A.C. Page
Platoon Commander	PSM Gordon

OC D Company	Major J. Dodge
2 i/c	Captain A.H. Salmon
CSM	Mr Satchwell
Platoon Commander	2/Lt J.H. Lavington
Platoon Commander	2/Lt R. Hammond
Platoon Commander	PSM Mullender
OC HQ Company	Captain R. Wasey
Signals Officer	2/Lt I.H. Battye
Motor Transport Officer	Lt R.D. Milton
OME	Lt D. Rae RAOC
CSM	Mr Butler
Platoon Commander	PSM Chilton

Note: this list is not exhaustive.

Table 5
Officers who sailed for France, April 1940

<u>HQ</u>
CO	Lt Col F.G. Parker
2 i/c	Maj. F.W. Walden (Fannie)
Adjutant	Capt. B.L. Bryar (Laurie)
IO	2/Lt E.P. Shanks (Ernest)
QM	Lt E.D. Knight MM (Rocky)
MO	Capt. J. Smith (John)
Padre	Capt. Revd F. Bennett

<u>HQ Company</u>
Company Commander	Maj. A.A. de C. Chimay
Transport Officer	Lt R.D. Milton (Ray)
Signals Officer	2/Lt J.H. Battye (Jim)

<u>A Company</u>
Company Commander	Capt. G.D. Paterson (David)
2 i/c	Capt. H.R. Mountford (Charles)
	2/Lt A.R. Meikle (Mike)
	2/Lt B.R. Wood (Reg)

B Company
Company Commander	Capt. E.W. Holding
2 i/c	Capt. R. Wasey (Ronnie)
	Lt P.F. Smythe (Peter)
	2/Lt F.S. Caulfield-Kerney

C Company
Company Commander	Capt. H.C. Padfield MBE
2 i/c	Capt. P. Beevor (Paul)
	2/Lt J.E. Walker
	2/Lt H. Page

D Company
Company Commander	Maj. J.B. Dodge DSO, DSC (Johnnie)
2 i/c	Capt. A.H. Salmon
	2/Lt H.J. Lavington (Jack)
	2/Lt R. Hammond (Ham)

First-Line
Reinforcements
	Capt. C.K. Williamson (Charles)
	2/Lt A.L. Burton
	2/Lt G. Kent
	2/Lt J.J. Evans (John)

Table 6
Some of the positions occupied July to August 1940

Position	Grid	Occupied by	Note
Greatstone on Sea	519415	10 Platoon	Under 135 Bde (temp)
New Romney	506434	12 Platoon	Under 135 Bde (temp)
Hampton	596860	7 Platoon HQ + 1 section	Under 1 Lon Inf. Bde
Swalecliffe	578858	7 Platoon 1 section	Under 1 Lon Inf. Bde
Bishopstone	653868	8 Platoon HQ + 1 section	Under 1 Lon Inf. Bde
Reculver	670874	8 Platoon 1 section	Under 1 Lon Inf. Bde
Sarre	699829	9 Platoon HQ + 1 section	
Minnis Bay	730877	9 Platoon 1 section	
Horton Park	565580	11 Platoon	2 Lon Inf. Bde mobile res
Broadoak	609796	B Company HQ	Moved from Hothfield Place

Rose Marie Café	Whitstable	C Company HQ	
Herne Bay pier		7 Platoon HQ +1 section	Moved from Hampton
Herne Bay prom-enade	646868	7 Platoon 1 section	Moved from Swalecliffe
Hampton	596860	10 Platoon (part)	Moved from Greatstone
Swalecliffe	578858	10 Platoon (part)	Moved from Greatstone
Whitstable harbour	649853	12 Platoon HQ + 1 section	Moved from New Romney
Lower Island (Whitstable)	640840	12 Platoon 1 section	Moved from New Romney
Herne Bay	623855	B Company HQ	Moved from Broadoak
Reculver	668873	B Company platoons	Under 1 Lon Inf. Bde
Reculver	654874	B Company platoons	Under 1 Lon Inf. Bde
Reculver	625866	B Company platoons	Under 1 Lon Inf. Bde
Reculver	615864	B Company platoons	Under 1 Lon Inf. Bde
West Cliff	810820	9 Platoon HQ + 1 section	Moved from Minnis Bay
Club House	796773	9 Platoon 1 section	Moved from Minnis Bay
Minnis Bay	730877	8 Platoon 1 section	Moved from Bishopstone
Upstreet	674816	B Company HQ	Moved from Herne Bay
Minnis Bay	730877	7 Platoon HQ + 1 section	Moved from Herne Bay
Westgate	776886	7 Platoon 1 section	Moved from Herne Bay
Reculver	667875	8 Platoon 1 section	
Herne Bay	614866	11 Platoon HQ + 1 section	
Herne Bay prom-enade	636866	11 Platoon 1 section	
Minster in Sheppey	402916	10 Platoon	To join mobile reserve
Hampton	596860	12 Platoon HQ + 1 section	Moved from Whitstable
Swalecliffe	578858	12 Platoon 1 section	Moved from Whitstable
Warden Bay Sheppey	467901	10 Platoon HQ + 1section	From mobile reserve
Leysdown, Sheppey	475891	10 Platoon 1 section	From mobile reserve
Westbrook		14 Platoon	Took over from 7 Platoon
Sandwich		15 Platoon 1 section	Took over from 9 Platoon
Pegwell		15 Platoon 5 section	Took over from 9 Platoon

51st (Highland) Division

The 51st (Highland) Division comprised the following units and formations on its move to the Saar in April 1940:

152 Brigade:
2nd Seaforth Highlanders
4th Seaforth Highlanders
4th Queen's Own Cameron Highlanders

153 Brigade:
1st Gordon Highlanders
4th Black Watch
5th Gordon Highlanders

154 Brigade:
1st Black Watch
7th Argyll & Sutherland Highlanders
8th Argyll & Sutherland Highlanders

OTHER DIVISIONAL TROOPS

17th Field Regiment RA
23rd Field Regiment RA
75th Field Regiment RA
51st Anti-Tank Regiment RA   51st Divisional Signals Regt

26th Field Company RE
236th Field Company RE
237th Field Company RE
239th Field Park Company RE
Divisional Postal Unit RE

525th (Ammunition) Company RASC

526th (Petrol) Company RASC
527th (Supply) Company RASC

152nd Field Ambulance
153rd Field Ambulance
154th Field Ambulance
13th Field Hygiene Section

Divisional Provost
Company

ATTACHED TROOPS (NOT BRIGADED)

1st Royal Horse Artillery RA
51st Medium Regiment RA
1st Battalion The Princess Louise's Kensington Regiment
7th Battalion Royal Northumberland Fusiliers
213th Field Company RE
7th Battalion Royal Norfolk Regiment
6th Battalion Royal Scots Fusiliers
Lothians & Border Horse Yeomanry

Appendix III

Senior Commanders

Maj. Gen. Victor Fortune	General Officer Commanding 51st (Highland Division
Lt Col Harry Swinburn	General Staff Officer 1
Brig. H. Stewart	Officer Commanding 152 Brigade
Brig. G. Burney	Officer Commanding 153 Brigade
Brig. A. Stanley-Clarke	Officer Commanding 154 Brigade
Lt Col F. Gordon Parker	Commanding Officer Princess Louise's Kensington Regiment
Gen. Lord Gort	Commander-in-Chief, British Expeditionary Force
Gen. Sir John Dill	Chief of the Imperial General Staff
Lt Gen. Sir Henry Karslake	Officer Commanding lines of communication troops
Lt Gen. J. Marshall-Cornwall	Liaison Officer with French Tenth Army HQ
Maj. Gen. A. Beauman	General Officer Commanding 1st Armoured Division
Maj. Gen. R. Evans	General Officer Commanding Beauman Division
Adm. Sir William James	Commander-in-Chief, Portsmouth
Vice Adm. Sir Bertram Ramsay	Flag Officer, Dover
Col Gen. Walther von Brauchitsch	Commander-in-Chief, German Army
Col Gen. Gerd von Rundstedt	Commander, Army Group A
Col Gen. Fedor von Bock	Commander, Army Group B

Col Gen. Hans-Gunther von Kluge — Commander Fourth Army

Gen. Hermann Hoth — Commander XV Corps

Maj. Gen. Erwin Rommel — Commander 7th Panzer Division

Gen. Maxime Weygand — Commander-in-Chief, French Armed Forces

Gen. Alphonse Georges — Commander-in-Chief, North-East Front

Gen. Robert Altmayer — Commander Tenth Army

Gen. Marcel Ihler — Commander IX Corps

ENDNOTES

Chapter 1

1 Ellis, Major L.F., *The War in France and Flanders 1939–1940* (HMSO 1957) Appendix 1, p.371
2 Linklater, E., *The Highland Division* (HMSO 1942) p.23
3 Collier, B., *The Defence of the United Kingdom* (HMSO 1957) p.73
4 Harpur, Major B.V.C., *The Kensingtons* (Regtl Old Comrades Assoc. 1952) pp.3–10, 374
5 Simmons, John, personal communication with author, 5 July 2011
6 Wood, Lt B.R., Diary, September–October 1939
7 Wood, *Ibid.*, 6 April 1940
8 Ellis, *Op cit.*, p.80
9 Ellis, *Ibid.*, p.326
10 Ellis, *Ibid.*, Appendix 1, p.369
11 Ellis, *Ibid.*
12 Wood, *Op cit.*, 25 April 1940
13 Wood, *Ibid.*, 26 April 1940
14 WO/167/759 Kensingtons' war diary, 27 April, 1940 (National Archives)
15 Two such maps are contained in the Kensingtons' war diary WO/167/759 (National Archives)
16 Linklater, *Op cit.*, p.12
17 Held in the Kensingtons' war diary file WO/167/759 (National Archives)

Chapter 2

1 Harpur, Major B.V.C., *The Kensingtons* (Regtl Old Comrades Assoc. 1952) pp.23–4
2 Linklater, E., *The Highland Division* (HMSO 1942) p.15
3 Linklater, *Ibid.*, p.15
4 Linklater, *Ibid.*, p.14

5   Wood, Lt B.R., Diary, 1 May 1940

6   Linklater, *Op cit.*, p.13

7   Wood, *Op cit.*, 4 May 1940

8   Wood, *Ibid.*, 5 May 1940

9   Wood, *Ibid.*, 6 May 1940

10 Wood, *Ibid.*, 7 May 1940

11 Wood, *Ibid.*, 8 May 1940

12 After the war Charles Frost was reburied in the Commonwealth War Graves Commission cemetery at Choloy, 17 miles west of Nancy (source: CWGC web site: www.cwgc.org/search/cemetery_details)

13 Author's conversation with Peter Gardner, son of Charles Frost's sister, 7 May 2010

14 Harpur, *Op cit.*, p.24

15 Royal Indian Army Service Corps

16 Wood, *Op cit.*, 9 May 1940

17 Wood, *Ibid.*, 11 May 1940

18 Wood, *Ibid.*, 12 May 1940

19 Harpur, *Op cit.*, p.24

20 Wood, *Op cit.*, 10 May 1940

21 Ellis, Major. L.F., *The War in France and Flanders 1939–1940* (HMSO 1953) p.251

22 Linklater, *Op cit.*, p.17

23 Commonwealth War Graves Commission web site: www.cwgc.org/search/casualty_details

24 Linklater, *Op cit.*, pp.17–20

25 Linklater, *Ibid.*, p.20

26 Linklater, *Ibid.*, p.21

27 National Archives WO/373/15, recommendation for honours and awards

28 *Ibid.*

29 Wood, *Op cit.*, 13 May 1940

30 Wood, *Ibid.*, 14 May 1940

31 Wood, *Ibid.*, 15 May 1940

32 Wood, *Ibid.*, 16 May 1940

33 Wood, *Ibid.*, 17 May 1940

34 Wood, *Ibid.*, 18–20 May 1940

35 Commonwealth War Graves Commission web site: www.cwgc.org/search/casualty_details

36 WO/167/759 Kensingtons' war diary, May 1940

37 Linklater, *Op cit.*, p.26

38 A Company started from Hagondange, grid 38632732. C Company started from St Michel, grid 40142700

39 Wood, *Op cit.*, 23 May 1940

40 Linklater, *Op cit.*, pp.27–9

41 Contained in the war diary for May 1940 WO/167/759

Chapter 3

1 Linklater, E., *The Highland Division* (HMSO 1942) p.32

2 Wood, Lt B.R., Diary, 2 June 1940

3 Ellis, Major L.F., *The War in France and Flanders* (HMSO 1953) p.265

4 Wood, *Op cit.*, 3 June 1940

5 Harpur, Major B.V.C., *The Kensingtons* (Regtl Old Comrades Assoc. 1952) p.30

6 Wood, *Op cit.*, 4 June 1940

7 Ellis, *Op cit.*, p.266

8 Harpur, *Op cit.*, p.31

9 Linklater, *Op cit.*, p.34

10 Harpur, *Op cit.*, p.30

11 Harpur, *Ibid.*, p.32

12 Linklater, *Op cit.*, p.39

13 Wood, *Op cit.*, 5 June 1940

14 Linklater, *Op cit.*, pp.44–5

15 Linklater, *Ibid.*, pp.52–3

16 Wood, *Op cit.*, 6 June 1940

17 Wood, *Ibid.*, 7 June 1940

18 Wood, *Ibid.*, 8 June 1940

19 Wood, *Ibid.*, 9 June 1940

20 Harpur, *Op cit.*, p.33

21 Other accounts say the front ran only as far south-east as Gamaches

22 Harpur, *Op cit.*, p.32

23 Harpur, *Ibid.*, p.33

24 Ellis, *Op cit.*, p.276

25 Linklater, *Op cit.*, p.59

26 Linklater, *Ibid.*, p.64

27 According to the war diary Battalion HQ, HQ Company and D Company had moved from Bois Ricard to La Chaussée, 5 miles west of the Bethune River, at 2030 hours on 8 June. The journey took six and a half hours and the force reached La Chaussée at 0300 hours on 9 June. La Chaussée is 7 miles south of Dieppe. A Company HQ with one section and B Company arrived at Longueville, 10 miles south of Dieppe, on 9 June. C Company withdrew to Bellengreville, 3 miles south-east of Dieppe, on 9 June. Forges is 2 miles south-east of Neufchâtel

28 Harpur, *Op cit.*, p.34

29 Linklater, *Op cit.*, p.65

30 Ellis, *Op cit.*, p.283. A clear indication of the bravery, tenacity and strong morale of these territorial units

31 Ellis, *Ibid.*, p.285

32 Ellis, *Ibid.*, p.284

33 Linklater, *Ibid.*, p.71

34 Harpur, *Op cit.*, p.35

35 Wood, *Op cit.*, 10 June 1940

36 Ellis, *Op cit.*, p.287

37 Wood, *Op cit.*, 11 June 1940

Chapter 4

1   Linklater, E., *The Highland Division* (HMSO 1942) p.74

2   Ellis, Major L.F., *The War in France and Flanders* (HMSO 1953) p.290

3   The report by Maj. de Chimay is set out here and can be found in the Kensingtons' war diary (WO/167/759)

4   Linklater, *Op cit.*, pp.76–7

5   Linklater, *Ibid.*, p.817

6   Linklater, *Ibid.*, pp.79–80

7   Ellis, *Op cit.*, p.289

8   Linklater, *Op cit.*, p.82

9   Harpur, Major B.V.C., *The Kensingtons* (Regtl Old Comrades Assoc, 1952) p.36

10 Harpur, *Ibid.*, pp.36–7

11 Harpur, *Ibid.*, p.37. Note that according to Lt Wood's diary for 12 June (below), Farlander, Haslam and Paley were killed on board a French destroyer that was bombed off St Valery shortly after 0800 hours

12 Commonwealth War Graves Commission web site: www.cwgc.org/search/casualty_details

13 Wood, Lt B.R., Diary, 11/12 June 1940

14 These moves reflect the shrinking perimeters. Anneville is 5 miles south of Dieppe. Ouville is 7 miles north-west of Anneville. Cailleville is 10 miles west of Ouville and 3 miles south of St Valery

15 Bradford, A., *Escape from Saint Valery-en-Caux* (The History Press, 2009) p.58

16 Harpur, *Op cit.*, p.39

17 Commonwealth War Graves Commission, *Op cit.*

18 21-year-old Robert Farlander's parents, Francis and Augusta, lived in Hornsea. Edwin Haslam was 27. Albert Paley was 35. His parents were in Leeds and he left a wife, Annie. Farlander and Haslam are buried in the war cemetery at St Valery. Albert Paley has no known grave. His name is listed on the Dunkirk Memorial which commemorates those whose final resting place is unknown. (source Commonwealth War Graves Commission, *Ibid.*)

19 Wood, *Op cit.*, Diary, 12 June 1940

20 Linklater, *Op cit.*, pp.87–8

Chapter 5

1   The force consisted of 4th Black Watch, 7th Argyll and Sutherland Highlanders, 8th Argyll and Sutherland Highlanders, 6th Royal Scots Fusiliers, 154 Brigade Anti-Tank Company, the Kensington Regiment (HQ plus HQ Company, B and C Companies), 204 Anti-Tank Battery RA, 75th Field Regiment RA, 17th Field Regiment RA, 154th Field Ambulance

and four companies of Royal Engineers. Also included was A Brigade of the Beauman Division (4th Border Regiment, 5th Sherwood Foresters, 4th Royal East Kents) and elements from the RASC

2 Ellis, Major L.F., *The War in France and Flanders* (HMSO 1953) p.285

3 This account relies largely on the Kensingtons' war diary (WO/167/759). Other sources are noted

4 Linklater, E., *The Highland Division* (HMSO 1942) p.68

5 Ellis, *Op cit.*, pp.286–7

6 Linklater, *Op cit.*, pp.92–3

7 From the war diary and from Lt Kent's account it is clear that B Company was on line A and C Company was on the inner line B, very close to Battalion HQ and HQ Company

8 Ellis, *Op cit.*, p.18 (sketch map)

9 Ellis, *Ibid.*, p.264

10 Ellis, *Ibid.*, p.296

11 Ellis, *Ibid.*, p.293

12 Contained in WO/167/59 Kensingtons' war diary, June 1940 (National Archives)

Chapter 6

1 WO/167/759 Kensingtons' war diary (National Archives)

2 Simmons, J., personal communication with author, 5 July 2011

3 Knott, V. (*née* Simmons), personal communication with author, 10 April 2011

4 With the final entry for June the war diary WO/167/759, covering the months April to June 1940, comes to an end. It was now a momentous time for the country, with the Battle of Britain about to start and all available troops placed on alert for the expected invasion. There follows an account of the part played by the Kensingtons in this new phase of the war

5 See Appendix I, Table 3

6 See chapter five

7 Collier, B., *The Defence of the United Kingdom* (Naval & Military Press 2004) p.125

8 C Company HQ already had 10 Platoon on the island and it is not clear why B Company HQ was sent there rather than C. It may reflect the fact that platoons rather than companies seem to have become the basic tactical unit of the battalion

9 See Appendix I, Table 6 for full details

10 WO/166/4350 Kensingtons' war diary, July 1940 (National Archives)

11 Advanced units

12 2 London Infantry Brigade operational plan 10 July 1940, in WO/166/4350 Kensingtons' war diary, July 1940 (National Archives)

13 Collier, *Op cit.*, p.179

14 Collier, *Ibid.*, p.219

15 Collier, *Ibid.*, pp.178–9

16 Collier, *Ibid.*, p.107

17 Collier, *Ibid.*, p.125

18 Collier, *Ibid.*, p.125

19 Collier, *Ibid.*, p.142

20 Collier, *Ibid.*, pp.143–4

21 WO/166/4350 Kensingtons' war diary, copy 1st Division op instruction 12, dated 25 July 1940 (National Archives)

22 Commonwealth War Graves Commission web site: www.cwgc.org/search/casualty_details

23 Collier, *Op cit.*, pp.222–3

24 Collier, *Ibid.*, p.245

Chapter 7

1 Wood, Lt B.R., Diary, 4–6 March 1941 (paraphrased)

2 Linklater, E., *The Highland Division* (HMSO 1942) p.94

3 National Archive file WO/373/60, recommendations for honours and awards

4 Harpur, Major B.V.C., *The Kensingtons* (Regtl Old Comrades Assoc. 1952) p.46

5 Commonwealth War Graves Commission web site: www.cwgc.org/search/casualty_details

6 Harpur, *Op cit.*, p.122

7 Linklater, *Op cit.*, pp.95–6

8 Ellis, Major L.F., *The War in France and Flanders* (HMSO 1953) p.326

9 Ellis, *Ibid.*, pp.327–8

BIBLIOGRAPHY

Secondary Sources

Bradford, A., *Escape from St Valery-en-Caux* (The History Press, 2009)

Bungay, S., *The Most Dangerous Enemy* (Aurum Press, 2000)

Collier, B., *The Defence of the United Kingdom* (HMSO, 1957)

David, S., *Churchill's Sacrifice of the Highland Division* (Brassey's, 2004)

Deighton, L., *Battle of Britain* (Jonathan Cape, 1980)

Doherty, R., *None Bolder* (Spellmount, 2006)

Ellis, Maj. L.F., *The War in France and Flanders* (HMSO, 1953)

Harpur, Maj. B.C.V., *The Kensingtons* (Regimental Old Comrades Association, 1952)

Horne, A., *To Lose a Battle* (Penguin, 1969)

Innes, B. (ed.), *St. Valery: The Impossible Odds* (Birlinn, 2004)

Linklater, E., *The Highland Division* (HMSO, 1942)

Longden, S., *The Men They Left Behind* (Constable & Robinson Ltd, 2008)

Lukacs, J., *Five days in London: May 1940* (Yale University Press, 2001)

Robinson, D., *Invasion, 1940* (Constable & Robinson Ltd, 2005)

Sebag-Montefiore, H., *Dunkirk: Fight to the Last Man* (Viking, 2006)

Takle, P., *The British Army in France after Dunkirk* (Pen & Sword, 2009)

Thompson, J., *Dunkirk: Retreat to Victory* (Sidgwick & Jackson, 2008)

Contemporary Sources

National Archives WO/167/759, Kensington Regt. War Diary April–June 1940

National Archives WO/166/4350, Kensington Regt. War Diary July–September 1940

National Archives WO/373/60, Mentioned in Despatches Pte F. Ford

National Archives WO/373/15, Recommendation for honours & awards Sgt R. Pratt

Wood, Lt Reg, Diary

INDEX